New Approaches to Socialis

History and politics titles from New Clarion Press

Lawrence Black et al., *Consensus or Coercion? The State, the People and Social Cohesion in Post-war Britain*

Keith Flett and David Renton (eds), *New Approaches to Socialist History*

Duncan Hall, *'A Pleasant Change from Politics': Music and the British Labour Movement between the Wars*

Anne Kerr and Tom Shakespeare, *Genetic Politics: From Eugenics to Genome*

David Renton, *Classical Marxism: Socialist Theory and the Second International*

David Stack, *The First Darwinian Left: Socialism and Darwinism 1859–1914*

Leo Zeilig (ed.), *Class Struggle and Resistance in Africa*

Forthcoming

John Carter and Dave Morland, *Anti-Capitalist Britain*

Mark O'Brien, *When Adam Delved and Eve Span: A History of the Peasants' Revolt of 1381*

New Approaches to Socialist History

edited by Keith Flett and David Renton

New Clarion Press

© Keith Flett, David Renton, Tobias Abse, Anne Alexander, Ian Birchall, John Charlton, Ralph Darlington, Neil Davidson, Andrew Dawson, Paul Grist, Dave Lyddon, Craig Phelan, 2003

The right of the above named to be identified as the authors of this work has been asserted in accordance with the Copyright, Designs and Patents Act 1988.

First published 2003

New Clarion Press
5 Church Row, Gretton
Cheltenham GL54 5HG
England

New Clarion Press is a workers' co-operative.

A catalogue record for this book is available from the British Library.

ISBN paperback   1 873797 41 9
      hardback   1 873797 42 7

Cover photo: Seattle World Trade Organization mass protest, 1999.
By Geoff Oliver Bugbee (www.geoffbugbee.com).

Typeset in Times New Roman by Jean Wilson Typesetting, Coventry
Printed in Great Britain by The Cromwell Press, Trowbridge

Contents

Contributors

Keith Flett is convenor of the socialist history seminar at the Institute of Historical Research in London. He has published numerous articles and monographs and is an active socialist and trade unionist. He is the co-editor, with David Renton, of *The Twentieth Century: A Century of Wars and Revolutions?*

David Renton is Senior Research Fellow in History at Sunderland University. An active socialist and anti-war campaigner, his books include *Classical Marxism: Socialist Theory and the Second International* and *Marx on Globalisation*. There is also a webpage dedicated to his research at http://www.dkrenton.co.uk.

◆ ◆ ◆

Tobias Abse is Lecturer in Modern European History at Goldsmiths College, University of London. He is the author of *Sovversivi e fascisti a Livorno: Lotta politica e sociale (1918–1922)* and numerous articles on Italian history and politics.

Anne Alexander works as a journalist specializing in the Middle East. She is currently a doctoral student at the Institute of Arab and Islamic Studies at the University of Exeter.

Ian Birchall, formerly Senior Lecturer at Middlesex University, is an independent writer specializing in the history of socialism. Recent works include *The Spectre of Babeuf* and *Sartre against Stalinism*. He is a longstanding member of the Socialist Workers' Party.

John Charlton is a writer and political activist living in the north-east of England. He has a strong interest in popular movements and is currently working on the roots of 1960s activism in north-east England.

Ralph Darlington teaches industrial relations at Salford University and is the author of *The Dynamics of Workplace Unionism* and *The Political Trajectory of T. J. Murphy*. He is a longstanding member of the Socialist Workers' Party.

Neil Davidson is the author of *The Origins of Scottish Nationhood* and *Discovering the Scottish Revolution, 1688–1746*. He is a member of the Scottish Socialist Party and an activist in the Public and Commercial Services Union.

Andrew Dawson teaches American history at the University of Greenwich. He has a forthcoming book, *Lives of the Philadelphia Engineers: Capital, Class, and Revolution, 1830–1890*. His new project looks at Hollywood's industrial relations.

Paul Grist teaches history in Bradford, where he is an activist in the local trade union and anti-racist movements.

Dave Lyddon teaches industrial relations at Keele University and is editor of *Historical Studies in Industrial Relations*. He is a longstanding member of the Socialist Workers' Party.

Craig Phelan is Lecturer in American Studies at the University of Wales Swansea. He has written biographies of three American labour leaders: Terence Powderly, John Mitchell and William Green. At present he is writing a comparative study of labour movements in northern Europe and the USA.

◆ ◆ ◆

The London Socialist Historians Group was formed in 1993 to promote discussion of new socialist approaches to history. It is concerned to develop an understanding of the past from the point of view of the working class, exploring history from both 'above' and 'below'. It is an open group, with members from outside of academia as well as professional historians.

Introduction: Socialist History beyond the Millennium

Keith Flett and David Renton

It has been widely suggested that socialist history is redundant and that the influence of left-wing ideas is a matter of past interest, but the chapters in this book tell a very different story. Indeed they suggest that interest in socialist history is as strong as ever. The chapters included here represent papers given at a one-day conference organized by the London Socialist Historians Group in May 2000 at the Institute of Historical Research in London. Around 50 socialist historians attended, some well known and with academic positions, others outside but with an abiding passion for historical research written from a radical, oppositional perspective.

Accounts of what takes place at meetings of socialist historians, why the meetings are held, and whether the papers meet with the approval of those attending are sparse, perversely given the subject under discussion. The most influential tradition, that of the 'British Marxist historians', goes back to the formation of a Communist Party Historians Group in the 1940s.[1] Eric Hobsbawm, Victor Kiernan, Dorothy Thompson and Bill Schwarz (among other writers) have provided us with a record of their meetings.[2] Yet, at least until the rise of Euro-Communism and for most practical purposes until the collapse of the Stalinist states in eastern Europe in 1989–91, the Communist Party Historians Group did not hold public meetings and events. To do so would have raised the possibility of open discussion and perhaps dissent from a party line.

The History Workshop movement, whose annual conferences started at Ruskin College in 1966, had no such problems. There was no fixed party line, or if there was, rather like old-style Labour Party conferences, it was not something that was much discussed at all. For example, the collective decided in 1976 to title their publication a 'journal of a socialist history', then in 1982 to add 'and feminist' to the masthead, and finally to drop the label altogether. None of these decisions was determined at the annual History Workshop conferences. Ideas and historical theories were open to the fullest possible debate, but the practical policy of the group was excluded from discussion.

Yet in other ways, this was a tremendously impressive movement. At the height of History Workshop conferences, thousands attended and hundreds gave papers, even if comparatively little made it into any subsequent publication. All sorts of activist histories flourished in this milieu. The account of Raphael Samuel, one of the founders of the movement, gives some sense of the original ideals that inspired History Workshop:

> History Workshop began life at a time when the cultural revolution of the 1960s was carrying all before it. In the universities, disciplinary boundaries were being challenged. In the schools, project work and 'learning by doing' were designed to break down the apartheid which separated the teachers and the taught ... At Ruskin, a college of mature students, recruited from working men and women, these ideas had a particular resonance, and the History Workshop was in the first place an attempt to replace the hierarchical relationship of tutor and pupil by one of comradeship in which each became, in some sort, co-learners.[3]

Sadly, this revolutionary élan did not survive the harsher conditions of the 1980s. The subject matter of the *History Workshop Journal* has been increasingly concerned with topics such as sexuality, dreams and psychoanalysis, a preoccupation with the personal psyche to the exclusion of economic and political affairs. While the first History Workshop publications were often memoirs of working-class life written by trade unionists and young workers from Ruskin, the drift of the journal has been towards more academic discussion of standard postmodernist ideas, cut off from lived, historical experience.

Although the old History Workshop is no more, socialist history remains alive and well. The attendance at our 2000 conference and the breadth of subject matter in the chapters of this book underlines the vitality of socialist history at the millennium. The mechanical certainties of history influenced by Stalinism have largely gone. Labour history remains (with some happy exceptions) deeply unfashionable, but there are still plenty of scholars working away in the archives and elsewhere who use socialist thought of some kind as their guide. Our conference took as its theme new research in socialist history precisely to demonstrate that, despite the many obituaries, socialist history is still very much alive, and that younger generations are now coming forward to take up the work of the old Communist Party Historians Group and others. Of the authors represented here, the majority are well under 50 and some are in their twenties. We are not against aged historians, but our point is that this movement is something of the present, not a hangover from the past.

The popularity of Francis Wheen's biography of Karl Marx suggests not only an interest in Marx himself, but a thirst for a left-wing history.[4] The history to be found in this book is different from Wheen's, in that ours is based on empirical research and rigorous historical method. The conclusions may not always be happy ones from a socialist perspective, but it is necessary to understand moments of defeat as well as victory. Sadly, the former have been at least as numerous as the latter where the left is concerned. The commitment to research is important and it is a debt that the group owes to History Workshop and to Raphael Samuel in particular.[5] His enthusiasm for returning to historical sources is a theme that underwrites all of the papers given at the conference.

Yet as Sam Ashman and others have argued, the History Workshop approach had its limits. The bigger picture became lost in ever more obscure research.[6] The papers given at our 2000 conference, therefore, while based on original research, also had to pass a test of relevance. Did the history they examined offer something of use for activists in the twenty-first century? This is meant not in what might (perhaps a little unkindly) be called the Tony Benn approach to history, which is to see all previous events as providing direct lessons for us today. Rather it uses a more generic focus, that the approach taken to the subject can illuminate wider questions of class, class consciousness and class struggle, whatever its period and specific content.

If there is one thing that many of the chapters in this book do take directly from the History Workshop tradition, it is the concept of rescuing lives 'hidden from history'. There are events and people who have, for a variety of reasons, been obscured from the historical record. What is concealed and what is not comes and goes. For example, three of the chapters, Ian Birchall's on Alfred Rosmer, David Renton's on Stafford Cripps and Craig Phelan's on Terence Powderly, examine labour leaders who were important figures but whose lives have not been recorded to any great extent. Labour history became a deeply unfashionable subject in Britain during the Tory years from 1979 to 1997 and it has made an uncertain return since. During the period of its fashionability a series of biographies of significant labour leaders, such as John Maclean and Tom Mann, were produced. All now, however, are long out of print.

The organizers of the conference did not run a separate labour leaders strand, preferring to keep the focus simply on new research in socialist history. It was felt that an important weakness of early labour history was that it tended to be very eurocentric, perhaps even anglocentric. We commissioned several papers on African labour leaders for the conference, following on from some successful seminar papers on this theme, but, alas, they did not arrive.

The relationship to tradition informed another strand of thinking around the conference: the question of whether the London Socialist Historians Group is an attempt at a successor to the Communist Party Historians Group. The answer, for most of those participating, is a resounding 'no'. We look to the serious work and the impressive publishing record of the CP Historians as an inspiration, but we have many differences. First, the LSHG is not a 'party' operation with a party line on history to follow. It contains members of the Socialist Workers' Party and the Labour Party, anarchists, Stalinists and lots of people of no particular affiliation. It also has a broad rather than a narrow definition of socialist history – and there is certainly no attempt to push a narrow party line.

Second, the London Socialist Historians Group is not just based in universities; in fact we positively welcome papers from historical enthusiasts who hold no academic position, and this book has contributions from several of them. Third, we do not see 'history' as a separate discipline from others, but as something that informs all kinds of areas. Hence the chapters of this book could easily be filed under social movement theory, industrial relations, economics and so on. Divisions between subjects are created for the convenience of the university system. They are not something that should preoccupy socialists. Finally we felt that the Communist Party Historians had a certain narrowness of view in what areas they actually looked at, and while we ourselves have a way to go, this book does represent a broad spectrum of history, rather than the traditional kind of subjects in which socialist historians are expected to be interested.

The chapters in this book have a further importance beyond that of demonstrating the vitality of new research in the field of socialist history. They are also a powerful counterweight to those who would argue that socialist history itself is redundant; that it lacks intellectual coherence and has nothing useful to say following the collapse of Stalinism. The definition of socialist history adopted by the LSHG is a broad one, but several of the historians represented in this book were strong critics and opponents of Stalinism for many years before its final demise. As a result of that shared background, members of the group have tended to argue for class as a key concept in understanding history, for a belief in progress in history and for a desire to study those movements and moments when people have tried to change society for the better, often in revolutionary ways.

There is no question that the existence of an organization of socialist historians, the insistence on the importance of socialist history and the ability to defend a coherent tradition of socialist history continue to draw fire from critics on the right and centre-left. Indeed, given the supposition that socialist history is dead, the virulence of the attacks on it is remarkable. Nicholas Fearn, reviewing Robert Conquest's *Reflections on a Ragged Century* in the *Independent on Sunday*, provided the following précis of Conquest's argument: 'The Western dupes of the Soviets were the idealists of nothing but their own egos, puffed up by intellectual vanity. There is a lot of mileage in the thought. Leading sit-ins at the LSE [London School of Economics] was always, one suspects, a good way of impressing the girls.'[7]

One figure that Conquest and Fearn had in their sights was Eric Hobsbawm. Most of those involved with the LSHG would disagree with the political tradition in which Hobsbawm stood concerning the nature of post-1927 Russia. His Stalinist perspective did not help his work as a Marxist historian. Even so, Hobsbawm has produced an impressive body of work which is firmly rooted in the classical Marxist tradition. There is much scope for debate and disagreement within the tradition; indeed, Chris Harman has considered some of the issues in a book produced from the papers of our 1999 conference.[8]

Themes

The biggest challenge that socialist history has had to face is that of postmodernism and the linguistic turn. Postmodernists have criticised the fundamental idea that history had a grand narrative, an understanding of the big picture of historical progress which historians had to uncover. The linguistic turn, pioneered in Britain by Gareth Stedman Jones, argued that it was above all the language that people used that was important for historians, not why they used it, or the situations they used it in. Over the past few years, the postmodernist attack has begun to fade. Even as recently as 1995, the editors of *Labour History Review* felt it necessary to publish a series of articles engaging with Patrick Joyce's linguistic analysis of British Chartism.[9] One member of our group contributed to the debate, suggesting that in Joyce's analysis, 'Everything is viewed as a static category, as if frozen in time, and people meant what they said, and nothing else must be allowed to come into it.'[10] Ironically, Joyce's defence appeared in *Past and Present*, a journal originally established by members of the Communist Party Historians Group, seeking to loosen their ties with party headquarters in King Street.[11] The recent turn-of-fashion against postmodernism has taken place partly because new styles of labour history have emerged, which are more confident to challenge postmodernism on the terrain of identity, gender and ethnicity.[12] It appears that the champions of the linguistic turn have lost interest in challenging history.

Yet while the chapters in the book are firmly rooted in the accepted disciplines of historical research, socialist history is not conservative in method. Rather it looks to new ways of approaching historical study. In Chapter 1, which sets the tone for the book, John Charlton looks at the moment when social movements explode into public consciousness. In comparing the Chartists, the New Unionism of the 1880s and the Seattle protests of 1999, he argues that when such moments arise is not predictable, but that the character of the movements involved, and also how they develop subsequently, is shaped by their pre-history. It is the task of the historian to try and piece together these pre-histories. Protest may appear spontaneous, but the participants bring to such protest much pre-determined strategy and ideas. Paul Grist, in Chapter 2, examines issues of rank-and-file organization, leadership and revolt in the wave of industrial protest that took place in Britain between 1911 and 1914. A second group of chapters address the theme of leadership in the working-class movement. In Chapter 3, Tobias Abse considers the role of the leading Italian Communist Palmiro Togliatti. Abse rejects the view of Togliatti expressed in much recent historiography, which described him as a founder of a more liberal Euro-Communism, and hence as a real alternative to Stalinism. In reality, Togliatti was one of the Comintern officials sent to supervise the movement during the Spanish Civil War. His actions in Spain and later in Italy show that Togliatti was more closely tied into the Stalinist project than those who have sought to rewrite his role have allowed. Craig Phelan considers the biography of Terence Powderly in Chapter 4. Powderly was the leader of the early American trade union federation, the Knights of Labor. Phelan's history is strongly rooted in the source material, and is generous in its appraisal of the relationship between Powderly and the rank and file.

In Chapter 5, David Renton addresses the career of Stafford Cripps, expelled from the Labour Party in the 1930s for his socialist views, but later the Chancellor of the Exchequer in the Attlee government. Cripps' trajectory prefigures the subsequent history of the Labour Party under Blair. Renton both defends and criticizes Stafford Cripps' politics, searching out the limits that explain his subsequent dash to the right. Ian Birchall, in Chapter 6, examines the history of the Red International of Labour Unions, a revolutionary federation established following the October Revolution in Russia. Birchall's story follows the biography of Alfred Rosmer, who was a revolutionary syndicalist and a prominent supporter of the Bolsheviks. Later Rosmer was a close confidant of Leon Trotsky. All in all, Rosmer was a more impressive figure than the other labour leaders considered in this book.

Chapters 7 and 8 are devoted to the theme of class and class politics in history. Anne Alexander describes how left-wing politics developed in Egypt in the years following 1945. The position of the left in the post-1945 period was strong. Small numbers of Communists were able to take positions of leadership in the workers' and the national movements, and thus gained an influence out of all proportion to their numbers. Alexander shows that the defeat of the workers' movement came about because the Communist groups failed to address crucial issues of poverty and injustice, leaving a vacuum of organization and leadership for others, including the Free Officers and subsequently political Islam, to fill. In Chapter 8, Andrew Dawson evaluates the class relationships that lay beneath the American Civil War, looking at the social development and politics of the northern manufacturing class. Far from radical defeat being inevitable, developments during the civil war were determined by the circumstances, personalities and organizations prevailing at the time.

The theme of the final two chapters is 'hidden from history': they consider episodes of working-class struggle that have generally been overlooked by more conventional historians. Dave Lyddon and Ralph Darlington, in Chapter 9, examine the year of crisis of 1972. They ask how labour disputes were organized, and what the role of the Communist Party was in shaping rank-and-file workers' activity. Finally, in Chapter 10, Neil Davidson looks further back to one of the first general strikes in history, which took place in Scotland in 1820. Both chapters relate back to the earlier contributions on socialist leadership. They consider how class organization took place, and the politics that informed the struggle.

The one session at the London Socialist Historians' conference of 2000 which is not represented here was arguably the most important. This was the final plenary when people were able to report back on points and issues raised in earlier sessions, to pose wider questions on what socialist historians should be doing and to make suggestions for future work. An open final session is preferred to one where a speaker sums up themes, precisely to emphasize not only the democratic but also the collective nature of the socialist historical effort when it comes to new research. Ideas and suggestions feed off each other, and while, of course, there is without question such a thing as the loneliness of the long-distance researcher, one purpose of a group like the London Socialist Historians is to contribute towards a milieu where a culture of socialist history can flourish.

These methodological issues are important, if the question of how best to popularize socialist history is to be answered. Other ways of focusing this debate also surfaced: in particular, whether socialist history as a dissident history, particularly in the age of New Labour, could find a space in schools and colleges. Both the Communist Party Historians Group and History Workshop were hugely influential in how school history was taught. There is now a considerable vacuum, which, again, in a modest way, the London Socialist Historians hope to be able to fill.

The generation of socialist historians who turned towards postmodernism in the 1980s did so under the influence of events – including the election of Margaret Thatcher and Ronald Reagan, and the defeat of the miners' strike in Britain in 1984–5. Often people would defend this turn with reference to a series of 'facts' in society – the idea that work itself was disappearing, or that protest no longer took place. Yet recent events demonstrate the falsity of such claims. New generations have entered the workplace. More people in Britain now define themselves as working class than at any time since records began. The cultural expression of class has changed, but the analytical significance of class endures.

Meanwhile, the rebirth of the global protest movement provides further evidence that the tide has turned in favour of an active socialist history. The history of the movement covered in John Charlton's chapter is contemporary. It began with the 50,000 workers, green activists, Lesbian Avengers and 'turtle kids' who took part in protests at Seattle in

November 1999, and continued through the efforts of thousands more who have demonstrated since then against globalization in Washington, Millau, Kyoto, Seoul, Prague, Genoa, Barcelona, Johannesburg and elsewhere. A new mood exists, a new style of protest, which will at some stage begin to reinvigorate the tradition of activist history, as well as achieving much more besides. This book aspires to present a synthesis between the history from below practised in the 1960s and the movement of today. It continues the tradition that Raphael Samuel spoke of in relation to a collection of History Workshop papers published over twenty years ago:

> We hope it will indicate some of the richness and variety of work being undertaken within or close to, the Marxist and socialist tradition; that it can introduce this work to students and first-time readers; and that it can encourage others to take part in the task of constructing a history which speaks to the condition of our time.[13]

1

The Pre-history of Social Movements: From Newport to Seattle

John Charlton

My interest in this topic was sparked by political activity in the 1990s. The socialist movement was deep in the long downturn that had lasted with few interruptions for nearly twenty years. Two questions regularly cropped up. Could the situation ever change? And, if so, how? To try to find answers I started to review my understanding of past situations in the history of mass movements in Britain. Two of these I had previously examined in detail: the Chartists and the movement that produced New Unionism at the end of the 1880s.[1]

As I was bringing my ideas together last autumn came the battle in Seattle where a mass demonstration brought a meeting of the World Trade Organization to a halt.[2] In our own times, was this the answer to the first question? Certainly, for the first time in a generation, American activists had produced an event the impact of which rang round the world. Of course, one swallow does not make a summer. However, Seattle itself was certainly a big event, which commentators at the time saw as a significant moment in the growth of an anti-capitalist movement. Understanding how it came about might throw light upon some general questions. By exploring a living movement, could we discover things hitherto unavailable to students of movements in history?

Of the three movements reviewed here, New Unionism and Seattle may help to answer the question of how movements appear suddenly, after long periods of apparent passivity. In contrast, Chartism came towards the end of two decades of rising struggle – from the popular reaction to the Peterloo Massacre, to mass campaigns for repeal of the Combination Acts, for Catholic emancipation, around the first parliamentary reform bill, for a free press, for the Tolpuddle Martyrs and against the New Poor Law. Nevertheless, in South Wales in the autumn of 1839 the workers' rising marked a qualitative shift in the scale and content of radical activity.

By the late 1880s, almost 40 years had passed since the last Chartist upsurge of 1848. The skilled craft unions ossified into elitist bodies of members led by cautious bureaucrats – notwithstanding periodic and sometimes lengthy economic struggles. In 1890 John Burns, attending the Trades Union Congress on behalf of a newly formed union, reported the contrasting appearance of delegates:

> Physically the 'old' unionists were much bigger men than the 'new', and that no doubt is due to the greater intensity of toil during the last twenty or thirty years . . . The 'old' delegates differed from the 'new' not only physically but in dress. A great number of them looked like respectable city gentlemen; wore very good coats, large watch chains and high hats – and in many cases were of such splendid build and proportions that they presented an aldermanic, not to say a magisterial form and dignity. Among the 'new' delegates not a single one wore a tall hat. They looked workmen. They were workmen. They were not such sticklers for formality or Court procedure but were guided more by common sense.[3]

The only mass political movement that emerged in the period was for suffrage reform in 1866–7, but it was ephemeral, withering soon after the 1867 Reform Act was passed. There were also periodic agitations in support of Irish nationalism, but otherwise it was largely a period of extreme political passivity among working people.

In retrospect we can see two main contributory factors to this passivity. There was the contained economic elitism of craft union members, many of whom both nationally and locally embraced Gladstonian liberalism. Then there was the apolitical passivity of the masses of unskilled labourers scrabbling for a marginal living. Observers from Thomas Wright in the 1870s to Charles Booth in the late 1880s noted both.[4] Negative evidence of the latter point is afforded by the state's lack of preparation for an upsurge of activity in summer 1889. The cabinet was never in session during the crisis; indeed, its members were enjoying their usual extended long summer recess apparently oblivious to the events. In contrast, during and immediately after the Chartist upsurge, both government and employers were very much alert to the 'dangerous classes'.[5]

Seattle has some of the character of the unexpected about it, although the forces assembled by the state might suggest otherwise. Those who run the modern state tend to leave nothing to chance. Yet in American conditions it is necessary to distinguish between the local and federal state, as separate responsibilities devolved on each.

For a few years the World Trade Organization (WTO) had been the source of a mounting antagonism. Direct action was certainly in the air – or on the internet. The surprise elements were the scale of the protest in terms of size and, crucially, the uncharacteristic behaviour of organized labour. Together this exposed the inadequacy of the local state's preparation, at least. The undisciplined violence of the Seattle police could be seen as evidence of this lack of anticipation. It might also be seen as a central cause of the Seattle events achieving such international celebrity. I will return to this point later in the chapter.

The local state was under-prepared to the point of pre-event complacency. In the week before the event there was coverage in the major daily paper, the *Seattle Times*. But the main pitch came from the Business Section's paeans to the WTO. In the two weeks before 30 November, the only reference to a law and order dimension was a report on 25 November of the Seattle school district's decision to close down the school system two hours early. The resignation of the Seattle police chief on 4 December, before the demonstrators had all gone home, indicates the deep shock that the local authorities had experienced.[6] A report by Californian police chiefs, commissioned by the mayor's office and published in May 2000, underlines the presumption of complacency in its listing of evidence of potential 'trouble' ignored by the authorities.

There is a different story when we look at the role of the military. There was a chilling collection of special units on standby in the Seattle area, but none of them intervened.[7] This must surely indicate that their presence was entirely related to a fear of international terrorism when so many prominent politicians were in attendance, including the expected arrival of President Bill Clinton and Vice-President Al Gore. It had little to do with predictions of the size and content of a mass demonstration.

Many of the demonstrators themselves were shocked at the scale of things. And why wouldn't they be? For all demonstrators under the age of 40, Seattle's scale and militancy were something quite different from anything sampled before. One of the important Seattle stories is that of coalitions assembled for the event. They consisted of many groups with long histories of activity, but virtually none had enjoyed the involvement of substantial numbers in one place at one time. Redwood Activists, for example, had camped out in the tree-tops of Oregon to some effect, but this necessarily involved small numbers of athletic and dedicated individuals. Admiration for them within the movement at large derived from their bravery rather than their numbers.

The history of US movements during the twenty years since the end of the Vietnam War bears strongly upon the response to Seattle. It has clearly been at a low ebb of activity. The large-scale anti war movement simply disappeared after the fall of Saigon, the student movement going down with it. The women's movement shrank as many of its leading lights found comfortable academic or media jobs. The Black Power movement, harassed and smashed by the state, was marginalized. The small socialist groups split and largely withered, leaving a legacy of hostility towards their often sectarian behaviour.

Any notion of the labour unions as a source of revitalization was also absent. They had been no friend of the movement in the 1960s and 1970s, sometimes militantly supporting state violence against demonstrators. The subsequent decades reported only decline and further depoliticization in the face of rapid deindustrialization, the central experience of the Reagan era. The election of Reagan was part of a global shift to the right, its belligerent confidence in the free market sweeping aside all but the most intransigent members of the counter-culture. Connection with the multifarious radical tradition of the 1960s was all but broken. Those who did survive with an alternative value system were largely marooned in a romantic past, 'doing their own thing': living in Haight-Ashbury, or the Village, having kids, eating, drinking, smoking, socializing in greying circles, going to school, teaching school, in Maine or Oregon, or a city college, doing 'community work', helping on literacy programmes or AIDS counselling. And for some there was employment in the new high-tech industries of the north-west, which in the late 1970s could still provide career opportunities relatively untainted by the odium of corporate power. Identity politics was the name of the game. The prospect of a return to mass politics seemed an impossible dream.

On the other hand, one movement (or series of movements), the motif of which was concern for the planet, had come to life from the mid-1980s as more and more evidence surfaced about the wanton depredations of corporations. Part of an international green current, its attentions were multi-focal, encompassing damage to rain forests, global warming, cruelty to animals, pollution of rivers and lakes, unnecessary road development, genetic modification, exploitative advertising, super-exploitation of labour in developing countries and Third World debt. Each campaign had a separate target. Such diversity may have been a merit in bringing noisy attention to an enormous gamut of issues, but the ecological movement was marginalized and regularly trashed by the mainstream media. It is against this background that Seattle surprised.

Thus it can be seen that the New Unionism of the 1880s and the anti-WTO demonstrations at Seattle had strong elements of surprise, hitting the consciousness of their worlds after long periods of apparent dormancy.

The revolutionary 'moment'

When we come to consider why movements occur when they do, all three examples have something to offer. 'The moment' seems to contain at least two elements: the immediate cause of the flashpoint and the build-up of forces that enables the flashpoint to occur at all.

Chartism had at least three flashpoints: November 1839, August 1842 and February 1848. In November 1839 miners, iron workers and sundry other workers assembled in their home valleys of South Wales to march on Newport.[8] They were reacting specifically to the incarceration of a Chartist lecturer, Henry Vincent, though for some time in a number of local communities there had been a swelling of anger deriving from extreme working and living conditions. Chartist lecturers had been touring the area for months, agitating on political and economic issues. This was the biggest mobilization of working people in British history to that date.

On 5 August 1842 an employer in Stalybridge imposed a wage cut and verbally insulted his workforce. The workers walked out of the factory, met on some wasteland, divided into squads of flying pickets and set off to parade through factory villages, pulling out factory after factory from Stalybridge to Manchester. In three weeks the strike spread across the north of England, the central band of Scotland and even had repercussions in the capital. As in South Wales earlier, workers in these areas had been suffering serial privation, during which Chartist activists had pressed their arguments, sold their papers and organized cells. Central to the action was a small group of working-class Chartist activists who seized the initiative after the first walkout, calling for immediate flying picketing.

In February 1848, left-wing Chartists meeting in a pub in central London heard news of the outbreak of revolution in France and Austria. They raced out on to the street to celebrate. Their high level of excitement was rapidly translated into a nationwide organizational drive for a new petition of Parliament, and two months later a mass demonstration was held at Kennington. As in both previous cases, groups were formed or revived, organizing through meetings and the circulation of papers and pamphlets.

In July 1888 three young women working at Bryant and May's match factory in Bow, East London, were accused of lying to the press, sacked and removed from the factory. The workforce, largely consisting of teenage women, followed them from the factory and ran nearly three miles to Fleet Street to seek a radical newspaper editor, Annie Besant. Thus began the match girls' strike. Only a week before the walkout Annie Besant, a middle-class socialist, responded immediately to reports of intense exploitation of young women in East End sweatshops by going down to the factory in Bow to speak to the women after work. The victimization they suffered was a direct result of the article she wrote for her little newspaper, *The Link.*

The women's cause was taken up by socialists who organized workplace and community collections to sustain the strikers. The women won and their success was to act as an inspiration to other workers throughout London's East End. It set in motion a militant movement that ultimately spread nationwide, creating the union drive known as New Unionism.

On 30 November 1999 the Seattle police set about clubbing and tear-gassing direct action demonstrators, who were attempting to halt the proceedings of the World Trade Organization in Seattle by locking on and blocking the entrance to the conference centre. The exceptional violence of the police enraged trade unionists taking part in a parallel demonstration against the same target. Despite the attempts of the labour union stewards to prevent their members joining the direct action contingents, the workers broke through their ranks to engage in shoulder-to-shoulder battles with the police. In the process, a new alliance was forged. It could be argued that the gratuitous violence of the police, flashed round the world via TV and the internet, was a key factor in the worldwide impact of the events in Seattle. Though fresh agendas remained to be written, this movement carried on in North America through the year 2000, registering further successes in Washington DC in April and Windsor (Ontario) in May, and at both nominating conventions in the summer. Subsequently it spread internationally to Millau, Okinawa, Melbourne, Prague and beyond.

In each of these examples, an accidental element intruded into specific situations, bringing about a qualitative change in antagonistic relationships. But there was also deliberate and determined action by militant activists. For the subordinate elements, at least, there appear to have been strong shifts in their mental landscapes. Confrontation with the state in 1839 brought an organizational shift towards workers' party building, in 1842 towards flying picketing and organized trade unionism, and in the defeat of April 1848 the first significant debate about *social* democracy. The match girls' dispute in 1888 taught both the need for the unskilled to enter civil society and the possibility of their doing so. The wider movement of New Unionism formed the basis of both general unionism in Britain and independent labour representation.

The Seattle effect is still provisional. Two things can be asserted. First, new alliances were apparently shaped on its streets. The disparate elements of the broadly 'green' movement achieved a common denominator: namely, anti-capitalism. In its first year the new movement relentlessly pursued the World Bank, the IMF and the World Trade Organization, the institutions that most clearly represent world capitalism in the new century. Secondly, Seattle and the subsequent events have spawned a new and widening debate on critical issues of strategy and goals for the anti-capitalist movement.

I have argued strongly for the significance of the accidental or surprise element in the trajectory of movements. This might just suggest a spontaneous character. But such a conclusion would be mistaken. There is a need to separate moments from process. Moments may contain 'accidental' elements that could not be prepared for. The belligerent arrogance of the Stalybridge factory owner in 1842, the Bryant and May manager/director who sacked the girls, and the indisciplined rage of the Seattle police are obvious examples. On the other hand, it is important to point out that factory bosses and police behave in these ways with great regularity without provoking a militant response. To understand what makes a difference at certain points requires an examination of the history of both subjective and objective factors that have their conjuncture in 'the moment'.[9] The subjective factors include determined initiatives by individuals who, in Huey Newton's language, 'seize the time' and the accumulated histories of grievances such as we see in the Chartist period. On the other hand, the factors might be quite obscure, or a mixture of the obscure and the obvious, as seems to have been the case with the match girls.

With the Chartist movement, obvious factors predominate in our understanding, though the obscure still play a significant part. When looking at Newport in 1839 it seems evident that columns of working men in various states of armed intent would at some point clash with the armed forces of the state. We also know that during the previous year Chartist lecturers like Henry Vincent had been touring the towns and villages of South Wales, spreading the message of the Charter. We also have evidence of economic fluctuations taking families to the edge of starvation. And there seems to have been a sophisticated network of committees rooted in the working-class communities and workplaces.[10]

In 1842 it is easier to trace the sinews of organization going back some years. Several of the known strike leaders had personal political histories extending backwards into the agitations of the late 1820s and the 1830s. It is also very likely that workers engaged in the mass strike had themselves participated in previous activities especially in the Manchester area, although the West Midlands, Potteries and West Yorkshire were also areas of strong radical and trade union traditions where meetings, pamphlets and working-class newspapers were already embedded in working-class culture. These were the areas where *The Northern Star* built the strongest base of its considerable readership between 1838 and 1842. Even after defeat and downturn in 1842, this culture did not disappear. Moving on to the ground temporarily vacated by militant suffrage organization in this period, the Chartist Land Association kept the political traditions alive despite state vigilance. When the tocsin of European revolution was heard in the spring of 1848, the dormant movement sprang to life.

When we look at the match girls' dispute, there are no such obvious signposts. There had been earlier struggles, the most recently uncovered being a brief strike for wage increases in 1886. A firmer piece of evidence relating to class struggle attitudes among the workers came from the episode of the Gladstone statue.[11] When Annie Besant met the girls in June 1888, among their complaints was the charge that George Bryant, the managing director, had levied a 'voluntary' contribution on the workers for the erection of a statue to the Liberal Prime Minister, W. E. Gladstone. It was reported as if it had taken place in the very recent past. The truth was that the episode had occurred some six years before the strike – when a substantial portion of the 1888 workforce was not old enough to have been employed. It appears that the episode, which had included some direct action by workers, had become embedded in the collective memory of the workers to be pulled out for service at an appropriate moment. However, it is probably not in direct class confrontation that the key to the match girls' rebellion lies. We must instead look to an Irish dimension that became clear only on the recent discovery of the factory's ethnic composition.[12] The labour force at Bryant and May was heavily Irish. The community in which they lived and worked was Irish. Irish nationalist politics was conducted at a high level of activity in the 1880s. It was very likely that many members of the workforce came from families involved in that activity. Anti-British sentiment was rife during the late 1880s. As recently as March 1888, a mass meeting to protest the arrest of nationalist leaders in Dublin had taken place at Tower Hill in London. It was attended by large numbers of people, who marched in columns from the local Irish community among which the Bryant and May factory was situated. The Irish character of all movements in the East End is an important key to understanding the upsurge of the unskilled, of which the match girls were the vanguard.

It is important also to register the importance of Irish people and politics in the emergence and growth of the socialist movement in the 1880s. Socialists had campaigned on the Irish question for most of the decade, selling papers and recruiting members to their organizations. It was not an accident that when the militant strikes began, strikers looked to socialist workers who, while not themselves Irish, were known to have Irish sympathies. These men, Tom Mann, Ben Tillett, Will Thorne and John Burns, had gained the confidence of the Irish communities, who looked to them for leadership in the industrial struggles that took place between 1888 and the early 1890s. Of course, their high profiles in campaigns over free speech and unemployment meant that their impact was not limited to the Irish section of the unskilled workers' community.

Seattle completes a new chapter of a similar story. The scale of the event and its impact came as something of a surprise to commentators. Yet, if those commentators had closely observed the situation running up to the event, they could have seen it prefigured in organizations and protests over the previous period. Environmental campaigners with a very wide range of causes had very long histories. Networks were extensive, if small in the numbers connected. So too were those campaigning from university campuses against the labour practices of the multinational corporations, especially as they affected people in the Third World. An interesting feature here was the way this activity transformed its participants from purely idealist fighters to direct action critics of the institutions of the USA when they revealed the murky business practices of the universities themselves. This helped to forge new relations with labour unions.

Labour unions were themselves transformed by attrition in the Reagan years. The old manual unions, robbed of membership by deindustrialization, had launched membership drives in the public sector and on college campuses, changing their composition and opening themselves up to debate. Although their leaders were largely eager to stifle any impulses to direct action in their rank-and-file membership, this proved impossible in the heady atmosphere of the crowds outside the WTO meeting.

So 'the moment' was important – indeed, critical – but attention must be given to the threads of activity which arrived at Seattle, all with a central target in view, though not necessarily with exactly contingent objectives. It would also be right to note a further specificity in Seattle as the location of the protest. As noted above, the Pacific north-west was an area with special attraction for those seeking lifestyle changes after the downturn in the 1960s movement. In the late 1970s the software industry was in its infancy. The region was, of course, to develop as a leading edge of the high-tech industry, one of the most powerful reasons for the WTO meeting to end up there. The Seattle movement had a high incidence of participants with first- or second-generation radical histories. Unlike the nineteenth-century examples, we can examine both the voices of participants and a minute blow-by-blow account of the run-up to the event and the event itself.[13]

At this stage it is possible to make only provisional assessments of the nature of the new movement of which the battle in Seattle was a significant moment. Retrospect may reshape our perspective. Tentatively we can offer these suggestions. Seattle was a moment 'waiting' to occur. The proliferation of campaigns against the excesses of corporate capitalism was a strong feature of the last decade of the twentieth century. Environmental protest had become a regular part of news bulletins across the world. Knowledge of the threat to the planet's future was encyclopaedic among a growing constituency of both older seasoned activists and newcomers from the college campuses. With job security a distant memory, workers too arrived in Seattle with scores to settle. The alliance formed on the streets of the city was far from problematic. As future events in North America would show, labour union leaders would still maintain their capacity to confuse and mislead members. By simply playing with the calendar, as they did in Washington DC in April, they could both bring their members on a protest and keep them away from the 'wider' constituency. However, as several local initiatives were also to show, the new openness between green forces and union workers could be carried on. Union locals were represented at Florham Park, New Jersey in March, DC in April, LA in August and most powerfully at Windsor, Ontario in June.

This chapter has attempted to achieve two main goals. First, it has argued against the concept of spontaneity by emphasizing the deep significance of varied histories preceding the event. Secondly, it has stressed the importance of moments which, while having the element of the accidental, also have encapsulated within them those varied histories. All confirm the experience of history in capitalist societies marked by injustice and inequality: struggle is endemic.

2

The Strange Death of Liberal Bradford

Paul Grist

This chapter tells the story of two strikes. The first is the Manningham Mill strike of 1891, which ended in a defeat for the striking textile workers. In the aftermath of the strike, the Independent Labour Party (ILP) was established in Bradford. The second is the textile workers' strike of 1910. This was a sharp confrontation between the district's textile workers and employers. These two strikes fit into broad movements known as New Unionism and the Great Unrest. There is a theme that links my account of these strikes: the assault on liberalism both as an intellectual current and as an organized political force. In his book, *The Strange Death of Liberal England*, George Dangerfield locates the decline of the Liberal Party in the inability of classical liberalism to cope with the social tensions generated by mature capitalism.[1] In Bradford during the nineteenth century, many of these tensions were played out in microcosm. The tensions and rebellions that Dangerfield describes brought to an end the Liberal Party's political hegemony in the town.

The economics of classical British liberalism

The Russian Marxist Leon Trotsky defined British liberalism as 'the political generalisation of free trade'. In his words, 'The Manchester School had occupied a dominant position from the time of the bourgeois, property-qualified, electoral reforms of 1832 and the repeal of the Corn Laws in 1846. Over the course of the next half-century the doctrine of Free Trade seemed to be an immutable programme. Accordingly the leading role belonged to the Liberals.'[2] The Manchester school of economics was founded upon the general economic theory of Adam Smith. David Ricardo, a stockbroker and Liberal politician, developed Smith's ideas, believing that labour was the source of value. Ricardo wrote that 'Labour, like all other things which are purchased and sold, and which may be increased or diminished in quantity, has its natural and market price.'[3] Classical political economists such as David Ricardo observed how the market had transformed labour into a commodity. 'Like all other contracts, wages should be left to the fair and free competition of the market, and should never be controlled by the interference of the legislature.'[4]

Liberal politicians argued that it was the duty of government not to impinge upon, but to set free, 'the invisible hand' of the market. By the nineteenth century, the unity of the Liberal Party was established on the platform of free trade and minimal government interference – a 'nightwatchman state'. They professed a belief that the pursuit of individual self-interest furthered the interests of society as a whole. The poverty and inequality that Frederick Engels highlighted in his book about the English working class would eventually be overcome as wealth trickled down.

Bradford was one of the northern towns that grew rapidly in the first half of the century as a centre of manufacturing industry. In 1801 the total population of the town was only 13,264. By 1851 this had risen to 103,778; by 1911, after the incorporation of Thornbury, Eccleshill, Idle, North Bierley, Wyke, Thornton and Tong, its population was 288,458.[5] An 'industrial aristocracy' made fortunes: it included Henry Illingworth, for example, who sent his son to Cambridge, from where he became Liberal chief whip in the 1906 Liberal government; Francis Willey, who bought Blyth Hall in Nottingham and became Lord Barnby in 1922; the dyer H. W. Ripley, who sent his sons to Cheltenham (they in turn sent their sons to Harrow); and the Listers, Amblers, Salts, Mitchells, Wards and Priestmans, all of whom acquired fortunes during the nineteenth century.[6]

It is not surprising, therefore, that liberalism established political hegemony among the district's manufacturers. Between 1832 and 1859, out of a total of eighteen MPs returned to Parliament, only five had been Tories. Between 1861 and 1886 the Tories did not return a single MP from Bradford. Then, in 1895, the Tories won every Bradford seat. The old certainties of liberalism, free trade and minimum state interference, were breaking down. The largest and most powerful empire in the world was beginning to experience the onset of relative economic decline.

The individual capitalist had been crucial in the growth of the British economy. In the eighteenth century, the improvements in infrastructure necessary for the growth of industry had been financed by private money. The pottery manufacturer Josiah Wedgwood, for example, invested heavily in transport such as canals, linking his factories with ports and coal. In the late eighteenth and nineteenth centuries, the British economy grew on the basis of self-sufficient small and medium-sized industrial and commercial capital. By the 1880s the competition had changed.

Germany became a unified state in 1871. Unification encouraged the development of infrastructure. This made it possible to exploit the rich potential for iron and steel production in the Ruhr valley. The new unified German state used protectionism to nurture German manufacturing. National banks were established, such as the Deutsche Bank in 1870 and the Dresdner Bank in 1872, closely linked to industry. These banks could then marshal the capital necessary for large-scale long-term investment. Bank representatives sat on the corporate boards in every major industrial sector. The new factories, which were still for the most part small and medium sized, had the finance to invest in the most modern technology. Coal and steel were supplied through the syndicates and cartels supported by the state. By controlling quotas and prices, the cartels encouraged expansion in the scale of the enterprise and massive concentration of capital.[7] One German economist, Heymann, writing in 1904, highlighted the direction in which Germany was moving:

> Pure enterprises perish, they are crushed between the high price of raw material and the low price of the finished product . . . There remain, on the one hand, the big coal companies, producing millions of tons yearly, strongly organised in their coal syndicate, and on the other, the big steel plants, closely allied to the coal mines, having their own steel syndicate. These giant enterprises, producing 400,000 tons of steel per annum, with a tremendous output of ore and coal and producing finished steel goods, employing 10,000 workers quartered in company houses and sometimes owning their own railways and ports are the typical representatives of the German iron and steel industry. And concentration goes further and further. Individual enterprises are becoming larger and larger. An ever-increasing number of enterprises in one, or in several different industries join together in giant enterprises, backed up and directed by half a dozen big Berlin banks. In relation to the German mining industry, the truth of the teachings of Karl Marx on concentration is definitely proved.[8]

The American Revolution, which threw off the yoke of British rule, and later victory for the North in the American Civil War, combined to clear the way for the prodigious expansion of US industry. Successive American governments had encouraged the development of infrastructure, handing out vast tracts of land to railroad companies. The rail network grew from 23 miles of track in 1830 to 208,152 miles of track in 1890. Apart from providing communication and transport, the railroads consumed iron and steel. Concentration of capital and the growth of industry proceeded hand in hand. In 1879 $2.7 billion was invested in US manufacturing; $8.2 billion was invested in 1899, which increased to $20.8 billion by 1914. Corporations were formed, many of which remain today among the largest US multinational companies. By 1900 the Standard Oil Company was worth $122 million and the United States Steel Corporation was worth $1.4 billion. Again, like the new German state, the government of the emerging United States pursued a protectionist policy, exploiting its own immense market and revenue from imported goods.[9]

Between 1860 and 1873 textiles boomed. Then in 1874 the French government imposed a 10 per cent duty on textile imports. In 1879 the largest continental market for Bradford's worsted goods was effectively closed as the German government imposed a 30–40 per cent tariff. Then in 1890 the American government introduced the McKinley tariff, reducing by 50 per cent the value of exports to the USA.[10] The textile boom turned into prolonged depression interspersed with short periods of growth. The intensification of competition translated into increased pressure on workers; productivity was increased while wages were cut. In 1888 the *Bradford Observer* reported that 'One weaver will now mind in two looms as much as 11,000 to 12,000 ends for practically less wages than were once paid for minding two looms with a matter of 800 ends each.'[11]

The Manningham Mill strike

Aware of the threatened imposition of the McKinley tariff, the Bradford millionaire mill-owner, S. C. Lister, put his workers on overtime. His aim was to stockpile in order to offset the impact of industrial action. He must have known, given the climate of New Unionism, that there was a good probability that his plans to cut weavers' pay by up to 33 per cent would be resisted by the workforce.[12] On Tuesday, 9 December 1890 notices of the wage cut, to take effect from the 24th, were plastered around the mill. The weavers responded by inviting officials from the West Riding Weavers' and Textile Workers' Association to a meeting to advise them on what course of action to take. The union officials advised caution, setting up a committee to negotiate with management. A meeting with management was hastily convened. Ben Turner, a Socialist League member from Leeds, accompanied the union officials to the meeting. The bosses refused to compromise.

When the officials reported back to the weavers, Turner injected a more militant tone. He pointed out that company profits for the previous year had been £138,000 whereas the wage cut amounted to £7,000 and argued that the bosses should be forced to cut profits rather than wages. A second meeting with management confirmed that the bosses had no intention of withdrawing the wage reduction without a fight. By the weekend 1,000 weavers were on strike. As they lacked financial reserves, a manifesto was drawn up appealing for solidarity and financial support. 'In the face of these low wages we are of the opinion that we should be doing not only an injustice to ourselves but to the whole of the textile industry in the West Riding of Yorkshire by accepting the proposed reduction . . . Help us fight this enormous reduction. Our battle may be your battle in the immediate future.'[13]

Speakers addressed meetings across the north of England and collections were taken. Mill workers also took collection boxes around the streets of Bradford and surrounding villages. Over £11,000 was collected. The strike was reported in the left-wing German newspaper *Volkstribune* and messages of solidarity came from the American Federation of Labor and French trade unionists. By March, against the advice of cautious union officials, the workers in the spinning departments had joined the weavers on strike. This action cut against the sectionalism of the union structures and brought the whole mill out on strike.

Regular weekly meetings and demonstrations were held, involving thousands of mill workers, their families and supporters. Attitudes hardened. Police protected scabs and fought against the strikers. By late February the Liberal authorities were openly intervening to try and break the strike. The Watch Committee refused to grant authorization for the use of public places for meetings. The chief constable instructed publicans not to allow strikers to use their meeting rooms. This had the effect of politicizing the strike and driving a wedge through working-class support for the Liberal Party. Through March and April the size of the meetings and demonstrations swelled to between 20,000 and 60,000.[14] For the workers involved it became increasingly clear that the whole of Bradford's social, legal and political establishment was united against them.

On Sunday, 12 April, Ben Tillett, a London dockers' leader, addressed a meeting at St George's Hall organized by the Trades Council. Outside the hall, the police attacked an overflow meeting that was being addressed by Turner. Rioting continued into the night. Not long after these 'free speech' riots, the strike was called off. The strikers, although having widespread support, suffered a demoralizing defeat, effectively starved back to work.

In the aftermath of the strike, trade unionists and socialists involved in the Socialist League met with the express purpose of developing an electoral alternative to the Liberals. The committee that was established at this meeting defined its purpose as furthering 'the cause of direct Labour Representation on local bodies and Parliament'. Despite the polarizing effect of the strike, the leaders of official trade unionism in Bradford showed an extreme reluctance to break with the Liberal Party. A month before the 1892 election the question of whether to support Tillett or the Liberal candidate in the Bradford West constituency was discussed. In order to have the question discussed at all, the pro-Tillett union representatives maintained that it was a non-political issue. In the end it was decided to support Tillett by the margin of 47 votes to 33. The Liberal sections of the local union leadership were furious, assuring Mr Tillett that 'his candidature in West Bradford has driven a knife into every labour organisation in town'.[15] Tillett eventually polled 2,749 votes.

Tillett stood again in 1895. His vote held at 2,264. By this time the Independent Labour Party had around 2,000 members across Bradford and 29 ILP groups or clubs.[16] In 1896 Keir Hardie stood in Bradford East, coming away with 1,953 votes.[17] At a time when many working-class men and all women had no vote, the combined ILP vote for Bradford East and West was around 4,000. Hardie's election campaign involved a huge rally at St George's Hall. On the platform along with Hardie were Tom Mann and the Pankhursts. Hardie's election leaflet suggested that a vote for Hardie was a hand up 'from industrial slavery to social freedom'. By 1900 there were six 'Labour' councillors sitting on Bradford's council. However, it is important to remember that the growth of the ILP in the 1890s corresponded to a period not of working-class revival, but of defeats in the face of an employers' offensive. The circumstances of its birth and development stamped themselves on the character of the ILP. Independent political representation was often argued for in terms of an alternative to the industrial militancy that seemed to have failed.

The employers' offensive and the Labour Representation Committee

A royal commission was appointed in 1891 to investigate 'relations between workers and employers'. The commission stated that 'Formal organisations of employers usually make their appearance at a later date than those of the workmen and arise for purposes of joint resistance, when individual employers find themselves too weak to cope with the growing strength of trade unions.'[18] New Unionism had clearly rattled the bosses and concentrated their minds on the problem of how to deal with the militancy. In 1895 engineers in Belfast and on the Clyde came out on strike, demanding a wage rise. The engineering employers refused to give into their demands and after three months they went back to work defeated. In the wake of this strike a National Employers' Federation was formed.

Two years after the Clyde and Belfast strikes, the engineers in London advanced the demand for the eight-hour day. Around a hundred small firms agreed to the demand but the larger firms decided to fight. The employers in London used the Employers' Federation to organize a national lockout, which involved a quarter of all workers employed in the industry. What had begun as an offensive battle for the eight-hour day turned into a defensive struggle to defend pay and conditions. The employers now not only refused to accept the eight-hour day but demanded that the engineers formally accept piecework and the principle of working overtime, abandon every rule that limited the number of apprentices and repudiate all claim to interfere in the management of the firm. Furthermore, the employers demanded the right to settle claims with their workforce directly without intervention from the union. On 28 January 1898 the employers' demands, slightly modified, were accepted. Thirty weeks of strike action had ended in 'the most serious defeat British Trade Unionism had received in living memory'.[19]

Following the engineers' defeat, the president of the Trades Union Congress (TUC) warned that 'For the first time in the history of the movement we had to face a mammoth combination of military-led capital, whose object, as openly stated by its leader, was to cripple, if not crush the forces of trade unionism.'[20] The employers were pushing the union bureaucracy towards developing their own voice in Parliament, independent of the Liberal Party. At the 1895 TUC conference the ILP had been attacked as 'an anti-Labour, anti-trade-unionist movement'.[21] At the 1899 TUC conference the proposal to support independent parliamentary representation was reconsidered. The conference voted by a narrow margin, 546,000 votes to 434,000, to arrange a special conference to discuss ways of increasing representation.[22]

The foundation conference brought together trade union, ILP, Social Democratic Federation (SDF) and Fabian representatives. Proposals from the SDF representatives that the new party should adopt a revolutionary standpoint were rejected, as were proposals merely to continue pressurizing the Liberal Party to adopt Labour candidates. In the end Keir Hardie's proposal for 'a distinct Labour Group in Parliament, who shall have their own Whips' was adopted.[23] But it was the Taff Vale judgment that really forced the hands of the TUC. In July 1901, the Lords judged that the Amalgamated Railway Servants Society was responsible for 'offences' committed during a strike a few years previous. The union was ordered to pay £23,000 damages. A legal precedent had been set which effectively outlawed industrial action and made unions financially responsible even if they condemned the action of their own members. Trade union leaders, who had so reluctantly embarked on the experiment of developing independent parliamentary representation, now began to put their weight behind the project. By the time of the second conference of the Labour Representation Committee (LRC) in 1902, affiliations had grown from 350,000 to 450,000, and by 1903 affiliations had risen to 861,000.[24]

ILP leaders like Keir Hardie, Philip Snowden and Ramsay MacDonald had all begun as Liberals. In 1892 Hardie had declared that 'I have all my life given an independent support to the Liberal Party . . . I am in agreement with the present programme of the Liberal Party.' Meanwhile Snowden maintained that he was 'cradled and nurtured in Liberalism'. In 1899, MacDonald and Hardie wrote that liberalism and the ILP were linked through 'the true line of the progressive apostolic succession'.[25] The ILP did not attempt to fashion itself into an explicitly socialist alternative, either as an independent party or as a platform within the Labour Party. At the 1902 LRC conference, Hardie argued against calling the Labour Party a socialist party, claiming that if Labour supporters, 'being Socialists, had insisted that all should be Socialists, there could be no such gathering . . . They had fixed upon a common denominator that, when acting in the House of Commons, they should be neither Socialists, Liberals, nor Tories, but a Labour Party. Let them have done with Liberalism and Toryism and every "ism" that was not Labourism.'[26] The ILP became known as the 'soul' of the Labour Party; its left wing.

Bradford during the Great Unrest

The first decade of the twentieth century was a time of hardship for Bradford's textile workers. Wages had steadily declined. The wages of unskilled and semi-skilled workers were particularly hard hit, falling steadily from as much as 24s in 1872 to 14s 8d in 1906 for male workers, while women's wages dropped from 18s in 1874 to 12s 6d in 1901.[27] Yet, by the end of the decade, business appears to have been good for many textile firms. In January 1910, Lister and Co. Ltd announced that it would pay out dividends of 5 per cent to all shareholders. During February the directors of the Holden Company and Bradford Dyers also announced dividends of 5 per cent. Woolcombers announced dividends of 7 per cent and claimed that during the previous year the volume of business was greater than in any previous year. In the 10 March copy of the *Yorkshire Factory Times*, 'Dyasman' wrote that 'The strike may be a barbarous means, but until the workman has some better means of securing his rights and employers are prepared to negotiate with workmen collectively, there is nothing left for the workman but to stop the job.'[28]

The headline in the next week's *Factory Times* declared the 'revolt of the Bradford woolcombers'. On the previous Thursday, combers working in the Illingworth mills (which had become part of the Woolcombers group) walked out on unofficial strike. The dispute came from management's attempts to make two workers do the job that had previously been done by three. The workers' union attempted to arrange a meeting with the Illingworth managers to resolve the strike. The managers, however, refused to meet with union representatives. It seems they believed the strike would be easily beaten and took a completely uncompromising position. They badly misjudged the situation and the mood of the workers.

The Woolcombers' Union called a meeting for the following Monday night. On the night it was reported that upwards of a thousand men and women from the 22 firms organized in the textile syndicate attended the meeting. A resolution was carried to bring out the combers working for Woolcomber Ltd. However, on the same evening workers at the Greenwood and Co. mills, a company not in the syndicate, downed tools and walked out. At another mill, workers who had just received a 5 per cent pay rise also walked out 'to express sympathy with the strike movement'. The following day the paper reported that 'gangs' of workmen paraded from mill to mill encouraging workers to join the strike.

On Tuesday night a second union meeting was convened. This time the resolution that was adopted demanded a general wage rise, a uniform night turn with two half-hour breaks and a closed shop to operate in all textile factories. On the same evening, the employers met to organize their response to what had begun as a dispute involving two workers in one mill, and was now threatening to become a general textile strike across the whole district. The *Factory Times* reports that there was a representative from practically every firm in the city at the meeting. Stunned by the speed and militancy of developments, they desperately wanted to bring the strike to a halt and were prepared to make a deal. They resolved to meet with union representatives on Thursday night.

Over the next couple of days the momentum of the strike grew as it spread across the city's factories. For example, the *Factory Times* reports that striking woolcombers demonstrated through Cottingly and Bingley. Cottingly Mill was still working, so a group of strikers went into the mill to encourage the workers to walk out. It appears that the employers had notified the police, and the strikers were forcibly ejected from the premises. Later in the same afternoon, a group of 200 strikers marched to the mill with the same purpose of closing it down. This time they were met with a much stronger police presence. The police may have been able to prevent the flying pickets from entering the mill, but they could not prevent the workers inside from walking out, and afterwards they were greeted by the applause of the pickets. Bradford mills were 'turned out'. Strikers from Bowling Green Mill in Bingley marched to the Stanley Mill and brought the workers out there. The *Factory Times* also reports that wool mills in Keighley were grinding to a halt.

While the factory workers were busy spreading the strike across the town, the union officials were meeting with the employers. By the Friday, only a week after the initial walkout, they had come to an agreement. The deal on the table stipulated that joint boards involving employee and employer representatives should be established to deal with all future disputes arising from pay and conditions. Secondly, there would be an immediate wage rise followed by a further rise in August. Thirdly, night shifts would be made uniform and would include two paid half-hour breaks. Finally the deal was conditional on an immediate return to work.

The signatures on the deal are evidence of the potential scale of the strike. On the employers' side the agreement was signed by representatives of Holden and Sons, Illingworth and Sons, Greenwood and Co., Woolcombers Ltd, Jowett and Sons, and Holden Burnley and Co. From the union side the agreement was signed by officials from the Amalgamated Society of Dyers, the Woolcombers' Union and William Barker, the Secretary of Bradford Trades Council. Initially the agreement was not put to a meeting of the workers themselves. The meeting between union officials and management took place in the town hall. After the agreement was signed, the Lord Mayor walked out on to the town hall steps, where he read out the terms of the agreement to a demonstration of strikers.

William Barber then went to report back to the Trades Council, which unanimously supported the deal. In his address Barber stated that the difficult task would now be to persuade the strikers to accept the settlement and return to work. He expressed his hope that no attempt would be made the following day to sow dissension among the workers. He also told his audience that it was appalling for any official to have to face a strike of such magnitude, the strikers being like 'an untrained army'. He said he felt a desire to commend the police for the good spirit and praiseworthy tact they had shown throughout the week. Barber got his way and the strike was wound down, although it took some time to end as minor disputes rolled on in various mills across the city. These short strikes ended in quick victories. Black Dyke Mills in Queensbury walked out. Several hundred workers at Drummond's Mill on Lumb Lane walked out and their demands were immediately met.

The events in Bradford were not unique. Similar protests and strikes were organized in textile and cotton districts all over the north, and this was just the start. Over the next three years national dock, railway and coal strikes rocked the Liberal government. At one point London was virtually controlled and run by a strike committee for a week. In the same period the Tories plotted sedition in Northern Ireland, making clear that should the Liberal government grant Home Rule in Ireland, they would support the Ulster Orangemen taking up arms. At its most extreme the suffrage movement used bombs, suicide missions and hunger strikes to campaign against an injustice that it was almost impossible for the Liberals to justify.

All the various elements of the unrest came together during August 1913. William Murphy, the owner of the *Irish Independent* newspaper and the Dublin United Tramway Company (and also an important figure in the Irish Home Rule Party), launched an all-out attack on the Irish Transport and General Workers' Union. Murphy sacked all the union members working in the dispatch department of his newspaper, and two days later sacked 100 men working in the parcel department of his tram company. As the union fought back, the employers united in locking out the workers. By the end of September, a general lockout gripped Dublin, which involved around 400 employers and over 25,000 workers.[29] Throughout the streets of Dublin, strikers fought running battles with the police.

Larkin appealed to British workers to take solidarity action. On 16 September, Liverpool railwaymen blocked all Dublin traffic. It has been reported that solidarity action was taken by workers in Birmingham, Sheffield, Crewe, Derby and elsewhere. In South Wales two rail workers were sacked for refusing to handle Dublin traffic and 30,000 workers struck in support.[30] In Bradford collections were taken in the streets for the Dublin workers.[31]

Larkin was jailed and on 1 November a meeting was held at the Albert Hall to demand his release. According to Dangerfield:

> That Albert Hall meeting on the night of 1st November 1913, presents
> us with a very convenient phenomenon, for on the speakers' platform
> sat, in serried ranks, the united grievances of England. For the first and
> the last time Irish nationalism, Militant Suffrage and the Labour unrest
> were met together . . . for what? . . . One thing, at least, is certain; the
> vigorous and passionate oratory, rising in increasing volume and a va-
> riety of accents beneath the roof of the Albert Hall, was not – as some
> people rather ingeniously imagined – merely the irritable expulsion of
> reformist steam. It resembled rather the gathering of a heavy cloud,
> caught up out of some teeming sea; for its strength was drawn from
> every factory, every workshop, mine, wharf and slum throughout the
> length and breadth of England . . . The workers of England . . . con-
> trived to project a movement which took a revolutionary course and
> might have reached a revolutionary conclusion.[32]

During the period of the employers' offensive, most ILP leaders had
become more and more distanced from attempts to use extra-parliamentary pressure to advance the interests of the working class. Indeed, it
had been the failure of militant action in the mill strike, and the behaviour
of Liberal politicians during that strike, that had convinced a majority on
the Bradford Trades Council to support an independent candidate. When
the pressure finally lifted the lid on the bitterness and anger that had been
accumulating, these ILP leaders were horrified rather than connected to
the militancy of workers. MacDonald claimed that 'Socialism must be
parliamentary or it is nothing', while the ILP's *Socialist Review* asked
'how is the nation to deal with a menace of such almost incredible coercion – a coercion which is altogether apart from the question of the
justifiability of the claims of the workers?' The ILP could no longer even
claim to represent the left of the Labour Party during the Great Unrest.
Whatever their betrayals and treacheries, the trade union leadership, due
to their position in society, were in many ways more sensitive to the mood
of their rank-and-file members than the ILP, shut away in municipal and
parliamentary committees. The ILP actually lost influence during the
strikes. Why was political representation necessary when strikes could
get the job done? But politics was necessary.

In 1912 delegations from the German SPD visited Bradford and frater-
nal greetings of solidarity were expressed all round. Later in the year
Bradford's Trades Council minutes reported correspondence from the
London office of the Second International, requesting that the council
vote on a resolution calling for immediate political strikes in the event of
war. The resolution was eventually raised and passed.[33] When war finally
broke out across Europe, a 'protest' meeting was called in Bradford.
Nobody at the meeting called for the strikes and demonstrations for which
the Trades Council had committed itself to call. Fred Jowett, Bradford's
ILP MP, expressed nothing but resignation and hoped only 'to bring
peace as soon as possible on a basis that will endure'.

Conclusion

The main beneficiary of the Liberal Party's demise was the Labour Party. Even the Labour Party's left wing, the ILP, restrained rather than developed industrial militancy during the Great Unrest. The ILP therefore failed to develop its influence and roots within the working class during the most revolutionary period in British history since Chartism. Consequently, despite its impressive municipal support in terms of council seats and votes, and despite the background of industrial unrest, the ILP was unable to mobilize industrial militancy against the war. The great Liberal project – free-market, laissez-faire capitalism – ended in catastrophe. Opposition to the war did eventually take root. When the war finally ended the Soviets were in power in Russia and Europe was gripped by revolution. The political and intellectual landscape would never be the same again.

3

Palmiro Togliatti, Loyal Servant of Stalin

Tobias Abse

Palmiro Togliatti died in 1964 but is still the subject of heated controversy in a way that British figures of a comparable era, such as Hugh Gaitskell and Nye Bevan, are not. The reason for this ongoing debate is that Togliatti has been the object of a cult on the part of large sections of the Italian left – political activists as well as intellectuals – for decades since his death. Here I am not just referring to Armando Cossutta and his followers in the Partito dei Comunisti Italiani (PDCI), whose nostalgia for Togliatti is no longer curbed by Bertinotti in the way that it was before their split with Rifondazione Comunista in October 1998. (The split was accompanied by atavistic and frenzied attacks on Trotskyists, allegedly the principal architects of Bertinotti's adoption of an anti-governmental line, that were reminiscent of Togliatti at his worst.) The cult extends far beyond the Cossuttiani and includes influential currents that are part of the political mainstream.

Former Prime Minister Massimo D'Alema regarded Togliatti as his political hero and role model. It could be argued that D'Alema was indeed a third-rate ersatz Togliatti in some respects, such as his devotion to the holding of power as an end in itself, his love of intrigue and his willingness to compromise with any force or personality that he regarded as possessing more power than he did – most notably Berlusconi, for whose political resurrection and election victory in May 2001 he is primarily responsible. Similarities might be detected in D'Alema's obsession with constitutional reform – his beloved Bicamerale, which he saw as equivalent to the Constituent Assembly of 1946–8 – at the expense of the social and economic questions that preoccupy organized labour, the pensioners and the unemployed; or in his willingness to prostrate himself before the demands of the Catholic Church, eager to attack the secular state school system with renewed vigour.

D'Alema failed to expand his party membership, despite fusions with other left groups and a second name change, from Partito Democratico della Sinistra (PDS) to Democratici di Sinistra (DS). Even more significantly, he failed to build a large and devoted personal following amongst the popular masses. So the resemblance to Togliatti had its limits, even supposing the methods of the 1940s and 1950s could have been successfully applied in Italy at the end of the twentieth century, which is clearly a very debatable proposition. However, my purpose in mentioning D'Alema's admiration for Togliatti is not to discuss the all too evident shortcomings of an ephemeral administration that staggered on from October 1998 to April 2000. Rather it is to substantiate my claim that a Togliatti cult, whose adherents are almost as impervious to rational argument as the proponents of Pius XII's sanctification, still exists in twenty-first-century Italy.

It is worth noting that the cult has a few British adherents, most notably Donald Sassoon, with whom I have engaged in a rather fruitless debate on the question of Togliatti and 1956 in an academic journal quite recently.[1] The problem with British writing on Togliatti is not the size of the group of fervent Togliattians – a handful of academics with a Euro-Communist past and close links with Italy. The problem is that the absence of English translations of any of the more critical works about Togliatti has allowed the Hobsbawm/Sassoon interpretation to shape the majority perception of a figure who has never aroused the interest of Anglophone academic circles in the way that Antonio Gramsci did 25 years ago, and to a much lesser extent still does.

The time has come to destroy the Togliatti cult for once and for all. The anti-Stalinist left should not be deterred from this key objective by the claim, often made by Togliatti's apologists, that any attack on Togliatti is an attack on the Italian Republic that arose from the Resistance. The sub-text of this claim is that to attack Togliatti is to ally oneself with neo-fascists or their revisionist fellow-travellers, such as Renzo De Felice.[2] First, the defence of the Resistance legacy does not entail the defence of a figure who, unlike Longo and Secchia, played no direct role in the Resistance, quite deliberately choosing to return to southern Italy and not northern Italy in 1944. Secondly, one can be well aware that some of the research on Togliatti carried out in the newly opened Russian archives may be motivated by old-fashioned Cold War perspectives without rejecting or ignoring valuable new empirical evidence unearthed by historians such as Aga-Rossi and Zaslavsky.[3] Aga-Rossi and Zaslavsky may have been pupils of De Felice, but their approach to documentary evidence has a seriousness that their master had abandoned by the end of his prolific career. Their tirades about totalitarianism or paeans of praise to the USA for allegedly safeguarding democracy in the world after 1945 may irritate socialist historians.[4] This is evident from what in my view was a slightly ill-judged response by Barbara Rossi in a recent issue of *Revolutionary History*.[5] But they do not invent or manipulate primary sources.

Lest this rather polemical introduction seem like an attack on straw men, it must be pointed out that the only recent full-scale biography of Togliatti, the one produced by Aldo Agosti in 1996,[6] represented a regression, not an advance on Giorgio Bocca's pioneering work of 1973.[7] Bocca's book was written by a journalist less than a decade after the death of its subject and was to a substantial degree dependent on secondary works and a wide range of oral testimony by Togliatti's contemporaries, in the absence of archival material accessible to a non-Communist writer. But it nevertheless represented a serious effort to unearth the truth. Agosti's recent life, despite its deployment of most of the apparatus of conventional historical scholarship and its pretence of objectivity, represents a stubborn and determined effort to salvage as much as possible of the old Communist historiography.

It would be impossible in the space available to deal with the entire career of Palmiro Togliatti, let alone the entire history of Italian Communism during his political lifetime. The fact that I am going to adopt 'a history from above' perspective in this account does not mean that there is not scope for 'history from below', as the work of Tom Behan among others has so clearly demonstrated.[8] Nor is it my intention to argue that the Partito Comunista Italiano (PCI), once it became a legal mass party with deep roots in Italian soil, remained uninfluenced by the society in which it worked. The PCI's gradual transformation from a fairly orthodox Stalinist party to a basically social democratic one, long before its dissolution in 1991, cannot be denied. Although this transformation only really gathered pace after Togliatti's death, paradoxically the tensions between Togliatti and Khrushchev – whose de-Stalinization did not meet with Togliatti's approval[9] – had the unintended consequence of opening up some space for debate within the Italian party. This was a development that a more consistent alignment with the new Soviet leadership would probably have prevented. Nonetheless, my starting point in this chapter is that Togliatti was a Stalinist politician, in all probability the greatest and most intelligent of all the western European Stalinist politicians.

When I say my aim is to destroy the myth of Togliatti, I do not mean to dispute his significance as a historical figure. My quarrel is with his supporters' interpretation of his significance as being allegedly the de facto founder of a specifically Italian Communism, a reluctant and half-hearted Stalinist who did his best to protect his own comrades from international Stalinism and surreptitiously preserved Gramsci's legacy. Togliatti was undoubtedly the most important figure in twentieth-century Italian Communism, leading the Italian Communist Party from Gramsci's imprisonment in 1926 until his own death in 1964. Indeed, in terms of practical politics rather than Marxist theory, Togliatti was far more significant than Gramsci. Gramsci's own period as party leader was very brief, about two years in 1924–6. For contrary to Stalinist mythology, subsequently repeated to wider non-Italian audiences by the Euro-Communists, the first leader of the Italian Communist Party was not Antonio Gramsci but Amadeo Bordiga, and Gramsci was heavily reliant on the Comintern in toppling Bordiga in 1924. The Como Conference of mid-May 1924 demonstrated Gramsci's abject failure to win over the party's leading cadres to the new line espoused by his recently formed Central Committee majority.

However, the fact that Togliatti enjoyed such a long and, in his own terms, successful political career does not mean that Togliatti was really *Il Migliore*, 'the best' of his comrades, as the cult has always claimed. Far from it. As the dates given above should clearly indicate, his years as a leading figure in the international Communist movement coincided with Stalin's years of absolute power and, to use an old cliché, it was no accident that this was the case.

In labelling Togliatti a Stalinist politician, I deliberately mean to emphasize both the adjective and the noun. As Togliatti's Stalinism will be discussed throughout the remainder of this chapter, I want to take this opportunity to justify my characterization of Togliatti as a professional politician, rather than a professional revolutionary like Lenin or Trotsky. Togliatti was not, except perhaps for a few years at the beginning of his career when he was influenced by Gramsci and Bordiga, a genuine revolutionary. The depth of his commitment to revolutionary politics even in those early years is open to question in the light of his behaviour in 1923, in the aftermath of the December 1922 fascist massacre of the Torinese left, a period when Gramsci was in Moscow and Bordiga was in prison. As Bocca asks, rhetorically: 'Was he ill from December 1922 to April 1923?'[10] Togliatti's sister told Bocca that, to the delight of their mother, a devout Catholic who had never had any sympathy with her son's involvement in left-wing politics, Togliatti returned to the family home after the December 1922 massacre, that he was not ill, that he had more or less abandoned political life and that he asked her to go to the university and enquire on his behalf about re-enrolling for his uncompleted philosophy degree.[11]

Terracini, left in effective charge of the party, after vainly making a series of private and indirect attempts to get Togliatti to return to an active role in the party, was forced to go to *Avanti*, the still legal daily of the hated Socialists, and request the publication of a communiqué announcing that 'Comrade Togliatti is invited to get back into direct relations with the Executive Committee of the Party immediately.'[12] Togliatti never really forgave Terracini for his public humiliation and was always eager to use sanctions against him when he opposed the Stalinist line on various questions in later years. Most notably, he expelled Terracini from the party in 1939 for opposing the Nazi–Soviet Pact and only re-admitted him to the party in 1945, rather than 1941. Camilla Ravera, another leading figure in the party in the 1920s, commenting on Togliatti's behaviour in early 1923, said: 'For Togliatti politics was the art of government, not revolutionary militancy.'[13]

In saying that Togliatti was not a genuine revolutionary, I do not mean merely that as a Stalinist he played an objectively counter-revolutionary role – although this was certainly the case in the two revolutionary or potentially revolutionary situations in which he intervened after 1919–20, namely Spain between 1936 and 1939 and Italy between 1944 and 1948. My argument is that he was never, at least after the *biennio rosso*, attracted by the notion of revolution in the way the more naively Stalinist Pietro Secchia clearly was in December 1947 and July 1948, to cite but two instances.[14]

In this context, given the importance of the First World War in dividing revolutionaries from reformists in the European labour movement, it is, to say the least, interesting that Togliatti was not a revolutionary defeatist, or even a pacifist, at any stage of the First World War. While Gramsci's own record during the Intervention Crisis of 1914–15 was, to put it kindly, ambiguous, Togliatti became a consistent interventionist and ended up volunteering for service during the war. In 1915 his short sight meant that he had to join the Red Cross rather than the armed forces but a change in the rules in 1916 allowed him to join the army, in which he remained until 1918. All the evidence suggests that Togliatti left the Socialist Party for the duration of the war.[15] It is perhaps equally significant that during the 1926–9 period, when Togliatti ceased to be under Gramsci's influence – refusing to forward the latter's letter of October 1926 to the Central Committee of the Soviet Communist Party – but had not definitively submitted to the influence of Stalin, he was a Bukharinite. In short, Togliatti sided with what appeared to be the most gradualist and moderate variant of Bolshevism.

Having marshalled some evidence that suggests Togliatti was a professional politician rather than a Communist revolutionary in his basic outlook, I want to turn rapidly to his Stalinism. This is because some of the material that I have already presented, while undermining his revolutionary credentials, might have had the side-effect of suggesting that he was a consistent proponent of a specifically Italian national and peaceful road to socialism. In other words, I might have unintentionally reinforced precisely the impression that the bulk of his latter-day apologists wish to convey.

Togliatti in the Spanish Civil War (1936–9)

Given the limitations of space, I will centre my case on two episodes in his career: his role in Spain between 1936 and 1939 and his alleged authorship of the *svolta di Salerno*, the Salerno turning point of March 1944. An examination of Togliatti's role in Spain is central to any judgement about the extent of his Stalinism and sheds a great deal of light on his conduct in Italy between 1944 and 1948. Any of Togliatti's actions in

Moscow in the 1930s might be seen by his apologists as actions under-taken under duress, with his willingness to accuse or even condemn others – such as the Polish Communists – in the course of Stalin's terror in the Soviet Union being excused as essential for his self-preservation or, in some versions, the preservation of the Italian party as a whole. The Span-ish case is different in that Togliatti was a protagonist in his own right on western European soil, in a context of political freedom rather than fascist or Stalinist dictatorship, taking the initiative and passing on instructions to others.

Many have portrayed Togliatti as the leading Communist in Spain during the civil war. Alexander Orlov, the chief NKVD (Soviet secret police) official in Spain from September 1936 until his defection in July 1938, included the following statement in his testimony to the US Senate Sub-committee on Internal Security in February 1957: 'Palmiro Togliatti was also in Spain . . . with me, and he had been a good friend of mine at the time. He directed the Spanish Communist Party and the Spanish Commu-nist military forces on behalf of Moscow.'[16] The Spanish Communist militia leader Valentin Gonzalez, better known as El Campesino, who es-caped from the Soviet Union after the Second World War, wrote in 1952: 'During the Spanish Civil War, the man who in effect directed the Com-munist Party was "Alfonso", the famous Palmiro Togliatti, one of the top-ranking figures in the Comintern . . . José Diaz and the entire Polit-buro did nothing more than carry out his directives.'[17]

Lest it be assumed that Orlov was too much under American influ-ence or that El Campesino, 'to all intents and purposes an illiterate',[18] was too readily swayed in his judgements by Julian Gorkin, the leader of the Partido Obrero de Unificacion Marxista (POUM) who helped him write his memoirs, it needs to be underlined that similar opinions about Togliatti's centrality were expressed by others who did not break with Moscow. For example, Enrique Lister, the prominent Spanish Commu-nist militia leader, who remained an unrepentant supporter of the Soviet Union, claimed in 1977 that Togliatti 'was the delegate in Spain of the Communist International whom the entire Politburo obeyed without a murmur'.[19] The American Communist John Gates, head commissar in 1938 of the Fifteenth Brigade, asserted in an unpublished manuscript about the International Brigades that 'Togliatti was the most powerful Communist figure in Spain. His responsibility was the whole policy of the Spanish Communists . . . The enormous growth of the Spanish Com-munist Party after the fascist revolt must be attributed in large part to his advice and leadership . . . Togliatti was a brilliant tactician, probably the most able in the Communist world.'[20]

Santiago Carrillo, who had been the leading figure in the Communist youth movement during the Spanish Civil War, wrote in 1971, when he was Secretary of the Partido Comunista de España (PCE) in exile, that Togliatti 'was an invaluable counsellor and, for many of us, who were very young and inexperienced, a veritable maestro'.[21] Fernando Claudin, a contemporary of Carrillo, who played a leading role in the PCE for three decades before his expulsion in 1965, wrote in 1970: 'Togliatti played a role of prime importance in the political guidance and even the political leadership of the PCE during the Civil War. Along with him were the Bulgarian Stepanov, the Hungarian Gerö, the Argentinian Codovilla and, of course, the eminent Soviet "advisers" both military and political'[22] – a statement that implicitly gives Togliatti primacy over all the other foreign Communists in Spain.

Alongside these testimonies from Communists and ex-Communists we have the recollections of Justo Martinez Amutio, the Socialist governor of Albacete, the headquarters of the International Brigades, who had personal dealings with Togliatti. In his memoirs published in 1974, Amutio claimed:

> He was the most skilful of all the agents sent by Stalin and the real director of Communist Party policy until the end of the war. I considered him . . . superior in intelligence and ability to Stepanov . . . The entire political orientation of the Comintern within the International Brigades was directed by this man, who together with Stepanov planned the domestic and military policies of the Communist Party . . . He was in the habit of asking questions courteously, insisting on details and learning through various channels about the personality of the most prominent political and military figures, wheedling out of his interlocutors their views. But, as far as he was concerned, no one could judge either from his gestures or facial expressions . . . what he was thinking or feeling.[23]

While one maverick British historian has recently attempted to minimise the influence of Togliatti and the Comintern over the PCE during the civil war,[24] the issue that has given rise to lengthy and bitter disputes is not Togliatti's influence in Spain but the date of his arrival there. The official version, first expounded in a hagiographical authorized biography by the Ferreras during Togliatti's lifetime,[25] is that Togliatti arrived in July 1937 – in other words, after the May events in Barcelona, the murder of the POUM leader Andres Nin and the successful Communist manoeuvres to remove Largo Caballero, the left-wing Socialist, as Spanish Prime Minister. But Togliatti's first serious biographer, the distinguished Italian journalist Giorgio Bocca,[26] did not subscribe to this version.

The controversy over the date of Togliatti's arrival in Spain had started during Togliatti's lifetime as a result of the memoirs of Jesus Hernandez being brought to the attention of the Italian public.[27] Hernandez was a leading figure in the Spanish Communist Party during the civil war and one of the two Communist cabinet ministers in both the Caballero government and the first Negrin government. As Julian Gorkin, a POUM leader who survived the civil war, explained in a letter to Bolloten: 'Palmiro Togliatti had his friends, the Ferrara couple, write that biography after I had denounced him at a meeting in Rome for his role in Spain and had the important daily newspaper *Il Messagero* publish long extracts from the book by Jesus Hernandez.'[28]

Bocca's opinion does not just rest on his belief in the credibility of Hernandez's controversial memoirs, a belief to which I will return in due course. Bocca also invokes the testimony of Scoccimarro, an important figure in the early leadership of the PCI. Bocca quotes Scoccimarro as saying of Togliatti that 'he was in Spain during the war and also before',[29] and argues that the degree of detail in Togliatti's articles and essays on Spain bears this out, citing various texts from 1934 onwards. More to the point, Bocca also cites a direct exchange with Scoccimarro in which he cross-examined the latter on the fundamental issue: "'Was he already in Spain in '36 or did he get there in '37?" And Scoccimarro says "He was there in '36. I am absolutely certain of it."'[30] The weakness of Scoccimarro as a source is that he was not present in Spain himself between 1936 and 1939 but confined to an Italian fascist gaol, so his recollection would have been based on conversations with other PCI leaders.

Bocca names the three leading Italian Communists present in Spain who backed up Togliatti's denials as Vittorio Vidali, Luigi Longo and Longo's wife, Teresa Noce.[31] As late as 1988 Paolo Spriano, the official historian of the Italian Communist Party, stressed that 'All the Italian Communist leaders who found themselves in Spain in 1936 have testified that Togliatti only arrived there in the summer of 1937',[32] as if this constituted a definitive rebuttal of Hernandez's claims. But he was sufficiently shrewd not to name these leaders. Since the trio in question were Vidali, a sinister figure widely believed to have been directly implicated in Nin's murder,[33] Longo, Togliatti's successor as party leader, and Longo's wife, the commonsense response, which Bocca did not feel the need to put on paper, is bound to be: 'they would say that, wouldn't they?' Moreover, Bocca, whose biography contains much evidence of Togliatti's dishonest accounts of many stages in his life, makes some specific points about Togliatti's unreliability with regard to his own record in Spain. He shows that Togliatti's comments to his biographers, the Ferraras, criticizing the infantile and sectarian position of the Spanish Communists in 1931 in the harshest of terms, make no sense given his own uncritical adherence to the Third Period line at the time, and that Togliatti's response in May 1962 to Hugh Thomas's book on the Spanish Civil War was dishonest.[34]

In addition to raising queries about Togliatti's reliability, Bocca discusses the Communist attempt to discredit Hernandez's testimony by personal vilification, quoting the claim by Francisco Anton, La Pasionaria's lover and a long-time Spanish Communist leader, that 'Hernandez invented Togliatti's presence in Madrid in the first months of the war on the advice of his CIA financiers to show that the Spanish Party was dependent on the Comintern.'[35] Bocca convincingly responds that, since Communist sources do not seek to deny the presence of the other four foreign Communists listed by Hernandez – the Argentinian Codovilla, the Bulgarian Stepanov, the Hungarian Gerö and the Frenchman Duclos – at the relevant meeting, adding Togliatti to the list would be superfluous and pointless in terms of what Anton claimed to be the objective of Hernandez and his alleged CIA controllers, namely showing the PCE to be taking orders from Moscow.

Destroying Hernandez's credibility has always been an essential goal for pro-Togliatti writers, given that no intelligent investigator of Togliatti's life and times could sincerely believe that Togliatti always told the truth about his own past, however vigorously they might assert the contrary in public for political reasons. Hence Spriano, whose intelligence and industry nobody would dream of disputing, but whose entire career rested on a privileged relationship with the PCI, resorted to every conceivable way of discrediting Hernandez as a source. Firstly, he cites Hugh Thomas and Gabriel Jackson's negative views of Hernandez's book.[36] The point here is not whether they have particularly convincing arguments to offer in favour of their positions, but that one is English, the other is American and neither is, or has ever been, a Communist. Secondly, Spriano approvingly cites a negative description of Hernandez in a book written by the POUM leader Julian Gorkin in 1941 when the former was still a Stalinist. It is a description whose vitriolic tone is hardly surprising given that Gorkin was living in Mexico where Trotsky himself had recently been murdered by a Stalinist agent. Thirdly, in the very next footnote Spriano attacks Gorkin for using Hernandez's 1953 book as his source for the claim that Togliatti went to the Soviet Embassy in Madrid to find out what the GPU (Soviet secret police) had done to Nin. Why Spriano should regard Gorkin, whom he would have seen as a Trotskyist, as a very reliable source in 1941 but completely unreliable subsequently is never made clear and smacks of blatant opportunism on Spriano's part. Spriano also shows no hesitation in distorting the circumstances of Hernandez's break with the PCE, saying that he left the Communist Party 'clamorously' when he reached Mexico after the Second World War, when the truth is that he was expelled in 1944.[37]

Perhaps the most colourful example of the endless Communist campaign to discredit Hernandez is provided by Bolloten's citation of the following passage from a work by Amaro del Rosal published in 1977: 'During a journey by train from Prague to Warsaw, Vicente Uribe informed me in detail of certain antecedents of Jesus Hernandez: an exploiter of women, a professional loafer and a filcher of alms boxes from churches.'[38] Why Uribe and other leading Spanish Communists should have given Hernandez a leading role in the party in the light of such a background is, needless to say, never explained.

Aldo Agosti's recent biography predictably backs Spriano against Bocca on the question of Togliatti's presence in Spain, leaving the uninformed reader with the impression that a definitive refutation of a journalist's libel has taken place. However, Agosti's anxiety to demonstrate a mastery of new sources unknown to other biographers leads him to undermine the ground beneath his feet. Agosti concedes that Italian diplomatic and police sources refer to a voyage by Togliatti to Spain between May and September 1936. One document originating from the Italian Consulate in Berlin gives a precise date for a meeting held by the Communist Party in Madrid – 29 August 1936. Agosti acknowledges that Togliatti did not attend meetings of the Comintern Secretariat in Moscow on either 20 August or 27 August, but Agosti points out that he was certainly in Moscow for a meeting by 5 September.[39] What Agosti quite deliberately does not choose to inform us of is that the date in the Italian diplomatic document fits the date of Hernandez's alleged first meeting with Togliatti perfectly; Hernandez did not give a date, but Bocca had worked out from contextual information that it must have occurred some time between 27 and 31 August 1936.[40]

Bolloten provides us with some further evidence of Togliatti's presence in Spain before summer 1937 that is not dependent on Hernandez's testimony. The first of these additional sources, while in other circumstances not the most substantial or significant one, is bound to offer considerable entertainment to any student of the defenders of the PCI faith, Togliatti, Spriano and Agosti. It is no less an authority than the Spanish Communist writer of the prologue to Palmiro Togliatti's *Escritos politicos*, published in Mexico City in 1971, before the non-Communist Bocca had written anything heretical that Spriano or Agosti needed to refute. Bolloten summarizes the prologue writer, Adolfo Sanchez Vazquez, as asserting that 'Togliatti was in Spain as a Comintern delegate during "practically" the entire conflict "from 1936 to 1939"'.[41] Bolloten's second source is Amutio, the Socialist governor of Albacete, the headquarters of the International Brigades, whose assessment of Togliatti was given earlier. He affirmed in 1974 that Togliatti was in Spain from September 1936 and recalled a conversation with him in December 1936 during which Togliatti tried to gain his co-operation in the 'purging' of the brigades of 'spies and undesirables'. If true, this conversation shows the depth of Togliatti's day-to-day responsibility for Stalinist repression against the dissident left in Spain.[42]

Given this range of evidence for Togliatti's early arrival in Spain, the absolute certainty that Togliatti was not in Spain before July 1937 demonstrated by E. H. Carr and Tim Rees is a bit hard to take and should on no account be allowed to congeal into a new orthodoxy comparable to the Togliatti–Spriano–Agosti line in Italy. In Carr's defence, *The Comintern and the Spanish Civil War*[43] was the last work of a dying man whose interest in the Comintern flowed from a deep knowledge of Russian, not Spanish, history and who made no claim to have read the earlier versions of Bolloten's book,[44] of whose existence he may well have been unaware; nor, for that matter, does Bocca's biography feature in the footnotes.[45]

Rees's completely cavalier approach to evidence is far more deserving of censure. Here we are dealing with a historian in his prime, a Hispanist and a man who has read Bolloten.[46]

Having shown that, contrary to the mantra endlessly repeated by Spriano, Agosti and their disciples, there is a prima facie case that Togliatti was in Spain before July 1937, the time has come to turn to the question of what Togliatti did there. Before citing Hernandez who gives the most detailed and substantial account of Togliatti's actions, it is perhaps more appropriate to cite Claudin, who was expelled by the Spanish Communist Party in 1965, not 1944, and whom nobody has accused of working for the CIA. As ought to have been apparent from the quotation given earlier, Claudin assigns to Togliatti 'a role of prime importance' in 'the practical leadership of the PCE during the Civil War', but never gives an explicit date for his arrival. Claudin refers to the report by Diaz, the leader of the PCE, to the Plenum of the Central Committee of the PCE on 5–8 March 1937 as 'a report *delivered* by Diaz, but drawn up in its main lines by the Comintern team which was overseeing the PCE'.[47] This amounted to a death warrant for the POUM written months before the May Days in Barcelona, and contained the following striking passage: 'Fascism, Trotskyism and the "uncontrolled" element are the three enemies of the people who must be removed from the political life not only of Spain but also of all civilised countries.'[48] Claudin had the honesty to acknowledge that 'the repression of the POUM, and in particular the vile murder of Andres Nin, constitute the blackest page in the history of the PCE, which acted as accomplice in a crime committed by Stalin's secret service'.[49] The implication of all this is that, if Togliatti was in Spain by this stage, he was involved in all this up to his neck, but Claudin chooses neither to confirm nor to deny Togliatti's presence in Spain before July 1937.

The evidence for Vidali's involvement in Nin's murder seems quite strong. One source directly links Togliatti to Vidali, and in any event, if Togliatti was present in Spain at the time, it is frankly beyond the bounds of credibility that he would not have known what an Italian Communist like Vidali was engaged in. It should now be apparent why Bocca placed no weight on Vidali's claim that Togliatti was not in Spain before July 1937; Vidali had as much to hide as Togliatti. By no means all the evidence against them comes from POUM or ex-Communist sources, as Spriano and his ilk try to suggest. Bolloten quotes an account of a discussion in the Interior Ministry in which Gabriel Moron, the moderate Socialist general security director, told his fellow Socialist Juan-Simeon Vidarte, Undersecretary of the Interior in the Negrin government:

> Since the premier is so determined to learn the truth, you can tell him that the abduction of Andres Nin was plotted by the Italian [Vittorio] Codovilla, by Commandante Carlos [Vittorio Vidali], by Togliatti and

by the leaders of the Communist Party including [Party Secretary] Pepe Diaz. The order to torture him was given by Orlov. Tell this to Negrin. If he wants to arrest them, I'll put them all in jail first thing in the morning.[50]

If the Socialists within the Interior Ministry understood the outline of the plot, it is hardly surprising that the most explicit accounts come from POUM and ex-Communist sources.

Julian Gorkin was naturally curious to establish as much as possible about the fate of his fellow POUMist and Bolloten points out that 'Julian Gorkin states that Enrique Castro, one-time member of the Communist Party's Central Committee, assured him, after he had left the party, that "the personal executioner of Nin" had been his former comrade in the Fifth Regiment, Carlos Contreras (Vittorio Vidali) and that Orlov had selected him as "his immediate collaborator in the case of Nin"'.[51] Bolloten also cites Hernandez's claim that 'Vidali simulated a Nazi assault to "liberate" Nin from his secret place of captivity in Alcala de Henares, the sham assault being executed by the German members of the International Brigade, who carried him off, leaving behind incriminating documents purporting to show his connection with the Nazi secret police.'[52]

In response to this allegation, Vidali told Giorgio Bocca: 'So many things have been said about me but this is a stupidity. Why put on that stage show? In those days, if an anarchist or a POUMist had to be executed, it was done without so much fuss, can you imagine then, why I was necessary?'[53] The elderly Vidali, talking to Bocca more than 30 years after the events, clearly chose to forget the element of show trial, as distinct from simple execution, that characterized the Stalinist campaign against the POUM, and that what he later called 'the stage show' was needed precisely because Nin preferred to die rather than act his role in the Stalinist script and make a false confession under torture.

Some reference to Berneri and Barbieri, two Italian anarchists murdered in cold blood in the immediate aftermath of the May Days of 1937 in Barcelona, seems essential in the interests of objectivity since many anarchists have held Togliatti responsible. Here the case against Togliatti, while by no means implausible, seems much weaker. The fact that both Bolloten and Bocca, who both believe the worst of Togliatti in other matters, concur in believing this might make the unconvinced less inclined to dismiss their carefully researched accounts as mere partisan polemics. Bocca believed Berneri to have been killed by the NKVD, but he did not find the attempt to link Togliatti to the murder convincing.[54] Bolloten's final edition goes further.[55] It emphasizes that at the time of the killings most sources sympathetic to the anarchosyndicalists attributed the assassinations to the Communists because of Berneri's criticism of the Communists' policy in Spain, in an Italian-language anarchosyndicalist periodical published in Barcelona since October 1936. However, it points out that it now seems equally possible that the murders were carried out by agents of the Italian secret police, the OVRA, with Italian archival evidence demonstrating that the OVRA had Berneri under surveillance. Furthermore, it emphasizes that there are clear similarities with the killing of the Rosselli brothers by OVRA agents in France shortly afterwards.[56]

The other equally important, if less gruesome, episode in which Togliatti, according to Hernandez, played a leading role was the removal in mid-May 1937 of Largo Caballero. Caballero was the left-wing Socialist Prime Minister who fell out with the Communists over a variety of issues linked to their attempt to roll back all the initial revolutionary gains obtained by the Spanish workers and peasants in July 1936. The crunch issue was the Communists' desire to persecute the POUM, a persecution that Caballero was not prepared to endorse, but the evidence suggests that the Communists had been looking for a means of removing him some time before the May Days in Barcelona. Claudin refers to pressures on Caballero from Stalin himself, citing Stalin's letter of 21 December 1936[57] and further unwelcome advice sent by Stalin at the end of February 1937 to proceed immediately with the unification of the Communist and Socialist Parties.[58] Claudin sums up the course of events as follows: 'Confronted with the stubborn refusal of Caballero to act like a good secretary of a national section of the Comintern, the only thing left for Stalin to do was to get rid of him, as was done with bad secretaries of national sections of the Comintern. The operation was accomplished by the end of May 1937.'[59] Although Claudin does not mention Togliatti by name, given Togliatti's role in the Comintern, the implication is clear.

Hernandez claimed that Togliatti not only pushed the Spanish Communist leadership into getting rid of Caballero, despite the reservations of Party Secretary Diaz and Hernandez himself, but also chose Caballero's successor: '"As for Largo Caballero's successor . . . I believe we should proceed by a process of elimination. Prieto? Vayo? Negrin? Of the three, Negrin may be the most suitable. He is not anti-Communist like Prieto, nor stupid like Vayo!"'[60] Referring to the summer of 1937, Bolloten argues: 'At that time Togliatti became the virtual head of the party, directing strategy and writing many of the speeches of José Diaz and La Pasionaria.'[61]

Although Caballero's removal was accomplished by peaceful means, the subsequent zeal with which he was deprived of any office within the Socialist Party, Parliament and the UGT trade union, as well as the gradual seizure of every newspaper supporting his political line and the ultimate ban on his speaking in public after October 1937,[62] suggest that his growing fears for his physical safety were by no means groundless. Togliatti played a central role in the silencing of Caballero and for this episode we can adduce Togliatti's own writings rather than the disputed recollections of Hernandez. It was early November 1937 before the last newspaper, *La Correspondencia de Valencia*, was taken from Caballero, but as early as

15 September 1937 Togliatti had complained in a letter to Moscow about the slowness of the PCE in throwing 'Caballeristas out of the regional leadership of the unions and out of the editorial staff of the paper'.[63]

The clearest account of the degree of control that Togliatti wielded over the second Negrin government, which resulted from Prieto's exclusion from the Defence Ministry in spring 1938, is provided not by Bolloten or Bocca but by Carr, who is generally anxious to convey a more favourable picture of Togliatti's role in Spain. Carr writes:

> The central committee of the PCE set up a commission, significantly headed by Togliatti and Stepanov, to draft a programme for the new government. The draft was submitted to a representative meeting of party leaders, as well as the leaders of other popular front organisations. After 'stormy debates' it was approved, and published in the party press on April 30 in the form of 'thirteen points'. It was designed primarily to maintain the independence and integrity of Spain. It promised the defence of democratic and civil rights, including the rights of property and the 'free exercise of religious beliefs'. A special clause, on which IKKI [Executive Committee of the Communist International] insisted and which caused some controversy, protected the property of foreigners, other than those who had helped the nationalists. Any element that could be labelled communist, or even socialist, was rigorously excluded. It was openly remarked that the thirteen points represented the transition from the 'popular' to the 'national' front.[64]

In a letter to his daughter dated 9 March 1939, Caballero's loyal friend Araquistain wrote: '[The Communists] have assassinated hundreds of Socialists and Anarchists. If they did not assassinate others such as Largo Caballero and me, it is because we left at the right time.'[65] By this stage a PCE document of 2 February 1939 had already denounced Caballero in terms eerily reminiscent of their party's attacks on the POUM: 'The Politburo specifically denounces the shameful flight from national territory of Largo Caballero who – surrounded by a small group of enemies of unity, of enemies of the Spanish people and of its organisations – has done everything in his power to sabotage the work of the government and destroy the unity and resistance of our people and now crowns his criminal career by fleeing.'[66] There is every reason to suppose that Togliatti helped to draft what amounted to a death sentence for Caballero; the impossibility of carrying it out does not excuse the blatantly murderous intent.

Togliatti in Italy: the origins of the *svolta di Salerno* (1944)

Having outlined the case for regarding Togliatti as Stalin's principal agent in Spain in 1936–9, the time has come to examine his record in Italy in 1944, in particular the *svolta di Salerno*. Togliatti's instructions to the Italian Communists on his arrival in Italy in late March 1944 to abandon their intransigent position of refusal to participate in Badoglio's government and their call for the king's abdication have traditionally been interpreted by Togliatti's apologists as evidence of an original strategy for Italian Communism devised independently of Stalin and the Soviet Union. Indeed, they have often been presented as the first step along the long and winding road to the PCI's eventual Euro-Communism. Given the chronological coincidence between the Soviet Union's unexpected decision to recognize the Badoglio government on 14 March and Togliatti's imposition on 30–31 March of a new more moderate line on the rather more militant Italian Communist leaders – many of whom had participated in the Northern Resistance and regarded the king and Badoglio with contempt after their ignominious flight from Rome to Brindisi on 8 September 1943 – contemporary observers including the Anglo-American Allied Control Commission and the liberal philosopher Benedetto Croce had assumed that the change in the PCI line was dictated by Moscow.[67] However, Togliatti claimed when he arrived in Italy that he had left Moscow in mid-February and, therefore, knew absolutely nothing of the Soviet Union's decision to recognize Badoglio's government.

Despite scepticism on the part of some historians, who were well aware of the almost identical policies being pursued by Communist parties in other countries at roughly the same time – in short, of the lack of any Italian exceptionalism in this case – Togliatti's version had until recently been accepted by the bulk of Italian historians and there was no firm evidence to disprove it. However, recent archival discoveries in Moscow brought to the attention of Italian readers by Aga-Rossi and Zaslavsky have shed considerable light on the issue, proving beyond reasonable doubt that Togliatti, far from showing any autonomy or originality, took his orders directly from Stalin himself in the most humiliating fashion imaginable.

Before entering into the detailed chronology that is essential to refute the myths of Togliatti and his apologists, it is worth pointing out that Togliatti's position since June 1941 had, unsurprisingly given that he was in the Soviet Union, been broadly consistent in calling for the widest possible unity against Hitler and fascism. Bocca cites a radio broadcast made by Togliatti in July 1941, which I will quote in Ian Birchall's translation:

> From the fall of Hitler we Italians have everything to gain. And understand me clearly: Italians of all social conditions! At least, those industrialists who see their business ruined by the brutal competition think so. The businessmen to whom today all the European markets are closed by the domination of the German invaders think so. The Catholics, who see in German fascism the enemy of their traditions and their

ideals of brotherhood, think so. Every Italian mother whose husband and sons are taken from her and sent to die under the flag of the swastika thinks so. The people, to whom the war means hardships, privation and hunger, thinks so. All Italians who aspire to be a free people think so.[68]

Therefore, in one sense the *svolta di Salerno* was not a bolt from the blue, but fitted very neatly into a pattern of pronouncements in favour of broad cross-class national unity against the Germans which Togliatti had delivered from Moscow for some years. More specifically, Togliatti had been in favour of Communist participation in the government of Badoglio, set up after Mussolini's overthrow on 25 July 1943, until December 1943. What is much more interesting is that at the beginning of 1944, Togliatti and Dimitrov, despite their general advocacy of cross-class coalitions of national unity at the European level, took up an anti-monarchist and anti-Badoglio position in the Italian case. This is possibly because they were aware that inside the Soviet Foreign Ministry itself, the opinion of the Russian experts on Italy was turning against Badoglio, for reasons that were not all that different from those that motivated the forces linked to the Resistance within Italy.[69] A Soviet Foreign Ministry memorandum of 19 November 1943 deplored the failure to introduce even 'the most minimal democratic reform' and correctly remarked that 'the middle and low levels of the state apparatus in Sicily and Southern Italy are full of fascists'.[70]

So on 24 January 1944, Dimitrov, probably acting on Togliatti's advice, sent a memorandum to Molotov entitled 'A Draft of a Reply to the Italian Comrades', arguing that the Italian Communists should not enter Badoglio's government but should instead support the creation of an alternative anti-fascist government of national unity and call for the immediate abdication of the king.[71] After Molotov failed to reply to Dimitrov's document, in February 1944 Togliatti drew up a memorandum 'On the Immediate Tasks of the Italian Communists', arguing that 'the Communists should ask for the constitution of a democratic provisional government . . . they should ask for the king's abdication . . . they should refuse to participate in the present government'.[72] Dimitrov sent Togliatti's memorandum to Molotov on 1 March, endorsing it with a supportive letter of his own.[73]

While Togliatti and Dimitrov finally succeeded in their objective of bringing the Italian situation to the attention not just of Foreign Minister Molotov but also of Stalin himself, they did not get the official endorsement they had hoped for. On the night of 3–4 March, Togliatti was received by Stalin in the presence of Molotov. The record of this fateful meeting has not yet emerged from the Soviet archives, but its substance is known to us from Dimitrov's recently discovered diary. Because of his close involvement in Togliatti's effort to change the Comintern's line on Italy, Dimitrov was telephoned by Molotov in the wake of the meeting to be informed of Stalin's views, and he also met Togliatti for a further discussion about it the following day. So there is no reason to doubt the general accuracy of his record, even though, unlike Togliatti, he was not actually present at the meeting with Stalin. For those remotely inclined to doubt that Stalin issued peremptory orders to longstanding Western Communist leaders in person shortly before their return to their native lands, it is certainly worth noting the existence of official minutes of an analogous meeting between Stalin and Thorez in the presence of Molotov and Beria on 19 November 1944, shortly before Thorez's return to France.[74] But to return to the meeting with which we are primarily concerned, Stalin made it crystal clear to Togliatti that 'the existence of two camps (Badoglio and the King against the anti-fascist parties) weakens the Italian people. It only favours the English who would like to have a weak Italy in the Mediterranean.'[75] As usual, Stalin was far more concerned with the real or perceived foreign policy interests of the Soviet Union than with the fortunes of the Italian anti-fascists.

Togliatti, accepting defeat, therefore immediately modified the February document 'On the Immediate Tasks of the Italian Communists' by hand, deleting the demand for the king's abdication and inserting one for Communist participation in Badoglio's government.[76] While there could be no clearer documentary proof of Togliatti's total subservience to Stalin, even when Stalin's views contradicted his own assessment of the balance of forces within Italy itself, Togliatti's hagiographer Aldo Agosti has indulged in a perverse reading of this document in a desperate effort to sustain his myth about Togliatti's autonomy from Moscow. Ironically, it was Agosti who first brought the document to the attention of the Italian public, publishing an Italian translation in the PDS daily *Unità* on 28 October 1991. His commentary proudly proclaimed that here was clear evidence that Togliatti had changed the document by hand, modifying Stalin's anti-monarchist line in the light of his own greater understanding of Italian circumstances.[77]

In 1991 it is possible that Agosti was genuinely unaware of the Stalin–Togliatti meeting and acted in good faith, albeit with an excess of zeal and in order to produce the secondary effect that he had wanted all along, namely a number of ill-informed sensationalist articles in the mainstream bourgeois press by journalists to whom the notion of a rather patriotic but somewhat dissident Togliatti who had won an argument with Stalin had some emotional appeal. Given that the twenty-fifth anniversary of Togliatti's death on 6 August 1989 had seen an attack on Togliatti as a Stalinist in *Unità* itself by a journalist close to Occhetto, such manoeuvres are less far-fetched than a British reader might imagine.[78] In particular, it has to be pointed out that Agosti's views were not as idiosyncratic, even in the early 1990s, as they might appear. Leading PDS intellectual Giuseppe Vacca, in his 1994 book *Togliatti Sconosciuto*, tried to claim that Togliatti's initial reaction to the fall of Mussolini –

exemplified by a letter of 14 October 1943 to Dimitrov that called on the PCI to become part of a broader-based Badoglio government – was 'an anticipation of the *svolta di Salerno*, conceived with extraordinary timeliness', and a policy that Togliatti had devised 'autonomously'.[79]

By 1996 when his biography of Togliatti was published, Agosti had realized that his 1991 position was untenable, given the appearance of two learned articles based on the newly released Soviet documents, one of them in Italian. Agosti therefore argued that it had been Dimitrov, not Togliatti, who had taken up an anti-monarchist position in 'The Draft of a Reply to the Italian Comrades' (24 January 1944), which Togliatti had for a brief period very reluctantly endorsed in the first draft of 'On the Immediate Tasks of the Italian Communists' (February 1944).[80] Agosti then muddied the waters still further by suggesting that the anti-monarchist line had been propounded either by Dimitrov or by 'somebody still higher than him'[81] – a convoluted innuendo worthy of the worst sort of Italian politician, say Andreotti or Cossiga. He managed to imply that it was Stalin himself who had been anti-monarchist, without actually saying so in an unambiguous way that might have invited rapid rebuttal.

Agosti's new account as elaborated in the biography is completely nonsensical. Firstly, Dimitrov did not have the authority within the Comintern to impose his own line on somebody as senior and experienced as Togliatti, especially on an Italian question; only Stalin could have authorized him to override Togliatti. Secondly, Agosti gives no explanation of why Stalin might have changed his position in February 1944, rejecting the cause of national unity in the struggle against Germany – a cause that he had maintained in a European, and not just Italian, context since the German invasion of the Soviet Union in June 1941, only to change his mind again and revert to his original position at the beginning of March 1944. Agosti's tortuous and unconvincing account of this episode seems to have been constructed for one purpose alone, namely to support an assertion based on no documentary evidence whatsoever that, in his meeting with Stalin, Togliatti played an 'active part, putting forward the arguments that he had advanced in the radio broadcasts in the first half of January'.[82]

Togliatti did not escape from Stalin's authority merely by entering the Italian government.[83] Aga-Rossi and Zaslavsky provide us with a great wealth of material indicating that Togliatti and other leading PCI figures made detailed reports to the Soviet Embassy on a virtually daily basis throughout 1944–7. This makes it impossible to argue with any conviction that Togliatti was exercising the degree of autonomy on policy – as distinct from organizational matters, where the Russians trusted his independent judgement – attributed to him by those apologists such as Sassoon or Agosti, who see him as a precursor of Euro-communism in 1944–7 before he was allegedly brought to heel by the Cominform.

Conclusion

To conclude, the depth of Togliatti's Stalinism has been under-estimated by the vast majority of writers sympathetic to the Italian left. The old claims that his involvement in Stalin's terror was confined to signing the death warrants of the Polish Communists under duress in Moscow, or that his career after 1944 was entirely distinct from the path he took between 1926 and 1944, are no longer tenable. Firstly, Togliatti played a leading role in implementing Stalinist policy in Spain, not only dictating the line and often the very words of PCE leaders, but also crushing an authentic workers' and peasants' revolution, led by anarchists, POUMists and left-wing socialists. He employed a variety of means including not just elaborate political intrigues that exploited the divisions in the ranks of other political forces but the importation of NKVD tactics of a hitherto unknown brutality on to the streets of cities such as Barcelona. Secondly, the *svolta di Salerno*, Togliatti's famous new strategy enunciated to the Italian Communists in March 1944, was the direct result of orders from Stalin, not the outcome of autonomous reflection. The Spanish and Italian experiences were closely linked, for the very notion of a parliamentary road to socialism in western Europe was first set out by Stalin in his December 1936 letter to Caballero.

Togliatti's loyalty and servility to Stalin did not mean that he was not an extremely intelligent and astonishingly cunning politician. He showed an extraordinary grasp of Italian reality in the years after 1944, turning the PCI into a mass party with deep social roots and a degree of electoral support unparalleled among western European Communist parties. Nor did it mean that he did not seize the opportunities offered by events to achieve some distance from Moscow between 1956 and 1964, although we need to acknowledge that his dislike of Khrushchev played an important role here. Togliatti was certainly not a mediocre Stalinist bureaucrat, but he was never *Il Migliore*. The Spanish Communists who worked with him in 1936–9 grasped the profound moral emptiness that lay behind his tactical genius, and it could be argued that the image conjured up by their descriptions is that of an intelligent psychopath, not the heroic figure of the Spriano–Agosti–Sassoon hagiography. El Campesino portrayed him as 'cold, cynical, without nerves and without scruples' and Enrique Castro was 'reminded of the words of his secretary in Spain: "He is the type of man that would make love to me just as coldly as he would have given orders to shoot me"'.[84]

4

Terence Powderly, the Knights of Labor and the Great Upheaval

Craig Phelan

Terence Powderly was the first American working-class hero of national stature. As Grand Master Workman of the Noble Order of the Knights of Labor, he presided over the most significant and ambitious labour organization of the Gilded Age during its most critical period (1879–93). In less than seven years after assuming office, at a time when employers and the public regarded labour associations with contempt, he helped to transform a weak and secretive body of fewer than 10,000 members into a powerful, public movement that effectively challenged corporate control at the workplace and the hegemony of the two major parties at the polls. His clarion call for the solidarity of all who toiled helped to rally more than three-quarters of a million workers from every conceivable background – skilled and unskilled, black and white, male and female, immigrant and native-born – to the banner of Knighthood in 1886.

No other American labour leader before or since has even approached the level of respect and adulation accorded Powderly. 'I have never seen or heard you but once,' gushed a Nashville furniture worker in a typical expression of unbridled admiration, 'but I fell in love with you, a love that will burn till I die.' Gilded Age working people of all descriptions wrote poems, songs and plays in his honour, hung his portrait in their homes and in their assembly halls, greeted his arrival in their communities as a triumphal celebration, and named their sons, their assemblies and even their towns after him. In the eyes of his many followers, Powderly epitomized the ideals of the movement he led – courage, manliness, honour and unswerving dedication to the principle of solidarity. He symbolized the promise of the Knights to combat the pernicious impact of industrial capitalism and to remake the nation along lines defined by workers themselves rather than corporate capitalists. Most agreed with the Indiana telegrapher who called him 'our Moses', the man chosen by working people to 'lead us through this "Valley of the Shadow" of cursed rock-ridden monopoly and wage slavery'.[1]

Building solidarity

His immense popularity rested in large part on an ability to articulate, forcefully and eloquently, the founding philosophy of the Knights. The Knights held that the periodic depressions and mass unemployment on a scale unknown before the American Civil War, the relentless efforts of employers to assume unilateral control over the labour process, and the increasing concentration of economic power in the hands of monopolists – all undermined the artisans' independent status by reducing them to 'wage slaves'. Unless checked, capital concentration would soon undermine the promise of the republic itself. Rather than a glorious expression of equal rights, equal opportunity and vigilant citizenry, America would become a land in which the degraded and pauperized masses were ruled by a handful of economic elites. In short, Powderly and the Knights tried to give voice to the righteous indignation of working people as industrialization convulsed their lives and their nation.

Challenging corporate power, Powderly argued, required new strategies and tactics. The methods of the past – organization of skilled workers along trade lines and striking for both higher wages and the maintenance of traditional rights at the workplace – were by themselves incapable of redressing grievances. The mass of unskilled workers must be brought into the fold, common problems facing all workers identified, and appropriate strategies hashed out through rational discussion in democratic fashion. Once such a grand 'army of the discontented'[2] was assembled, informed, disciplined and committed to a course of action, he believed, no power could resist it. The ideals of America's revolutionary heritage would at last be safeguarded and made real.

But Powderly understood all too well that working-class resistance rarely proceeded along such rational lines. Indeed, his career and that of the Knights were both made and unmade by the two greatest paroxysms of industrial discontent in the nineteenth century. Although founded in 1869, the Knights only became a national organization in the wake of the great railroad strikes of 1877, when the accumulated animosities of the depression erupted in the most ferocious display of spontaneous strike action the world had yet seen. In a dozen cities across the nation, railroad workers, miners and many other wage earners fought corporations, the state militia and at times even federal troops. The upsurge was remarkable, but the resulting loss of property and life weakened the labour movement for years by convincing employers, politicians and mainstream journalists that a sinister, alien ideology lay behind the disturbances. All labour organizations were tarred with the brush of radical un-Americanism. In Scranton, Pennsylvania, the imposition of martial law and the destruction of unions led workers to express their anger through the ballot, and in February 1878 they elected Terence Powderly to the first of his three terms as mayor.

The peak years of the Knights of Labor coincided with an even more impressive demonstration of worker militancy, the Great Upheaval of 1885–7, when an unparalleled wave of strikes, boycotts and local labour party activity washed over the nation. Although recognizing that this out-pouring of frustration had swelled the ranks of the Order and made it a force to be reckoned with, Powderly rightly worried that the Knights were still too weak and divided among themselves to unify their attack and strike a decisive blow. With frightened employers and politicians com-bining for a powerful counteroffensive, Powderly did his best to appease the forces of repression and maintain unity and discipline within the orga-nization. But events were far beyond the control of any one man. Although the Order was crushed soon thereafter by industrialists and statesmen fearful of the growing might of his forces, Powderly's vision lingered for years as a vivid reminder of the unlimited possibilities inher-ent in an all-inclusive workers' crusade for empowerment.

Although Powderly's followers regarded him as a genuine and pro-gressive labour leader valiantly struggling to create working-class solidarity, historians have painted a dramatically different portrait. While agreeing on little else, virtually all historians insist that Powderly is unworthy of our respect and attention. Those who were reared on the classic accounts of the Knights – the works of Selig Perlman, Norman Ware, and Gerald Grob – learned long ago that Terence Powderly was a grotesque bumbler whose antiquated notions, incessant meddling in the affairs of subordinate bodies, and lack of fitness for office helped to ensure the Order's consignment to the dustbin of history. The revolution in Knights' scholarship that began in the 1970s has done little to rehabili-tate his image. Recent findings have in fact dramatically elevated the seriousness of his 'crimes'. The Order is now recognized as having possessed an eminently viable 'movement culture' with enormous poten-tial to transform the social and economic landscape. The Great Upheaval is now viewed as a critical moment of class struggle, and 'American industrial relations and labor politics are exceptional because in 1886 and 1887 employers won the class struggle.'[3] Thus Powderly now appears more sinister than a mere bumbler. By failing to take advantage of the opportunities presented by the upheaval, we are told, he undercut the dream of solidarity and helped to shunt the labour movement down an exceptionalist path. He was a saboteur of an alternative America.

This is a peculiar legacy indeed for a leader who, far more than any other figure, struggled to make the dream of solidarity a reality, personified the promise of Knighthood, and structured the Order to accommodate working people from almost every conceivable back-ground. Powderly was undeniably the Gilded Age's most charismatic and eloquent advocate of class-wide solidarity, and as two recent scholars have concluded, 'The identification of the Knights of Labor with the organization of the entire working class was the Order's unique and indisputable achievement.'[4] From 1874, when he threw himself into the labour movement as Industrial Congress organizer, he championed its pledge to unite 'every department of productive industry' and thereby overcome class segmentation based on craft identity and skill. As a rising star in the fading Machinists and Blacksmiths International Union, he battled against divisive craft elitism by rebuking the 'aristocratic' machinist for allowing his 'airs and graces' to deny fellowship to less skilled boilermakers. Upon the collapse of his local trade union, he launched a Knights' assembly that welcomed machinists, blacksmiths, boiler-makers, patternmakers, grinders, moulders, labourers and helpers as equals. And throughout his years as Grand Master Workman, he preached in stirring tones the need for unity among all who toiled:

> The machinist goes to his home, the moulder to his, the carpenter to his; all go to the trades unions on their way; each one is so thoroughly self-ish as to never look beyond the limits of his organization; none ask whether any other men had rights. We said to ourselves this is igno-rance on the part of workingmen's trade unions; it is a crime and strong steps must be taken to remove this cause. Something must be done to bring these people together, so that they may know that a blow struck at labor in one place affects those in another; that the evil is felt every-where men live, from the rising to the setting of the sun.[5]

Craft identity was certainly not the only source of division within the working class, and Powderly continuously implored his contemporaries to shed their traditional attitudes towards race, ethnicity, religion, gender and party affiliation that kept them from exercising collective power. 'Brothers, Protestant and Catholic, I call upon you . . . to join hands in the amelioration of Labor,' he beseeched his Scranton comrades in early 1877 when religious intolerance jeopardized the health of Knighthood in that city, 'for God knows we have enemies enough arrayed against us in the ranks of Capital without our creating new ones among ourselves.' Thirteen years later he was preaching the same message to embattled mineworkers in another part of the state. 'Here we have Englishmen, Irishmen, Italians, Welshmen, Scotchmen, Germans and every other kind of mortals.' Operators hoped to keep them 'separated by the accursed fiends of national prejudice and religious intolerance'. But 'you are bound together' through labour, he insisted, and 'should always stand to-gether as men of one blood in the cause of industrial emancipation'.[6]

Not only did the Knights appeal to an astonishing variety of working people, each with their own traditions and agendas, but also to reformers and activists of every description – Irish Land Leaguers, staunch trade unionists, co-operative enthusiasts, third party advocates, feminists, ritualists, eight-hour champions, anti-monopolists, currency reformers, anarchists, Marxists, agrarians, temperance campaigners and numerous others. How to maintain harmony within this singularly diverse organization, how to placate each faction, how to pursue the dozens of often competing programmes advanced – these were just a few of the monumental problems inherent in the practice of solidarity.

Powderly understood that effective solidarity was not something that could be imposed from above. In a heterogeneous nation, 'you cannot make any society tie its members to a strict line of brotherhood,' he counselled. 'We must take men as we find them.' As with any other skill, solidarity needed to be learned and practised by members themselves. To this end he embraced the principle of local autonomy, hoping that through frank discussion in the sanctuaries, participation in Knight-sponsored cultural activities, and joint action on matters of mutual economic and political interest the working people of a particular community would eventually overcome their antipathies and identify their common grievances. The budding of meaningful solidarity thus necessitated freedom of action for local assemblies to pursue whatever objectives they deemed capable of uniting the workforce within their jurisdictions. 'Each District and Local Assembly should be permitted to enact its own laws', Powderly stressed throughout his tenure. 'In doing so there should be as little interference from the General Assembly as possible.'[7]

Out of both democratic principle and necessity born of diversity, Powderly erected the Knights upon the bedrock of local initiative and local control. He espoused what came to be known as 'horizontal unionism', a grass-roots, community-based approach to union building that some labour scholars contend is far preferable to the centralized, bureaucratic structures that have dominated the movement since the 1930s.[8] In the 1880s, when workers in communities across the nation rose in protest against the ruthless impositions of corporate capitalists, Powderly's horizontal approach and rhetoric of solidarity won large numbers of adherents. Knighthood did not miraculously materialize out of thin air in 1886, as a decentralized and democratic focal point of resistance; for years Powderly had devoted his boundless energies to the construction of a remarkable 'house of labour' able to accommodate all who toiled.

Lost opportunities?

Yet, despite some initial victories, this grand and unprecedented experiment in solidarity all went horribly wrong during the upheaval, and Powderly has been held accountable for much of the damage ever since. Some suggest that he abruptly abandoned local control and arrogantly imposed himself on self-sufficient locals and districts, undermining their efforts to exercise effective solidarity at the community level. Others insist that his ideological opposition to strikes intensified dramatically, quickly discouraging new recruits and damaging the spirit of resistance. Some believe that he developed an abiding hostility towards radicalism of any kind, which was manifested in his refusal to speak out for the anarchists accused of the Haymarket bombing, and claim that this single act split the movement at all levels. And still others argue that he became the prisoner of arch anti-trade unionists in the Home Club, which soon resulted in the defection of skilled workers and the creation of the American Federation of Labor (AFL). For one or all of these reasons, we are told, Powderly contributed to the decimation of the Order, the sabotaging of the upheaval, and the shattering of the very class-wide solidarity he had done so much to foster.

Despite all that we have learned in the past quarter of a century, Powderly is still required to play this preposterous role of class traitor. While great strides have been made to understand all other facets of the movement in their complexity, Powderly remains a caricature of the timid and fearful 'misleader' of labour who lost touch with the rank and file and betrayed the workers' interests. Implicit in many of the recent criticisms of Powderly is the belief that, had he only trusted the militant spirit of workers, had he exhibited a greater appreciation of class conflict, had he maintained his commitment to horizontal unionism, had he joined hands with Samuel Gompers and the trade unionists, and had he thrown the weight of the Order behind the Chicago anarchists' clemency campaign, then somehow the outcome of the upheaval may have been different, and somehow America today might be fundamentally different.

One of the most peculiar, pervasive and erroneous images of Powderly during the upheaval is that of the intrusive dilettante who imposed his will on flourishing locals and districts to the detriment of the cause. Once his final term as mayor of Scranton expired in February 1884, he found himself with plenty of time on his hands, which, unfortunately, according to Bruce Laurie, led to his divisive and 'constant interventions into local union affairs'. Judith Goldberg has argued that the increased 'interference' of Powderly and the executive board was the most important and 'disastrous' change in the Order in these years.[9]

In truth, Powderly and other board members had neither the time nor the desire to force themselves on self-sufficient locals and districts because they were inundated by thousands of desperate pleas for intervention from locals and districts incapable of handling their own affairs or resolving crises that arose within their jurisdictions. Rather than an arrogant and ill-informed intruder, Powderly was the harried fire marshal of the Knights, constantly asked to manage conflagrations that local leaders could not control.

A sense of Powderly's predicament can be gleaned by examining the appeals sent to him on just the first two days of a six-week board session in February and March 1886, even before the maelstrom of activity surrounding the May Day strikes. The vast majority of supplicants not only required national financing of their emergencies, but also desired, and usually demanded, that Powderly return with them to gain first-hand knowledge of the facts.

In those two days alone, Powderly reckoned with poorly managed strikes, critical lockouts involving as many as 3,000 workers, complex boycotts, friction with trade unions and crippling jurisdictional strife involving Troy stove mounters, workers on the Atcheson, Topeka and Sante Fe Railroad, female shoe operatives in Lynn, Massachusetts, textile operatives in Lewiston, Maine, cigar makers and wagon makers in Homer, New York, farm implement factory workers in Toronto, knitters in Amsterdam, New York, St Louis typographical workers, New York City's railroad employees, Danville, Pennsylvania steel workers, Little Rock railroad workers, wire makers in Des Moines, coal miners in Earlington, Kentucky, machinery workers in Springfield, Ohio, and glove makers at Gloversville, New York.[10] From Montreal came the disturbing news that the Catholic Church was about to condemn the Order officially, and from Chicago came urgent appeals for board intervention in two conflicts, one in which enthusiastic strikers had committed murder, and the other an ominous-sounding lockout at McCormick Harvester Works.[11]

The question of whether Powderly's intervention was an unwarranted and unhealthy imposition on subordinate bodies or the response to desperate pleas from them is central to any appreciation of the possibilities of the upheaval. The former suggests that the spirit of resistance, tempered only by the self-imposed discipline of the local Knight assembly, had the potential to establish lasting solidarity and effectively combat corporate capital. The latter implies that the spirit of resistance, while the source of the Order's strength, was by itself insufficient for either purpose. Without adequate controls, militancy often lapsed into squabbles within and between subordinate bodies or led to doomed confrontations with better-prepared and equally militant corporations.

Another article of faith is that Powderly was an anti-strike zealot. Both old and new labour historians, without exception, argue that Powderly, as a result of his 'parochial perspective', was 'indifferent to the plight of striking members', and pursued a 'bankrupt policy' that resulted in a 'conflict between the leadership and the rank-and-file'.[12] Acknowledging that virtually all Gilded Age labour leaders sought to impose administrative controls on the right to strike, Powderly is singled out for his supposed ideological antipathy to work stoppages. He 'went beyond . . . conventional wisdom' and resisted 'support for nearly all strikes, apparently unwilling to recognize that strikes had often been forced on workers'.[13]

Nonsense. Powderly approached strikes in much the same way as other labour leaders of the era, including John Mitchell, field general of the titanic 1902 hard coal strike. Although both men learned from bitter experience to be wary of conflicts in which the union lacked adequate finances, clearly defined goals and a solid chance of success, both recognized that strikes constituted an essential weapon of last resort and could be an effective means of organizing the unorganized.[14] 'Legitimate strikes', Powderly declared during the height of the counteroffensive, 'cannot be opposed by any fair minded man or body of men if entered upon as a last resort and in accordance with our laws.'[15]

As for his opposition to 'virtually all appeals for strike assistance',[16] in the summer of 1886 alone he issued appeals for Rhode Island Knights when manufacturers systematically began to discharge them, Pittsburgh street car employees, Allegheny county miners, lime workers in Rockland, Maine, the tanners and curriers of Salem and Peabody, Massachusetts, textile workers in Augusta, Georgia, female operatives in the carpet mills of Wesson, Mississippi, and dozens more equally deserving cases. In early September he issued a general appeal for especially hard-pressed Knights in eight states (Delaware, Georgia, Maryland, Massachusetts, Mississippi, Montana, New Jersey and Pennsylvania).[17]

It was not Powderly's ideology that precluded the possibility of adequate financial aid. Resisting all efforts to centralize the Assistance Fund, local and district leaders even denied him a viable system of compulsory assessments. The voluntary appeal was thus the only means at his disposal to offer financial support. In the early days of the upheaval, the appeal could be effective, raising $86,000 for the south-west strike, but its effectiveness decreased in proportion to the number issued. The three-quarters of a million Knights contributed the pathetic total of $14,000 to the September 1886 appeal on behalf of all their locked-out brothers and sisters across the nation.[18]

Unable to finance those locked out, prevent strikes that could not be sustained, or control organizers who continued to make absurd promises of financial assistance to new assemblies, Powderly found himself in a hopeless situation. Along with other board members, he sorted through the endless requests and made difficult choices. When subordinates were denied funds, their battles and their local organizations often collapsed, and they invariably blamed Powderly for their woes.[19] Even when the board issued an appeal, the trivial amounts they could offer did little more than foster resentment. When the leaders of the disastrous Augusta, Georgia textile walkout received just $2,000 to sustain over 3,000 strikers, they attacked Powderly on the floor of the Richmond General Assembly, charged him with failure to hand over all the funds collected and accused him of an anti-southern bias.[20] This cycle of defeat, disillusionment and recrimination was repeated on countless occasions.

The Knights, like the labour movement generally in both America and Europe at this time, were, in the words of Eric Hobsbawm, learning 'the rules of the game'. Like every skill, 'industrial solidarity must be learned'.[21] Especially among the semi-skilled and unskilled who flocked to the banner of Knighthood, strikes represented an outlet for pent-up frustrations. Many began in a festive atmosphere without preparations or coherent goals; sometimes they succeeded but more often they failed. Untutored members had yet to learn how to pick their fights and martial their resources. They had yet to recognize the need at times to subordinate local concerns for the greater benefit of the movement as a whole. Working people caught up in the excitement could not be expected to adhere to rules they did not yet understand, but equally true is that Powderly could not sustain all struggles, transform inevitable defeats into victories, or turn water into wine. Certain trade unions in the 1880s created structures that demonstrated a deeper understanding of the nature of industrial conflict, even if they did lack the same commitment to solidarity. The Knights failed to emulate them, not because Powderly abhorred strikes or trade unions, but because he was unable to channel the passions of workers through mere words. He paid a heavy price for this failure, for he was forced to watch helplessly as his beloved Order fell victim to the counteroffensive.

Factional strife

Leading Knights ably assisted the employers' campaign through ruinous internal dissent, and Powderly of course has been held accountable for much of the damage.[22] Factionalism had been a feature of Knighthood since the first General Assembly in 1878, but during the crisis atmosphere of the counteroffensive it escalated exponentially. By 1887 infighting had become truly labyrinthine as a startlingly diverse assortment of individuals and factions divided into pro- and anti-administration camps. Most cliques employed dirty tricks and none had a monopoly on truth, and although Powderly had the political savvy and sufficient support to engineer pyrrhic victories until 1893, the damage caused by the factional wars sealed the Order's fate.

Throughout all the complex episodes of intrigue, three ironic features stand in bold relief. First, while Powderly will always be remembered for his ceaseless red-baiting after 1886, the reactionary character of his attacks has obscured the fact that his principal opponents were self-styled anarchists and revolutionary socialists who happily embraced the roles of obstructionists and slander-mongers in their quest to gain control. Powderly had endured so many bitter experiences with the radical fringe since his first election in 1879 that his shift from toleration to truculence was all but inevitable. The machinations of E. A. Stevens, Theodore Cuno, P. J. McGuire, Burnette Haskell, A. J. Starkweather and Victor Drury and his District Assembly (DA) 49 henchmen – all had caused considerable disruption and had undermined democratic practice before 1886. And those who spearheaded the drive against the union administration beginning in that year – Burnette Haskell of San Francisco, Joseph Buchanan of Denver, Joseph Labadie of Detroit, and Tom Barry of the executive board – were all self-professed anarchists and radical socialists who employed similar tactics. Such was Powderly's experience that he and many others within the movement came to appreciate fully the warning of the Order's founder, Uriah Stephens: 'You must not allow the Socialists to get control of your assembly. They are simply disturbers . . . having driven all decent men away, they are supremely happy in the delusion that they have spread their ideas still farther.'[23]

Second, the anarchist Victor Drury had made New York City's DA 49 so odious, not only to Powderly but to many Knights on the East Coast, that hatred of Drury's Home Club became a focal point for the radical opposition in 1886. Opportunistically exploiting the myth of Home Club control of the executive board, the anarchists and radical socialists who challenged Powderly after Richmond sought to forge links with trade unionists embittered by the tactics of the anarchist element in New York. In the incendiary war of words that erupted, Powderly found himself in the crossfire. Little wonder that he grew somewhat paranoid about the disruptive potential of red and black flag wavers.

Third, no issue proved more divisive after 1886 than the fate of the Haymarket anarchists in Chicago, who were convicted that August after a sham trial. In the minds of Powderly and many Knights, these men had talked foolishly of dynamite and bloodshed, and whether or not they were associated with the bombing, they had helped to cultivate a national hysteria – America's first Red Scare – that not only made a fair trial for themselves impossible but was turned against the Order with such vengeance that its very survival was jeopardized. In the supreme irony, the effort to commit the Order to the clemency campaign united the radicals of DA 49 and their equally radical opponents. But even when acting in concert they failed to convince a majority of delegates, despite the fact that the latter accused the former of controlling the Order.

The factional wars also highlighted Powderly's political mastery. For one invariably depicted as weak, he was able to defeat all his challengers for another seven years with relative ease. He triumphed even though he lacked many of the bureaucratic controls routinely exercised by his more successful trade union counterparts – the appointment of organizers and their use as administration boosters, control of strike funds, and the ability to manipulate conventions – which made them increasingly impervious to internal dissent.[24] When power struggles took place, he was vulnerable, protected in large measure only by the prestige of his office, the popularity of his policies and his abundant political skills. By early 1888, however, the radicals' campaign had caused such disruption that Powderly, in an effort to protect himself and the organization he led, adopted autocratic measures to expel his enemies and thereby crippled the very democracy he was trying to safeguard.

As we have seen, virtually all of the charges levelled against Powderly fail to hold up to even a cursory look at the evidence. Powderly did not deviate to any great extent from his commitment to local autonomy in 1886. Even during the upheaval, his attitude toward strikes was by no means resolutely hostile, and he worked feverishly to support tens of thousands of Knights engaged in strikes and lockouts. Until the unleashing of the employer counteroffensive, radical Knights such as Joseph Buchanan and Joseph Labadie were among his most ardent admirers, and the clemency campaign proved so divisive at the 1887 General Assembly that the majority of delegates opted not to go beyond the Order's year-old appeal for mercy on behalf of the condemned. The Home Club did not hold him prisoner, he actively opposed the expulsion of Cigar Makers' International Union members at the 1886 General Assembly, and he struggled valiantly to overcome the structural problems that the trade union impulse presented within the Order. In short, Powderly was a far more progressive, tolerant, aggressive and competent leader than we have been led to believe.

The repetition of old stories regarding Powderly's ineptitude and betrayal, despite overwhelming evidence to the contrary, illustrates the impossibility of understanding the Knights through an exclusive focus on the community. Recent sympathetic studies of national institutions in the twentieth century, especially the Congress of Industrial Organizations, and national leaders, most notably Sidney Hillman and Walter Reuther,[25] remind us that large labour organizations are far too complex to be understood through a single methodological lens. National leaders in any era have valid perspectives, operate under pressing bureaucratic constraints, face a variety of internal and external threats that often stay their hands, and have to take into account national social and political realities as well as the interests of each subordinate body. The wealth of knowledge gleaned from the community study is truly remarkable, but the attempt to view the Order solely from the bottom up has perpetuated a whole host of myths and misconceptions about the leadership and the organization as a whole.

Only from a national perspective can we truly grasp the principal irony of the Order: that the very basis of its popularity – community control – also proved its greatest weakness. Although local autonomy was an inherently attractive and functional approach to managing an organization with a startlingly diverse membership, it was ill suited for the major battles of the upheaval, which pitted the enthusiasm of neophyte Knights, many of whom had never been active in a labour organization, against intransigent employer associations in major industries such as railroads, textiles and meatpacking. Time and again, Powderly found himself asked to intervene in large-scale strikes that had been started in a celebratory spirit at the local or district level without adequate organization, without clearly stated strike demands, without unity or discipline in the ranks, and without the possibility of adequate financial assistance from other assemblies engaged in their own expensive wars. All too often such strikes were waged against well-financed, single-minded and merciless employer groups that were formed for the sole purpose of eradicating the Knights in their industries; associations that could rely, if necessary, on powerful political and judicial allies. Only when it proved too late did Powderly address this dilemma. The various proposals that he introduced at the two General Assemblies in 1886, including the establishment of strong State Assemblies (with control over the strike activities of local organizations and districts within their jurisdictions) and the election of examining organizers (who would supervise the activities of the organizing corps within each state), indicated his desire to impose a measure of centralized authority without running roughshod over local autonomy. His inability to move in that direction sealed the Order's fate.

Powderly certainly had his faults. Among other shortcomings, he mirrored the ugly anti-Chinese prejudice of his generation, developed an hysterical hatred of extremists whom he believed unnecessarily antagonized the public by preaching propaganda by deed, whined incessantly about the burdens of his office, droned on about his favourite reform topics, especially land reform and temperance, whenever he feared tackling controversial issues at the annual gatherings, and lacked a sophisticated comprehension of collective bargaining issues such as the closed shop. His principal failing, however, was a naive faith in the rationality of collective action. In his eyes, the Order was far more than a mere labour organization. It was the genesis of a new worker-controlled society that would be free from economic exploitation, gender and racial discrimination, and political manipulation by elites. Knighthood did not provide a blueprint for the new society, but rather a forum in which all relevant issues could be studied and debated, in which tactics and strategies could be hammered out in democratic fashion at the local level. If a local assembly deemed strike action necessary, Powderly asked only that the members of that assembly made certain 'That the cause was just', 'That every reasonable means had been resorted to avert the strike', 'That the chances of winning were at least as good as the prospect of losing' and 'That the means of defraying the expenses of the strike and assisting those in need were in the treasury or in sight of it.'[26]

Powderly's confidence in such rational decision making was misplaced. By and large, unskilled and semi-skilled working people in the 1870s and 1880s learned the art and science of resistance through repeated and often disastrous confrontations with their employers rather than quiet reflection, a careful weighing of the alternatives and systematic preparations. Although the strikes of the upheaval 'lacked the insurrectionary quality' of the 1877 outbursts, many strikers in the mid-1880s nevertheless 'poured forth pent-up fury, roaring approval of Social Revolutionary speakers who denied that workers owed any allegiance to a society that made them all outcasts, storming the fortifications of factories whose employees had failed to strike, and defiantly boasting their triumphs'.[27] The pivotal south-west strike, as we have seen, began in a festive atmosphere against virtually insurmountable odds, with the district treasury already in the red, and with the knowledge that the railroad brotherhoods would not lend their support. The aborted packinghouse strike was a similar affair, as were hundreds of others. Although some strikers, especially in the spring of 1886, caught their employers off guard and wrested victories, a far greater number quickly found themselves in desperate straits. Only at that stage did hard-pressed strikers turn to Powderly, begging him to come to their rescue with a magic formula that could produce non-existent funds and turn certain defeat into victory. When funds were not forthcoming or his furious bargaining efforts proved ineffective, Powderly became an easy scapegoat for local leaders and historians ever since.[28]

Because he grappled with the consequences of such spontaneous eruptions on a daily basis, Powderly did clearly recognize where the upheaval was headed long before most local leaders or the rank and file. A veteran of the great railroad strikes of 1877, he had seen how quickly working-class enthusiasm in Scranton and elsewhere had led to vicious repression, martial law, public hostility towards labour and the decimation of the labour movement. Even before the May Day strikes in 1886, Powderly had ample evidence to indicate that the upheaval was generating an even more aggressive employer counteroffensive of national proportions, which was far too powerful for the decentralized Order. He feared that unless members tempered their passions with a commonsense analysis of the forces arrayed against them, a spiral of defeat and decay would be set in motion that would spell the total collapse of the movement. His worst fears were soon realized.

The savage employer campaign that killed the Knights in the late 1880s was itself cruelly ironic. Powderly had believed that as soon as workers had overcome their deep-seated divisions and joined him in his crusade for empowerment, then all things would at once become possible, all opposition would be humbled, and industrial emancipation would be realized. And to a degree that would not be repeated until the 1930s, hundreds of thousands of American workers did embrace his vision for a brief moment. The upheaval was a truly magnificent spectacle that would inspire future generations of activists. But rather than gaining emancipation, Powderly and the Knights succeeded in frightening, unifying and emboldening their corporate foes. Having temporarily overcome some of the fragmenting impulses within the working class that had stymied the creation of an all-powerful and multi-faceted labour movement, Powderly and the Knights helped to foster what is now recognized as the chief obstacle to such a movement in America – a powerful, ruthless, sophisticated and viciously anti-union capitalist class. The Providence

Manufacturers' Association that was organized soon after Powderly's visit in February 1886 and which spearheaded the drive that crippled the Order in Rhode Island, the new National Knit Goods Manufacturers' Association that smashed flourishing Knighthood in Amsterdam and Cohoes, New York, the new Southern Manufacturers' Association that defeated the Knights in the Augusta, Georgia mills and precipitated a series of setbacks across the south, and the new Packinghouse Association that was itching for a fight to the finish against Knights in the Chicago stockyards – these were representative of the organizations that survived the upheaval, wielded enormous influence in the political arena and the judiciary, and set the tone for labour relations in the decades that followed.

As the strike defeats and lockouts escalated, the bubble of solidarity burst and those who did not abandon the Order altogether engaged in endless rounds of recrimination and factional intrigue. Powderly continued to preach the gospel of solidarity until 1893, but he, like hundreds of others at the local and district level, resorted to dubious tactics to shield himself from his growing number of enemies within the declining movement, and his promise of liberation through solidarity now fell on deaf ears. Even before the depression of the 1890s, working people had largely reverted to the fragmenting impulses of ethnicity, craft identity and geographical parochialism.

That the Knights were unable to wrest victories in the major industries is hardly surprising, since the history of the movement for decades after the upheaval is littered with the wreckage of failed strikes against concentrated capital. The AFL unions survived the depression decade largely by shunning the organization of volatile unskilled workers, refusing to engage in pitched battles against superior opposition in the major industries, and establishing stricter control over their subordinate bodies' right to strike. The pivotal strikes of 1894, including the American Railway Union-engineered Pullman boycott, were 'preceded by widespread organization' and were 'centrally called and directed', and still they ended in disaster.[29] Not until the 1930s was the labour movement able to crack the nut of concentrated capital and erect viable industrial unions in mass-production industries, and only then with the dramatic, if temporary, New Deal shift in federal policy towards labour.

Powderly was not, as was once believed, a starry-eyed, middle-class utopian groping for impractical alternatives to industrial capitalism. Nor was he, as many recent scholars imply, a pusillanimous destroyer of a world that might have been. He was a flawed but worthy hero to tens of thousands of Gilded Age workers because he articulated their collective vision, encouraged them to jettison their sense of fatalism, and promised them that they could remake the nation if they stood as one before their oppressors. His clarion call for the solidarity of all who toiled, his confidence in working people's ability to shape their own destiny, his vision of a labour movement that would be all things to all people – all these mark him as the personification of progressive labour leadership. Rather than undermining an alternative America, the Grand Master Workman helped to shape our vision of it.

5

Socialism as Sacrifice: The Life and Politics of Stafford Cripps

David Renton

The invention of New Labour since 1995 provides a challenge to socialist historians. When Tony Blair suggests that the Labour Party should never have been formed, the first response must surely be to remember the alternative voices, the radical trade unionists, the old-style social democrats, the feminists and the pacifists, the Guild Socialists and the occasional revolutionaries, who all existed within the Old Labour camp. Having celebrated the diversity of historical predecessors to Blairism, the second task is to examine these past models in a critical way. One factor in Blair's continuing ascendancy is precisely the political and strategic weakness of these traditions, which his faction has displaced at the head of the Labour Party. This chapter will examine these themes through a discussion of the life and politics of Stafford Cripps, first the radical insider of the 1930s left, and later the custodian of orthodoxy as Attlee's Chancellor of the Exchequer from 1948 to 1950.

This chapter was first given as part of a session on labour leaders. At first glance, its subject may seem incongruous. Surely there are many more obvious leaders to write about. Even if they were to restrict their choice simply to figures from British working-class history, most people would think of Harold Wilson, Clement Attlee, Aneurin Bevan, Ramsay MacDonald, Tom Mann or Ben Tillett, before they named Sir Stafford Cripps.[1] Even today's Chancellor, a man most likely to nominate Stafford Cripps as his socialist hero, preferred in his youth to write a biography of James Maxton, the Independent Labour Party (ILP) rebel whose 'proto-Keynesian programme' offered 'to banish unemployment and poverty, and to create socialism quickly and without catastrophe'.[2] For a socialist audience Cripps' story lacks the romantic appeal of Tom Mann's, while even as a renegade Ramsay MacDonald constitutes a more obvious choice.[3] The fascination of Cripps is the speed of his conversion from left to right. Expelled to the left from the Labour Party in 1939, Cripps promptly found allies among marginal Conservatives. Within days, he had placed the left speech making of the Socialist League behind him. Within months of his expulsion, he had been appointed to a new post as ambassador to Russia. Back in the Labour Party after 1945, promoted to the Chancellorship and at the head of the British economy, Stafford earned the nickname 'Austerity Cripps', a sobriquet that derived from his conservative, deflationary budgets.

How was Stafford Cripps able to progress so seamlessly from anti-capitalist rebel to champion of the status quo? There have been three recent biographies of Cripps, but none answers this question satisfactorily. For Chris Bryant, a Labour councillor in Hackney and chair of the Christian Socialist Movement, the interest of Stafford's life is in his attempt to marry Anglicanism with a watered-down reformism. Bryant observes no crisis, no transition to be explained: Cripps was a socialist in the 1930s, and again fifteen years later.[4] The same is true of Simon Burgess, for whom Cripps' early radical ideas were 'irresponsible drivel' waiting to be swept away. Burgess's biography is uninterested in Stafford Cripps' radical years, preferring to tell the story of his time as Chancellor. It is the deflationary Chancellor and champion of fiscal rectitude who appeals to the biographer in these New Labour times.[5] Finally, the most recent (and best-researched) biography by Peter Clarke follows Burgess in slanting its account towards the 1940s – although in his case this includes a detailed study of Cripps' involvement in the negotiations surrounding the granting of independence to India, as well as the previous interest in Cripps' economic policies.[6]

Given the breadth of Sir Stafford Cripps' economic vision in the 1930s, why were Labour's economic policies so limited after 1948? Part of the answer must lie outside the figure of Cripps. The Cold War closed the space for radical alternatives, not just in Britain but in many other countries, from autumn 1947 onwards. Throughout the Western bloc, radical voices were marginalized and the upturn in protest which had accompanied the end of the Second World War was brought to an end.[7] Yet part of the answer must also lie within Cripps' socialism. In the Socialist League, Cripps claimed to espouse a socialist third way standing between social democracy and Stalinism. Yet in practice Cripps' socialism shared the worst of both worlds: it combined the admiration for Moscow found among Communists with the top-down politics of the Labour leadership. It is the limits of his alternative that explain the speed with which Stafford Cripps' politics turned right after 1939. In order to explain his right turn, therefore, this chapter is divided into two sections. The first describes Cripps' career, while the second focuses on the key moment of 1939.

Stafford Cripps: life and career

Stafford Cripps was born in April 1889. His was a stately-home family, southern England, landed and conventionally Christian. Cripps was duly sent off to Winchester public school, where his contemporaries included his later friend, fellow lawyer and Socialist League supporter D. N. Pritt. From Winchester, Cripps attended University College London and the bar. This was a solid, English, ruling-class upbringing, neither brilliant nor eccentric, but steady and straight down the line. Cripps' marriage to Isobel Swithinbank, heiress to the fortunes of Eno's Fruit Salts, did nothing to dispel this image – but did equip Stafford with a modest fortune. Like others of his background, Cripps was an Anglican, and he acquired from the Church a vague sense of duty, respect for his father and the Establishment. Otherwise, there is no sign of Stafford expressing any original views at any time before his thirtieth birthday. Here is Cripps himself on his upbringing:

> Brought up in a traditionally Conservative middle-class family, seldom meeting anyone other than Conservatives, I accepted that environment quite naturally, and from time to time participated in some election or political activity in the same way that I engaged in any other sort of social event. I was neither aware of democracy nor of politics in any real sense of the word.[8]

The radical of the 1930s was not born a socialist; instead he was the product of these chaotic times.

What first brought Stafford Cripps into the Labour Party was the parliamentary career of his father, Charles Alfred Cripps, who became Lord Parmoor. Cripps senior began his career as an upper-class Tory MP, and as late as the 1910 election was still furiously denouncing the socialistic schemes of the Liberal government. But Parmoor was a consistent Christian. Appalled by the terrible slaughter of 1914–18, Cripps senior called for a negotiated end to the war, and allied himself with the Liberal left in Parliament. Having taken this step, he became a leading figure within that left-leaning Christian milieu, whose members organized and ran the League of Nations Society, the World Alliance, the Life and Liberty Movement, Fight the Famine and Save the Children. As Lord Parmoor, he was one of a number of independents to be offered a seat in MacDonald's first minority government. Before accepting the offer of a Cabinet position, Parmoor consulted with his son Stafford's former headmaster, Hubert Burge, then Bishop of Oxford. Burge offered the following measured advice, 'I have taken into account the possible difficulties in which you might find yourself, as for instance if, to appease the extremists, Government measures were introduced which seemed rather recklessly to interfere with fundamental rights of property.'[9] In 1923, these were the concerns of an entire class: not just Burge, but Parmoor and indeed Cripps also. Despite such worries, Burge advised Parmoor to accept, and he duly became Lord President of the Council, MacDonald's deputy in Foreign Affairs.

While his father was enjoying this promotion, Stafford was making a name for himself at the bar, and became the youngest King's Counsel in the land in 1926 at the age of 37. Cripps shared his father's Anglicanism, with its associated morality of duty and discipline. With his father serving in the cabinet, alongside Stafford's step-uncle Sidney Webb, it was only a matter of time before Cripps would join the Labour Party. Prompted by Herbert Morrison, he signed up in 1929. Within months, a seat was found for Stafford Cripps, and he joined the cabinet in 1930 as Solicitor-General. More than one Labour Party activist complained about the promotion of rich lawyers over trade unionists and other working-class activists. In all fairness, Cripps' sudden promotion was less an example of MacDonald's very frequent deference to the rich than a logical conse-quence of Labour's determination to do everything by the book. As Burgess records, 'there were four barristers on the Labour benches in the Commons, and only one KC'.[10] If not from the Cripps family, then where else would Labour fill its quota of law officers?

Having joined the Labour Party, Stafford was not yet a socialist. Indeed for his biographers, Stafford Cripps' conversion to a full-bodied socialism was largely a matter of chance. Chris Bryant suggests that once Stafford's father had joined MacDonald's first government, the son was sure to follow at some stage. More convincingly, the left-wing journalist Paul Foot argues that the central event in the creation of Cripps' socialism was the betrayal of the Labour Party by Ramsay Mac-Donald in 1931. Pressed by the banks to cut unemployment benefit as the solution to economic crisis, MacDonald chose to form a National Government with Liberals and the Conservatives. As Foot writes, 'The debacle of 1931 forced the Labour Party to re-think and reject the "gradualist" approach which had led up to it.' Cripps' organization, the Socialist League, 'demanded that the betrayal of 1931 should never be allowed to happen again. To defend itself against future treachery, Labour had to develop a thoroughgoing socialist programme and a de termination to ensure that the programme could be passed into law without capitalist disruption.'[11]

Stafford Cripps' several biographers largely seem to have forgotten the extent of the popular outrage that marked MacDonald's defection to form a National Government with the Conservatives. Outside Parliament, the winter of 1931–2 was not quiet. Sixty thousand unemployed workers rioted in Glasgow and a further 30,000 in Manchester. The ILP disaffili-ated from the Labour Party in disgust, its 17,000 members forming their own party to the left of Labour. One trade union branch even unstitched the eyes from the portrait of Ramsay MacDonald that had been embroi-dered on its banner.[12] Elsewhere, in the single month of December 1931,

20,000 marched in Newcastle against the means test, while seamen and dockers prepared for a strike against wage cuts, and huge marches in the Potteries, Bootle and Keighley won concessions for the unemployed. Wolsey's struck against the infamous Bedaux time-and-motion system of managerial supervision, and 15,000 protested in the Vale of Leven for winter relief. Finally, that month 12,000 unpaid sailors in Cromarty Firth protested, leading to the Invergordon mutiny.[13]

So the Labour Party that Cripps joined was a party rapidly in ferment. The leading members of the party pledged to learn from MacDonald's betrayal; Labour must have a plan to turn socialism into effect. Moving to the left, the rising figure of Clement Attlee promised a war to the death against capital: 'The moment to strike is the moment of taking power when the Government is freshly elected and assured of its support. The blow struck must be a fatal one.' Herbert Morrison demanded that 'Labour must move to the Left in the true sense of the term – to the real Socialist left.' Even Hugh Gaitskell saw the need to 'smash the economic power of the upper class. When they had the power he believed they would be in a position to carry into action measures which were essentially revolutionary.'[14]

It is this context that explains Stafford Cripps' conversion to socialism. The key text is his 1932 pamphlet, *Can Socialism Come By Constitutional Methods?* According to its author, socialism could come through Parliament, but only if Labour would defend the spirit of democracy against the letter of parliamentary convention.

> The Government's first step will be to call Parliament together at the earliest moment and place before it an Emergency Powers Bill to be passed through all its stages on the first day. This Bill will be wide enough in its terms to allow all that will be immediately necessary to be done by ministerial orders. These orders must be incapable of challenge in the Courts or in any way except in the House of Commons . . . the Socialist Government would make itself temporarily into a dictatorship until the matter could again be put to the test at the polls.[15]

Elsewhere Cripps proposed emergency powers to be used against the throne – even in the Labour Party of the early 1930s, this was not the language on which a career could be built.

Despite such language, it would be wrong to exaggerate Cripps' radicalism. Given that the British Parliament has always been an institution that existed to manage society in the interests of the privileged, those socialists who have emerged from Parliament with the most credit to their name have necessarily been rebels – people like Victor Grayson and Bernadette Devlin – who found the air of compromise impossible to breathe. Stafford Cripps cannot be counted in their number. Roger Spalding cites a debate held in the House of Commons on 14 April 1932, at the height of the depression, and at the zenith of Cripps' left turn. The House was discussing the direction of investment capital, and Stafford Cripps chose this opportunity to make the general case for planning. In his words,

> The view that I take of this matter is based upon Socialistic principles, but at the moment I am on the basis that any appeal of this sort to hon. Members opposite would obviously not meet with any response, besides which it would raise questions of legislation which cannot be discussed tonight. What I am suggesting is that within the present system, circumstances being as they are, and tariffs being in existence, there is still ample scope for a planning arrangement.[16]

So Stafford Cripps still believed that it would be possible to introduce socialist planning without having first achieved a socialist transformation of the economy, the latter condition being impossible to achieve due to the limitations of the parliamentary timetable.

In October 1932, a number of left intellectuals and MPs came together to form the Socialist League. Their numbers included George Strauss, Clement Attlee, William Mellor, Ellen Wilkinson, Harold Laski and D. N. Pritt. Cripps took the chair, while the one-time prominent Communist J. T. Murphy was elected secretary, promising that the League would be an 'organisation of revolutionary socialists . . . for the purpose of winning [the Labour movement] completely for revolutionary socialism'.[17] Yet it would be wrong to take the revolutionary declarations of the founders of the Socialist League at face value. The League remained wedded to the goal of achieving change from above, through Parliament. Its policies represented an attempt to protect an elected Labour government from extra-parliamentary sabotage. This gave it a different strategy from its left-wing competitors, including the British Communist Party. The difference between the League and the Communist Party is apparent in their different attitudes to the unemployed riots of 1932. The propaganda of the Communist Party made clear that it supported the struggles: 'The events of Birkenhead and Belfast were rousing the fighting spirit of the British workers, and with their support the Hunger Marchers were breaking through to London, overcoming all obstacles.' By contrast, when Stafford Cripps was asked what he thought of the unemployed protests, his response was much more equivocal:

> What are we to say to the unemployed of Bristol who point to Birkenhead? We who are daily trying to persuade them that they will achieve nothing by rioting . . . are met at once by the argument 'But what happened in Birkenhead?' Only a few weeks ago I was asked by the unemployed in Bristol to lead a deputation and I refused, because I was not going to associate myself with the rioting I knew would probably result.[18]

The League is best known today for its Unity Campaign of the late 1930s, although to be understood fully this campaign must be placed against the background of the rival Popular Front campaign then being waged by the British Communist Party. This in turn was shaped by the British Communist Party's new line after 1935.[19] Following Dimitrov's announcement of the Popular Front strategy, each Communist Party throughout the International was asked to attempt a complete revolution in its tactics. Having formerly denounced the Labour Party from the left, the British party was now instructed to seek a permanent alliance with it. Indeed, the Communists would henceforth only be allowed to criticize Labour from the right. Under the flag of the Popular Front, Communists should seek alliances with Liberals and left-leaning Tories as well as Labour. When its proposed electoral pact with Labour was turned down in 1936, the Communist Party applied for outright affiliation. By June 1936, over 900 trade unions, activist groups and other left-wing bodies had passed resolutions supporting the party's campaign.

So while the Communist Party was trying to seek a Popular Front with Labour and the Liberals, with the goal of entering the Labour Party, the Socialist League was attempting a very different Unity Campaign of its own. This was not conceived as a Popular Front, but as a militant United Front, an alliance strictly between workers' parties. Such Labour lefts as Barbara Betts (later Barbara Castle) stood out against the Popular Front as a 'travesty of Lenin'. Her friend William Mellor was sacked as editor of *Tribune* because he would not accept the Popular Front. Indeed, with Labour, the Socialist League and the Independent Labour Party all rejecting the Popular Front approach, this Unity Campaign was the broadest organized unity that the Communist Party could achieve. The Socialist League actively backed the Unity Campaign, with Cripps and Aneurin Bevan speaking on platforms at Communist Party events. Indeed, so firm was its support for unity, that the League was itself expelled from the Labour Party in January 1937.[20]

Caught between the two strategies for unity, Cripps' role was to argue the Communist line within the Socialist League and the Labour Party. In September 1938, and following Hitler's annexation of Austria, the Communists called for a 'Peace Bloc' headed by Winston Churchill. Within three weeks, Cripps was singing the same tune. Stafford declared that it was 'necessary to reconsider one's opinions and decisions in light of changing events'. Again in January 1939, Cripps sent a memorandum to the Labour Party, calling for a Popular Front. At Labour's National Executive Committee (NEC), the memorandum was opposed by 17 votes to 3. When he attempted to take the campaign to Labour's rank and file, the NEC finally voted to expel Cripps, by 13 votes to 11.[21]

From 1936 onwards, it seems that Cripps was following Communist Party advice. According to Simon Burgess, it is the watered-down Stalinism of the Socialist League which explains the twists and turns of Cripps' 'erratic odyssey' through the 1930s, from supporting general disarmament, to pro-Soviet interventionism. Certainly it is clear that Stafford

Cripps' socialism was shaped by a series of personal friendships, and in a similar vein to Burgess, Chris Bryant makes much of Stafford's admiration for Harry Pollitt. Outside Labour, Cripps had an extraordinary chance to build a new socialist organization. He was one of the most popular figures in the Labour Party, a regular first-place in elections to Labour's NEC. The logic of his position impelled Stafford to build a new left-wing current, but instead Cripps chose to keep himself in Parliament. Even in Parliament, his conduct was surprising. Instead of organizing with the lefts in the Communist Party and the ILP, Cripps attempted to use his family ties to the dissident Conservatives around Churchill. His first strategy was to create a Popular Front for war, his second goal to secure a position for himself. These attempts were successful. Cripps spent the years from 1939 to 1942 in transit, first attempting a diplomatic journey to India and China, and then as the ambassador to the Soviet Union. After 1942, Stafford Cripps returned to Britain, his career boosted by his time in the Soviet Union. Invited into the war cabinet, Cripps served as Leader of the House and then (having been demoted from the cabinet) as Minister for Aircraft Production.

The last years of Stafford Cripps' life were spent in office. Invited to rejoin Labour, Cripps was Attlee's Economic Minister (1945–8) and then Chancellor (1948–50). In the latter role, Cripps had several achievements to his name. First, he expanded the department, making it responsible for economic planning, and using the fiscal authority of the Exchequer to dominate the cabinet for the first time. It is for this reason that Chris Bryant dubs Cripps 'the first modern Chancellor'. Second, Cripps was the first Labour Chancellor to make incomes policy a strategy for government. Introduced in 1948, Cripps' 'Statement on Personal Incomes, Costs and Prices' argued that 'In present conditions, and until more goods and services are available for the home market, there is no justification for any *general* increase of individual money incomes. Such an increase will merely raise costs of production, without making more goods available, and so can only have an inflationary effect.'[22] Cripps' policy blazed a dismal trail for successive Labour Chancellors to follow, 'Iron' Chancellors like our own, cutting wages while leaving profits intact.

Towards the end of his biography, Simon Burgess endorses the verdict of Labour's *Daily Herald* that Cripps was Britain's 'Minister of Recovery'.[23] In contrast to the received wisdom, he suggests that the image of 'Austerity' Cripps was black propaganda on the part of Conservatives. But the truth is that the language of austerity originated with Cripps himself. Take, for example, the Cripps speech broadcast to the nation in September 1949:

> We must at all costs avoid anything that increases costs of production. Indeed, we must continue with as much or even more vigour than ever, the drive for greater efficiency and lower costs of production. This change is not instead of the policies which we have been following to

earn more dollars, but in addition to them, because they of themselves have not been enough.[24]

Nor was this only a matter of language. Cripps stuck to the most fastidious of habits, rising at four to take a cold bath, walking at seven, taking roughage at eight with his breakfast. A lifelong teetotaller, 'his two meals a day consisted of raw fruit or vegetables, soured milk, brown bread and butter with the occasional baked potato thrown in as a luxury'.[25] He was a propagandist for the Alexander technique and vegetarianism.[26] Keeping to such tight routines himself, Cripps expected to find the same forbearance demonstrated by the entire British people. For Sir Stafford Cripps, austerity was not merely a policy of expediency; it was a reflection of his – indeed the nation's – personal relationship with God. Stafford lectured the Church of England's Lambeth Conference on financial crises, which were not economic in origin (he claimed) but 'the outcome of a profound moral disturbance in the world'. Douglas Jay, then a junior minister at the Treasury, records Cripps' belief that his decisions were 'directly dictated' by God.[27] Under his Chancellorship, Labour's early reforming burst was stopped. There were no further nationalizations, no further reforming bills on the scale of 1945–7; Cripps was adamant, the state must pay its way.[28]

Tired, Stafford Cripps' face showed the toll of years of overwork. He resigned as Chancellor in the winter of 1950 and disappeared from public view. After a brief illness, Cripps died on 21 April 1952.

From left to right: 1939

Having discussed Cripps' life in the first half of this chapter, the second section addresses Stafford's conversion to gradualism. Having been a radical in 1932, why did he later shift so fast to the right? Indeed, having left the Labour Party in 1939, why was he unable to build a consistent socialist organization, in Parliament or outside? And having rejoined Labour in 1945, why did Stafford Cripps so quickly become such a respectable figure – what happened to the former radical voice of the left? One explanation is suggested by the photographs of 1940s-era Stafford Cripps. Always impeccably attired in glasses, white shirt, tie and three-piece pin-stripe suit, Cripps appeared every inch the successful industrialist. Given enough industrial experience running the war economy, it would seem that Cripps returned inevitably to the values of his early years. Our hero simply went back to the class of his birth. Such an account was widely believed at the time, for there were always members of the Labour Party who distrusted their landed ally. Related by marriage, Beatrice Webb could see the limits of his politics clearly. 'For leadership in the labour movement Stafford had a most unfit upbringing.'

Meanwhile, Peter Clarke tells the story of one trade unionist petitioner whose letter to Cripps began 'Dear Sir and Comrade'.[29] Even as late as 1948, Cripps' Bristol East Constituency Labour Party only reaffirmed him as their candidate by 15 votes to 14, a close enough vote to suggest that such class suspicion never went away. Yet such a fatalistic account can make no sense of Cripps' 1930s-era socialism. Surely it was more principled, more deep-rooted, than this line would indicate?

One alternative approach would be to look more closely at the events of 1939. Having been expelled from the Labour Party, Cripps remained within the House of Commons. Why did Cripps fail to organize against Labour from without? Why did he restrict himself to parliamentary man-oeuvres? One half of the answer is that Cripps did actually try to organize outside the Labour leadership. This is the very crime that was punished with his expulsion. Having lost the vote for a Popular Front at Labour's NEC in January 1939, Cripps published his 'Manifesto' as a petition. Over half a million copies were printed, and several large public meetings held, under the aegis of the Left Book Club. Yet although Stafford Cripps' Popular Front campaign received the backing of the *Manchester Guardian*, the Communist *Daily Worker* and the liberal *News Chronicle*, the campaign failed to gather momentum, and Stafford's petition did not achieve the planned mass support.

The other half of the explanation for Stafford's limited conduct in 1939 is more a question of tactics. Cripps' major ally was the Communist Party, and Simon Burgess suggests that Stafford Cripps had been flirting with Communism since at least 1932, when he confided in George Lansbury that he was considering joining the Communist Party.[30] Yet by 1939 the Communists could have little use for a figure like Cripps. Their strategy was to seek Communist affiliation to Labour, and to achieve this the Communist Party needed every ally within the Labour camp it could muster. There is no record of Pollitt's response to Cripps' expulsion, but the overwhelming likelihood is that he was not pleased. The original voice arguing with Cripps to disband the League had been Pollitt's. Faced with the very first ultimatum from Labour's NEC, and acting (according to the ILP) on Communist advice, Cripps closed the League down. This decision was not supported by the League's membership, and if it had been taken to a vote, Cripps could easily have lost. If Pollitt argued with Cripps to remain within Labour in 1937, then Cripps had still less to offer his ally in 1939. Indeed, when another fellow-traveller on Labour's exec-utive, D. N. Pritt, moved to back Stafford's petition in 1939, it was the Communist Party that advised against. In effect, Cripps was left alone and without organized support.[31]

The fact that Stafford Cripps was left without options in 1939 still does not explain the permanent right-wing transformation that marked his pol-itics from then on. In the longer term, other options remained open to him. Aneurin Bevan, expelled at the same time as Stafford, remained wedded to Parliament, yet in later years Bevan was a far more consistent opponent of privilege than Cripps. As Paul Foot remarks, 'Whether Cripps junked all his 1930s ideas alongside his former Stalinism is not clear, but clearly something happened during the war which drove him back into conventional politics.'[32] According to Simon Burgess, it was Cripps' time as ambassador to Moscow which disabused our hero of his earlier allegiance to Communism. The biographer quotes a 1942 Bristol sermon, in which Cripps denounced Stalin as a 'dictator betraying socialism in a regime indistinguishable from Hitler's Germany'.[33] If this is correct (and Burgess's reference is remarkably vague) then Cripps' odyssey does take on a greater logic. Without the prop of the Soviet Union to bolster up his socialism, Cripps turned to religion to fill its place. The notion of a planned national economy was supplanted by a personal devotion to duty. In turn, the Protestant work ethic became the socialism of austerity.

One argument follows from this incident. In order to explain more fully the decline of Cripps' radicalism, more needs to be said about Stafford Cripps' socialism at its height. To understand the Cripps of 1948–50, we must understand the Cripps of 1932. Compared to many other figures in the Marxist tradition (to which Cripps was then linked, if only in the minds of his audience), Stafford Cripps' socialism was always a matter of intellect, and never an affair of the heart. The following is taken from a 1932 speech, widely quoted (especially by his opponents) as an example of Sir Stafford's republicanism:

> When the Labour Party comes into power they must act rapidly and it will be necessary to deal with the House of Lords and the City of London. There is no doubt that we will have to oversee opposition from Buckingham Palace and other places as well. It is absolutely essential that it should be made perfectly clear to the people exactly what it is we ask for the power to do. There must be no time to allow the forces outside to gather and to exercise their influence upon the legislature before the key parts of capitalism have been transferred to the control of the state.

When it comes to interpreting this passage, three points stand out. First, Cripps' socialism was logical and articulate. Stafford Cripps was trying to answer the real problem of how to bring about a different society. He sought to bridge the gap between the short-term activity and the long-term goals of the Socialist movement. Second, in 1932 Cripps remained hostile to the rich and the powerful. By the end of the decade such class hostility would be downplayed in favour of foreign policy concerns. After 1940, it would disappear altogether. Only for the time being did Stafford Cripps still place himself on the side of the dispossessed. Third, even at its best, Cripps' socialism was analytical and passionless. Always in his language socialism was something that would be achieved from above. 'It will be necessary', he said, 'there is no doubt', 'it is absolutely essential'.

Such impersonal verbs left a hole where the working-class movement should have been. What force could bring about socialism? Who else would introduce the 'necessary' change?

Perhaps the Labour politician of 1932 was hostile to the task of socialist persuasion. Propaganda and the articulation of belief had been the skills of Ramsay MacDonald, and his was no path to follow. For whatever reason, Cripps' was a chess-player's socialism, concerned with means and process, indifferent to ends and results. If Cripps had taken sides in the arguments among German Social Democrats in the 1890s, then he would have stood with Edward Bernstein's argument against Rosa Luxemburg. The socialist movement was what mattered to Cripps; it was everything to him, the goal was nothing.

Reading again the quotation from Cripps above, I am reminded of a passage from the 1970s activist and East End doctor David Widgery. He was concerned to attack the routine, grey and humourless attitudes adopted by so many figures on the British left, to make a virtue out of political isolation. Widgery's criticism was of a different incarnation of such doleful socialism, in his own age, but the point could be made for an earlier generation as well: 'If socialism is transmitted in a deliberately doleful, pre-electronic idiom, if its emotional appeal is to working class sacrifice and middle class guilt, and if its dominant medium is the printed word and the public procession, it will simply bounce off people who have grown up this side of the 1960s watershed. And barely leave a dent behind.'[34] If Widgery is correct, then the decline of Stafford Cripps' radicalism was well-nigh inevitable. The result of such an austere and moralistic socialism could only be defeat.

Conclusion

At the opening of this chapter, I suggested that in evaluating our own tradition, socialist historians must attempt to make two moves. First, we need to celebrate the diversity of non-Blairite voices within the Labour movement – in contrast to the narrow celebration of power shown by Blair's clique. Second, we must also speak critically of those voices that failed to establish a thoroughgoing alternative to the status quo. Without their failure we would not be where we are today. For the author of this chapter, the most important rule is that it does not have to end like that. Cripps, the young rebel, was limited both by the paucity of his own vision and also by external factors. These included the sterility of the Communist Party, which was such an influence on Cripps, and also the difficult political conditions, which limited the space for a truly democratic socialism, once the curtains of the Cold War had started to come down. Yet there are other socialist visions; Cripps' decline was not the only possible outcome. This chapter has mentioned David Widgery's condemnation of 'working class sacrifice and middle class guilt'. One plausible way to read Stafford Cripps' career is as a twenty-year vindication of Widgery's rule. If socialist organizations are built on a celebration of misery, then the result will be neither pleasure nor socialism.

6

Alfred Rosmer and the Red International of Labour Unions

Ian Birchall

Alfred Rosmer (1877–1964) does not easily fit the stereotype of a working-class leader. Although he remained an intransigent revolutionary from his first association with the *Vie ouvrière* group in 1909 till his death in 1964, it was only for a period of some four years, from 1920 to 1924, that he played a leadership role, both in France and in the newly founded Communist International. For the rest of the time he was a journalist, historian and activist in small groupings.

The history of the labour movement is full of leaders who have come up, like scum, on the surface of the rising waters of class struggle, and have then clung on to their elevated position as the tide receded beneath them. Rosmer was a leader of a very different type. As such, he was representative of a new type of leadership which began to emerge in the early years of the Comintern, until it was stifled by Zinoviev's 'Bolshevization'. Rosmer thus deserves to be rescued from the obscurity in which his life and work have remained since the triumph of Stalinism.[1]

Alfred Rosmer

There are several reasons why Rosmer's role as a labour leader remains shadowy. One is personal modesty; in his memoirs he lists the leading positions he held in the Comintern, adding, 'I never took personal pride in these positions. Most of them were imposed on me; I accepted them reluctantly, and I was never happier than when I could get rid of them and return to the ranks.'[2]

Rosmer was known for his discretion; he lacked 'oratorical talent'.[3] Lenin is reputed to have said: 'Rosmer is a man who knows how to keep his mouth shut in several languages.'[4] This was not simply a question of Rosmer's 'character', but of the milieu he came from. The syndicalist grouping around *La Vie ouvrière*[5] put great stress on moral qualities, as was normal on the 'anti-authoritarian left'.[6] It was in *La Vie ouvrière* that Albert Thierry had advanced the idea of *le refus de parvenir* (the refusal to make a career).[7] This implied a generalized distrust of intellectuals, parliamentarians and assorted aspirant leaders, and hence the attempt to develop a new style of leadership.

Rosmer's approach can be seen in his articles on the Couriau affair in 1913. Madame Couriau, of Lyons, had taken a job in the printing industry. The union would not accept her into membership, and instructed her husband to tell her to abandon her job; when he refused, he was expelled from the union. Rosmer wrote five articles for the syndicalist daily *La Bataille syndicaliste*.[8] In the first four he interviewed various union officials to establish the different views about female labour held within the union. Only after carefully listening to the various opinions did Rosmer set out his own position – a devastating attack on the bourgeois family that put him on a level with the most advanced feminists.[9] It is easy to see why Rosmer found himself at odds with an authoritarian demagogue like Zinoviev. He was already developing into the sort of leader he was to recognize in Lenin: 'Just because he knew a lot, he was able to fill out his knowledge when the opportunity arose, and also, an unusual thing in a "leader", to recognise that he had quite simply been wrong.'[10]

Rosmer's obscurity also owes something to his subsequent development. After expulsion from the French Communist Party in 1924 he remained a lifelong anti-Stalinist. He is ignored by Stalinist historiography.[11] For anti-Communists, who see Bolshevism as a monolithic conspiracy, the complex interaction of tendencies in the early years of the Comintern is an unnecessarily distracting subtlety.

Rosmer – like Victor Serge – was a dissident among dissidents. Initially he played an enthusiastic role in Trotsky's attempt to build a left opposition; his lifelong partner Marguerite wrote to Trotsky with pride about their efforts to 'deintellectualize' young recruits by making them do early morning paper sales.[12] But he broke with Trotsky over the latter's preference for Raymond Molinier, whom Rosmer believed would never 'understand anything about Marxism'.[13] In 1951 he endorsed Natalia Sedova's break with the Fourth International, arguing that 'the people who see themselves as the faithful followers of Trotsky, and who are at present in the leadership of the Fourth International, have lost any right to speak in his name', being 'sometimes . . . more Stalinist than Stalin'. He characterized Russia as 'nothing but a great power, military and militaristic, . . . distinctive only by the brutality of a totalitarian regime'.[14] It was, however, Rosmer, together with Maurice Nadeau, and not the organized French Trotskyists, who took on the job of finding new publishers for Trotsky's writings in France after the Second World War.[15] Even at the height of the Cold War, he maintained his strict independence of both Washington and Moscow, breaking with his old friends on *La Révolution prolétarienne* because they were diverging from a Third Camp position.[16]

The Red International of Labour Unions

Even for the independent anti-Stalinist left, the tradition with which the London Socialist Historians Group aligns itself, Rosmer poses certain problems. These derive from the fact that one of his main jobs in Moscow in 1920–1 was the preparation of the Red International of Labour Unions (RILU – also sometimes called the Red Trade Union International or the Profintern.)

The RILU has not had a very favourable treatment from historians of the anti-Stalinist left. For Walter Kendall its very existence was a threat to the International Federation of Trade Unions (IFTU), and hence to workers' organization:

> In Moscow during 1921 the Russian Bolsheviks had set up a Red International of Labour Unions (RILU), the main membership base of which was the Russian unions under tight communist control. The RILU was specifically created to smash the IFTU. Those unions which could not be captured from within were to be split, or, if this was impossible, destroyed.[17]

The account is tendentious. The RILU repudiated any attempts to split unions, and aimed to 'destroy' IFTU unions only in the sense of winning the leadership by superior politics.[18]

Tony Cliff and Donny Gluckstein are far more positive in their evaluation of the intentions of the Bolsheviks, but are almost equally damning in their judgement of the achievements of the RILU. They speak of 'the error and the complete fiasco of the enterprise', and argue that 'the trouble with the whole concept of RILU was not merely that it was ambiguous, but that it was fundamentally wrong'. They claim that the RILU 'ignored the difference between parties and collective organisations such as unions', that the Bolsheviks failed to understand the nature of trade union bureaucracy and to recognize the deep-rootedness and durability of the bureaucracy in the western world, and that 'instead of attempting to build a trade union international at an official level' the RILU should have encouraged 'rank-and-file movements'.[19] Ralph Darlington's recent biography of J. T. Murphy – who played an important role in the Founding Congress of the RILU – follows the same analysis as Cliff and Gluckstein, seeing the 'whole concept of the RILU' as 'fundamentally defective'.[20]

The history of the RILU is a complex and tortuous one,[21] and it would be difficult to claim it as one of the most brilliant successes of the

Comintern. But while Cliff and Gluckstein undoubtedly make valid points, they are too negative in their judgement of what was an improvised response to a contradictory situation. A re-evaluation, seeing the experience from the point of view of Rosmer (rather than from that of the British labour movement, a perspective that dominates in the case of all the aforementioned critics) may provide a different interpretation and draw some lessons for the future.

The RILU experience must be placed in the context of the concern of the Bolshevik leaders, especially Lenin and Trotsky, to draw the anti-authoritarian left into the orbit of the Communist International. In Russia anarchists had played a significant role at the time of the revolution, and Lenin in particular had always found time to discuss with representatives of anarchism and syndicalism, within Russia and in the international movement.[22] Lenin went out of his way to hold meetings with anarchist and syndicalist delegates before the Second Comintern Congress.[23] Rosmer recalled that, prior to the Second Comintern Congress, a Spanish delegate had declared: 'We are waging a pitiless struggle against the anarchists', to which Bukharin replied sharply:

> What do you mean by fighting against the anarchists? Since October, there have been some anarchists who have come over to the dictatorship of the proletariat. Other have come closer to us and are working in the soviets and in the economic institutions. It's not a question of 'fighting' them, but of discussing frankly and cordially, seeing if we can work together, and only abandoning the attempt if there is an irremovable obstacle.[24]

In the case of the French labour movement this was a vital consideration. In 1920 the Comintern had high hopes of winning the majority of the Socialist Party (SFIO).[25] But it also needed support in the main trade union body, the CGT. In 1920 the CGT had two million members, as against the SFIO's 180,000.[26] Not just quantity was at stake, but quality. The anarchists and syndicalists had been the first supporters of the Russian Revolution in France, when most members of the SFIO were hostile or indifferent.[27] The SFIO was stuffed out with parliamentarians and careerists who were willing to affiliate to the Comintern because it was currently popular.[28] The revolutionary syndicalists around Rosmer and Monatte were, precisely because of the moralistic tradition from which they came, of far higher calibre, and would be needed to play a role in the party leadership as well as serving as a bridge to the best militants in the CGT. As Henri Guilbeaux said at the Second Comintern Congress: 'Until there is a Communist party in France that the supporters of Comrade Loriot and the syndicalists around Rosmer and Monatte will join, we will not have won the masses. It is not by artificially transforming the French Socialist Party into a Communist party that we will win over the French masses.'[29]

Hence the warm welcome Rosmer received in Moscow in 1920. Trotsky, who had known him in Paris during the war, greeted him with a 'friendly reproach': 'Well, you were in no hurry to come and see us! Revolutionaries and journalists have come from everywhere except France.'[30] Somewhat later Lenin confided in Trotsky that he wished the whole leadership of the French party could be ousted and replaced by the group around Rosmer and Monatte.[31]

Contrary to the conspiratorial view often presented, the Bolsheviks did not have a clear, ruthless strategy for capturing control of the world's trade unions. In the first years after the revolution, their position was vague and erratic.[32] Trotsky's Manifesto for the First Congress of the Comintern in 1919 argued that 'the old parties, the old organizations of trade unions have in the persons of their leading summits proved incapable not only of solving but even of understanding the tasks posed by the new epoch.' It was implied that trade unions were now outdated and that the soviet, 'a broad organization which embraces the working masses independently of trade or level of political development already attained', would replace them.[33]

By the summer of 1919, revolutions in Hungary and Bavaria had gone down to defeat, and it was clear that the struggle would be a longer one than had been expected. Many authentically revolutionary militants were arguing that Communists should leave the reactionary unions and establish new bodies. This perspective had to be firmly rejected, but with the aim of winning rather than repelling its advocates. In this context, Lenin wrote *Left-wing Communism, An Infantile Disorder*, distributed to delegates to the Second Congress, in which he argued that revolutionaries must stay in the trade unions, if necessary by subterfuge.[34]

This left the Comintern with the problem of developing an organizational form whereby it could reach trade-union militants, in particular those influenced by various forms of syndicalism.[35] The RILU may not have been the ideal model, but what were the alternatives?

The Second Comintern Congress

At the Second Congress various approaches emerged. The simplest came from Paul Levi,[36] who effectively argued that nothing need be done; the anti-authoritarians were backward and could be ignored:

> It seems to me that clarifying the differences between communism on the one hand and the anarchist views of the Spanish comrade on the other is quite out of line with the tasks of this congress, nor does it serve the interests of what the world today is demanding of the Communist International, namely, fully defining a course of action. We get no closer to carrying out this task by focusing the discussion on a question

that the majority of the western European working class settled decades ago.[37]

Zinoviev's solution also had the merits of simplicity. In the report of the Executive Committee, he argued that the Comintern should 'revive the tradition of the First International', whereby trade unions as well as parties could affiliate.[38] It was not a very plausible proposal. This was the same Congress that was imposing the Twenty-One Conditions on affiliates. While it is true that the Spanish CNT and the Italian USI did vote to join the Comintern, it is unlikely that many other trade union bodies would do so. And the suggestion apparently made by Zinoviev, that the Twenty-One Conditions would not apply to unions,[39] would have created a situation whereby there were two classes of affiliates in the International, those who accepted the Twenty-One Conditions and those who did not.

Zinoviev followed this up by introducing the debate on the role and structure of Communist parties with a speech notable for its triumphalism and ultimatory style. The syndicalists were bluntly told that they were not 'ultra-lefts' but rather the bearers of bourgeois ideology:

> Sometimes comrades who oppose the need for the party fancy themselves the 'left' opposition. In my opinion that is not the case. That is not opposition from the left but quite the opposite. This antiparty mood expresses a vestige of bourgeois influence on the proletariat. The bourgeoisie drinks wine and exhorts the proletarian to drink water.
>
> Every good bourgeois belongs to a political party by the age of twenty-one. But to the workers they give propaganda against joining parties and catch workers on that hook rather often . . .
>
> Let us now take up the roots of this rejection of the party. We see that its deepest roots lie in the impact of bourgeois ideology.[40]

Such a stupidly patronizing diatribe could only provoke the indignation of those it was meant to persuade. The Spanish syndicalist delegate Angel Pestaña protested vigorously; the task of drawing him in was certainly not made any easier.[41]

Zinoviev rounded off his performance with typical rhetoric, invoking the Russian experience as universally valid, something he later put into practice in the disastrous 'Bolshevization' of 1924: 'Had we not had a centralized party built along military lines, with iron discipline, organized over the course of twenty years, by now we doubtless would have been defeated twenty times over.'[42] Though the Bolshevik experience was undoubtedly heroic, the party's fortunes had been rather more complex;[43] there had been little sign of 'iron discipline' in 1917 when Zinoviev opposed insurrection in the non-party press. The whole lamentable affair concluded with language more suitable for a church: 'To the advanced Russian worker the party is sacred; it is the best of all that exists, more precious than life, dearer than all else, the highest, the guiding star.'[44]

It was left to Lenin and Trotsky to salvage something from this appalling mess. They adopted a very different strategy. Rather than insulting and denouncing the syndicalists, they sought to draw them closer by pointing to what they had in common with the Bolshevik tradition. Lenin referred to the syndicalist concept of the 'active minority', which was very close to the idea of the party, as the most advanced element in the class; hence he argued that syndicalists should accept party organization. But he recognized that many syndicalists were anti-party because of their experience of corrupt parliamentary organizations.[45]

Trotsky too sought to conciliate rather than to estrange. Responding to Levi, he pointed out that the likes of Scheidemann might accept the principle of the 'party', but that he had more in common with 'American or Spanish or French syndicalists who not only want to fight against the bourgeoisie but who, unlike Scheidemann, really want to tear its head off.' He recalled his days in Paris during the war: 'I felt myself a comrade among comrades in the company of Comrades Monatte, Rosmer and others with an anarchistic past.'[46]

Trotsky developed similar arguments in a letter to Rosmer's close comrade, Pierre Monatte, then in jail. Here he set out the case for the revolutionary party, not with Zinovievite bluster, but with closely reasoned argument. He began with the fact that the CGT was led by the pro-war, pro-bourgeois Jouhaux; for the syndicalists to argue for the political 'independence' of the unions in fact meant abstaining from the struggle to replace Jouhaux.

He went on to discuss the question of organization: 'But as you know, within the working class itself all elements are not equally conscious. The aim to be achieved by the revolution appears clearly and in its entirety only to the most conscious revolutionary minority of the proletariat.' The syndicalists recognized the need for a 'guiding minority' to educate the mass of workers and provide them with a programme for action: 'What would you call this guiding minority of the proletariat, grouped into a homogeneous bloc by the communist programme and eager to lead the working class in the decisive assault on the citadel of capitalism? We call it the *communist party*.'

He concluded in conciliatory style. Forms of organization were secondary; what mattered was the revolutionary goal: 'The trade union, co-operative and political organizations, the press, the clandestine groups in the army, the parliamentary platform, the municipalities etc., are only varieties of external organization, partial methods or bases to be defended. The struggle remains one in its content, whatever may be the sphere in which it is taking place.'[47]

With the Bolsheviks themselves confused and divided, the Congress could hardly come to a clear conclusion. A Provisional International Council of Trade and Industrial Unions was established, with Rosmer as one of its members. That such a militant, who could have played an invaluable role in the establishment of the French Communist Party, was retained in Moscow is testimony to the shortage of leaders which bedevilled the Comintern.[48] Now Rosmer had to pick up the pieces.

The tradition of syndicalism

If the concept of the RILU was far from ideal, it was perhaps the least bad alternative. Critics like Kendall, Cliff and Gluckstein and Darlington often look at the RILU from an anglocentric standpoint. Syndicalism was far from uniform; it meant very different things in different contexts.

Thus Darlington writes that 'one of the most important limitations of Murphy's syndicalist outlook' was his anti-political stance in relation to opposing the war, which he blames on a syndicalist tradition of separating politics and economics.[49] But if this is fair criticism of Murphy, it could scarcely be directed at Rosmer, who opposed the war from day one and took the struggle into the heart of the labour movement.

Thus in the spring of 1915 Rosmer had been involved in one of the first public actions against the war. The metalworkers' union had decided to bring out a special issue of its newspaper for May Day. Rosmer worked closely with Merrheim, a leading member of the metalworkers' union. Government censorship strictly controlled any published material that was critical of the war. Merrheim and Rosmer prepared an issue with a number of articles against the war, including a piece by Rosmer about the strikes on the Clyde in February 1915, of which French workers knew nothing. The proofs were submitted to the censors, who demanded the removal of the offending articles. Then a few papers were run off with the appropriate blank spaces, and a large number with the full version. They were carefully packed with the censored papers at the top and the rest underneath, and posted. Some 17,000 papers were distributed to members of the metalworkers' union and former subscribers to *La Vie ouvrière*.[50]

The traditions of the French syndicalist movement were widely admired and imitated on an international scale. Moreover, French trade unionism was very different from British; in 1912 the CGT had just 400,000 members (as against 2,232,446 in the TUC);[51] thus the French union was much less inclusive than the British, far more a case of the 'active minority' giving leadership to the unorganized masses.[52] The Italian USI and the Spanish CNT were even smaller. Thus any international structure would have to accommodate a wide variety of national organizations.

The RILU is also said to have been a contradiction, because of 'the incompatibility of the proposal to call on communists to work within the existing Amsterdam trade unions, whilst at the same time calling on these unions to split from the Amsterdam International in favour of Moscow'.[53] But at the risk of abusing the dialectical method, it may be pointed out that the contradictions were in reality. There was no simple formula that could solve the complex problems of the situation. After all, it could be argued that it was 'contradictory' for the Comintern to fight to split the social democratic parties, and then almost immediately proceed to call on them to join a united front. Once again the contradiction lay in reality.

Amid these contradictions Rosmer had to carry through the work of preparing for the founding of the RILU, a process that took considerably longer than originally hoped.[54] There was a major effort to produce publications to extend the influence of the proposed new body.[55] Rosmer had to organize translations amid difficult circumstances and staff shortages; on one occasion he recruited a Menshevik woman to assist him.[56] He also found himself in a buffer position, as one of the few intermediaries trusted by both the Bolsheviks and the anti-authoritarians in Russia and abroad. Thus Rosmer was chosen to speak for the Comintern at Kropotkin's funeral, perhaps the only Comintern representative not liable to provoke the anger of the anarchists, some of whom had been temporarily released from jail to attend. Contrary to the myth of monolithic Bolshevik control, he was given no instructions, merely told that the Comintern had 'confidence' in him.[57]

It was Rosmer who was approached by representatives of the Russian anarcho-syndicalists who wanted to exploit the Comintern's desire to influence foreign anti-authoritarians in order to raise the issue of repression against anarchists in Russia. Maximoff, one of the syndicalists, noted that 'Rosmer was friendly and promised to examine our statement'.[58]

Rosmer had to deal with Zinoviev's arrogant and ignorant manoeuvring. When it was decided to address an appeal to the IFTU, 'Zinoviev merely let fly a broadside of insults, often in pretty bad taste, against "Messrs. Scab leaders", etc.', showing total ignorance of the labour movement and the principles of united front activity.[59]

The Founding Conference

The Founding Conference of the RILU was held in July 1921. Rosmer opened proceedings with the report of the Provisional Council. Unwisely he claimed total membership of the RILU as seventeen million workers; he was immediately challenged by J. T. Murphy and the Hungarian Kiraly, who argued that the figures failed to distinguish affiliated unions and minorities within reformist unions. Rosmer concluded his introduction by recognizing the problem of the trade union bureaucracy: 'Two enemies had to be conquered – the capitalists and their servants, the reactionary officials of the union movement.'[60]

The next item was an economic report by Eugene Varga, who provided the rationale for the RILU line of staying within the reformist unions; as Murphy reported:

> We are in for a period – it may be a long one – of persistent struggle, in which the Unions will be called upon to play an important part. It was therefore necessary to push on rapidly with the work of revolutionising them, and he believed that to do that the best policy was that of working with the Unions rather than attempting to build new competitive organisations.[61]

Then came the touchy subject of the relations between the RILU and the Comintern; it was not easy to find a formulation that would be acceptable to the syndicalists, with their long-standing opposition to political intervention in the unions. It had been planned that Zinoviev should give the main report, and be followed by Rosmer. At the last moment Zinoviev lost his nerve; as Rosmer reports: 'Only just before the Congress did he notice that there wasn't much affection for him there; rightly or wrongly the syndicalists didn't like him. As a result he decided to abandon his report and to withdraw from the Congress.'[62]

Instead Rosmer gave the introductory report, though he was highly reluctant to do so, since he believed that appearing as the Comintern spokesperson would undermine his personal efforts to create reconciliation. He was followed by Tom Mann.[63] Rosmer began by recognizing 'strong hostility on the part of the trade unions towards the political parties'. In order to mollify those who felt such hostility, he stressed his rejection of the traditions of the Second International, in opposition to which the syndicalist current had grown up:

> The Second International stands on the point of view that the decisive role belongs to the political parties, that they must take all political questions into their hands, and that they alone are capable of prescribing the general direction for the movement of the proletariat. The unions were pushed into the background as organisations which must confine themselves to the area of purely trade union questions.

He defended the need for the revolutionary party, using language very different from Zinoviev's, and stressed the need for a positive approach to the unions:

> The party is the soul of the working class. I do not mean to say thereby, that the trade unions should be subordinated to it. Absolutely not. The party must show a particular willingness to meet the unions halfway. The unions must serve as a point of support to the party in the realisation of socialism. Here there are no second-class 'comrades', and we cannot tolerate any arrogance by one group of fighters towards another. The syndicalists are just as good Communists as we are. We must, however, vigorously reject what has been called 'the theory of the equality of the parties who are in agreement'. This theory does not correspond to the truth. This is the direct legacy of the decrepit, thoroughly rotten and mendacious Second International, whose principle was as follows: 'You shall concern yourself with political matters and we with

economic matters; don't stick your nose in our affairs and we won't worry about yours'. No. We must tear this theory out by the roots from the consciousness of politically aware workers.

Rosmer went on to contrast the alleged subordination of unions to party command with what was in fact the Comintern position, the need for Communists to organize in the unions to fight for their policies and to win the support of their fellow-workers:[64]

> In Russia the Communist Party included the revolutionary elements and always differentiated itself from the political parties of other countries, both by its doctrine and by its action. Its members had to be in the front ranks of those fighting for the proletariat, wherever that struggle might be. They had to permeate all the labour organisations. Its members strove to achieve the dominant influence in the unions, and their claim to do so was completely justified and normal.
>
> The representatives of various tendencies, movements and parties, the different groupings fighting inside the unions, all make efforts to win a dominating influence. That is perfectly justified and acceptable.

He then, tactfully but firmly, distinguished himself from Zinoviev's position, arguing that he had been wrong to accuse the CGT and the Amiens Charter of 1906[65] of 'neutralism':

> But the *Charte d'Amiens* is a far more important document than it seems to be to comrade Zinoviev. In order to grasp its full meaning, one should not confine oneself merely to reading the text; one must be aware to what stage of the history of the syndicalist movement it belongs, and why and under what conditions it was adopted. It was elaborated at the time when syndicalism had taken firm root in France. It grouped around itself elements of the most diverse origins, former anarchists and those who had earlier been members of a range of socialist parties; the third category was formed of the new elements, who can be regarded as true syndicalists. These diverse elements were united by the same concept of the final goal, the abolition of capitalism and wage labour. They were not so very concerned about the elaboration of a new method of struggle. And even if they succeeded in elaborating one, can it be deduced from this that the CGT was completely neutral? And has it at any time been neutral? No, and the attempt to ascribe to the *Charte d'Amiens* this neutralism as a characteristic feature of syndicalism is a vulgar error.

Rosmer then developed the same argument that Lenin and Trotsky had developed at the Second Congress, namely that the CGT in fact functioned as a 'party', and that its anti-party stance was no more than a question of terminology:

> It has never been the intention of the CGT to confine its tasks to the purely trade union sphere, it has always taken part in all the questions

of the politics of the current time, and not only in specific cases but precisely in all matters.

In fact before the war the CGT was an authentic political party, but a party of a quite particular form. But when, at the Amiens Congress, the 'charter' which has become so famous was discussed, the revolutionary syndicalists had to fight against two groups. On the one hand against those who belonged to the socialist parties and defended the conceptions of the Second International. These people, moreover, endeavoured to ensure that the French unions which belonged to the CGT should not step outside the framework of a purely trade union activity and should leave political work to them. On the other hand the revolutionary syndicalists had to deal with some elements who showed a certain organisational strength and who almost exactly corresponded to the English trade unionists. These workers were mainly represented by the federation of workers in the printing industry. So among the revolutionary syndicalists there were two opposed groupings. On the one hand the trade unionists, who were concerned exclusively with questions of wages, the length of the working day, etc., and on the other hand the Socialists, who declared: 'Yes, we are revolutionaries too, but only the political parties and not the CGT should concern themselves with the revolution; the latter should in no circumstances carry out revolutionary propaganda.'

He concluded by arguing for a 'permanent link' between the RILU and the Comintern, while disavowing any 'desire to subordinate the RILU to the Communist International'.[66]

Rosmer's speech was one of his major contributions to the theory and practice of the Comintern. Three basic themes emerge:

- A defence of the syndicalist tradition. Rather than claiming universal validity for the Bolshevik model, Rosmer insisted that what had been positive in syndicalism should be maintained and incorporated into the Comintern.
- A vigorous rejection of any attempt to separate the political and the economic. If such separation was always to be rejected, it was a positive absurdity in a period of potentially revolutionary crisis.
- A rejection of formalism. Syndicalism and Bolshevism had different traditions and used different language; what was important was what united them.[67]

The concrete balance sheet of the Congress was at best ambiguous. The vote was won – but it could scarcely have been lost. There was a large Russian delegation, and the electoral balance was further assisted by the admission of sympathetic delegates representing minorities in reformist unions, who were allocated votes according to the number of unionists they claimed to represent.[68] (How far Rosmer personally was involved with such sharp practice is impossible to say.)

The majority for the formulation that established a link of an 'organic and technical' nature was large: 285–35. The French delegation was split, but some weeks after the Congress a meeting was held with the recalcitrant French delegates, and they agreed to support affiliation to the RILU.[69]

In fact the formalities turned out to be not that important.[70] The Second RILU Congress in 1922 revised the statutes to give a rather more flexible formulation, 'permitting the RILU Executive to make agreements with the CI Executive, to hold joint meetings, to issue appeals and to organize combined action with it'.[71]

Conclusion

Had it all been futile? Wayne Thorpe has given a highly negative assessment of Rosmer's achievements in the RILU:

> Rosmer's effort to deflect a debate on theoretical issues, to minimize ideological differences by characterizing the question of relations between the CI and the RILU as merely one of organizational form, could succeed only temporarily and only in the confines of a communist-dominated congress. For Rosmer concluded that the CI–RILU linkage was solely an issue of organization by proceeding syllogistically, in effect, from the major premise that if there were no significant theoretical differences between syndicalists and communists, the question of CI–RILU relations could only be one of organization. But his minor premise was fundamentally flawed, since profound theoretical differences survived between the syndicalists and communists in the summer of 1921; they could not be explained away, however adroitly. By their very nature organizational issues form one of the most direct and immediate linkages, a chief nexus, between theory and practice. Where theoretical differences survive, to turn to organizational questions is not to bridge, but to provoke, heighten and sharpen those differences. It fell to the hapless Rosmer, an earnest revolutionary and sincere supporter of labour unity, not only to be the spokesman in the RILU congress for a resolution whose language he found needlessly provocative, but to undertake a task that by its very nature in the circumstances of 1921 could not, as he hoped, reconcile and unite.[72]

Thorpe, whose sympathies are clearly with the syndicalists rather than the Bolsheviks, makes some valid points. It is easy to see Rosmer as powerless in the situation, his evident good intentions rendered null by the sectarianism of both the Bolsheviks and his fellow syndicalists. Yet that may be too fatalistic a way of seeing things. The Bolsheviks did not form a homogeneous bloc; there was a huge gulf between Lenin's leadership style and that of Zinoviev. As Rosmer himself wrote:

> Even before Lenin died a split had occurred inside the leadership of the Communist Party. On one side were the men who wanted to continue

his work, to maintain his policy of free discussion inside the party, of revolutionary audacity with the possibility of mistakes which could be corrected. On the other side were those who claimed that such a policy was no longer possible, that it involved too many risks, in short that it was too difficult. In their view, it was now possible to govern only by relying on a repressive police apparatus.[73]

The outcome was not settled in advance; if the International of Lenin, Trotsky and Rosmer had won out over the likes of Zinoviev and Levi, history might have taken a different course. In the face of the challenges of the epoch, the differences between Bolshevism and syndicalism were minor.

In 1922 Victor Serge addressed an appeal to French workers to show solidarity with the impending German revolution:

> When the barricades go up in Berlin, what will you do, knowing that the defeat of your German brothers will confirm, perhaps for another generation, your enslavement? When you are called up either to co-operate with their capitalist masters in making an exhausted people 'pay', or to put down their revolt, what will you do?
> Are you a Communist, a syndicalist or a libertarian? I haven't enquired, for in face of the practical conclusions – or better to call them obligations – imposed by this situation, I don't think that your personal opinions are of any great importance.[74]

That rejection of sectarianism based on tradition and organizational form is precisely the spirit of Alfred Rosmer and of the best of the Bolsheviks.

By 1924 the die was cast. Lenin was dead; the German revolution was lost; Rosmer had been expelled from the French Communist Party. Zinoviev's 'Bolshevization' had subjected the Comintern to 'mechanical and slavish imitation of Russian methods'.[75] The interaction of subjective and objective factors was complex, but subjective factors did play a part. Defeat in the particular form it took was not inevitable.

In the period after the Seattle WTO demonstration, some of the lessons of the RILU are acquiring a new relevance. Socialists from the Marxist tradition find themselves coming into contact with 'anti-capitalists' who have emerged from very different traditions. If joint action and serious political dialogue are to be established, then the political style of Alfred Rosmer will be much more appropriate than that of a Zinoviev or a Levi. The fetishism of organizational form can only be an obstacle.

Many people today have a legitimate disgust with politics, which they identify with the opportunism and corruption of the parliamentary system. Often their hostility extends to revolutionary socialists also, who are seen as being 'politicians' like the rest. Yet the issues that concern such people are profoundly political.[76] Meanwhile the Labour Party and trade union bureaucrats still try to impose the artificial distinction of 'economics' and 'politics' (keeping 'politics' out of trade union branches), although such distinctions are meaningless in a globalized world.

For these reasons the early years of the Comintern repay study, though not in the spirit of 'mechanical and slavish imitation'. For such study, there could be few better guides than Alfred Rosmer.

7

From National Liberation to Social Revolution: Egypt 1945–53

Anne Alexander

Saturday, 26 January 1952 has gone down in history as 'the day Cairo burned'. Tourist guidebooks still point out the damage in some of the city's older cinemas which dates from the riots and protests sparked by the massacre of Egyptian policemen by British troops in the Suez Canal Zone. 'Black Saturday' was not an isolated incident; it was the culmination of eight years of growing political and social crisis – the day the old order finally lost control. Jean and Simonne Lacouture give a vivid description of some of the forces at work:

> The crowd, in which police and soldiers with unbuttoned tunics were standing with their arms around students' shoulders, shouted at [the Minister for Social Affairs] with unusual familiarity . . . the mass of listeners, unsatisfied by the minister's brilliant denunciation of the British, the purpose of which was clearly to gain time and calm the mob, produced a list of 'People's demands'. They called for an absolute boycott of the British; the despatch of armed forces to the Canal, and a treaty of friendship with the Soviet Union. Thus like some Popular Front meeting, the dialogue between the minister and the crowd went on for almost three hours. Were these the opening scenes of a 'red revolution'?[1]

Elsewhere in the city other organizations were at work: the Muslim Brotherhood directed its activists against such symbols of corruption as bars and liquor stores. They poured bottles of whisky, brandy and rum on to broken furniture piled up on the pavement before setting it alight.[2] Symbols of colonial wealth and power also came under attack: 'Barclays' was on fire, The Twentieth Century French Art Gallery was on fire, and so was Chrysler's . . . increasing numbers of poor folk could be seen slipping into the still smoking department stores – Cicurel, Robert Hughes, Adès . . .'[3]

The events of 'Black Saturday' reflect in microcosm the contradictions of the entire period 1945–53. A genuine mass movement had coalesced around the nationalist demands for an end to British occupation. Yet this was not a nationalist campaign led by lawyers and professional politicians, but one in which the most dynamic force was the organized working class: a movement that was already half aware that its greatest enemy was the ruling class at home. Rather than depend on unreliable middle-class politicians, the nationalist movement was beginning to produce its own orators, organizers, agitators and fighters. Official politics could no more contain the mass protests of this period, than the Minister for Social Affairs could convince the sceptical crowd to disperse from beneath his balcony. The groups that had the most direct influence had no representation in parliamentary circles. At one end of the nationalist political spectrum stood the Muslim Brotherhood, advocating national liberation through Islamic salvation, while at the other were the small groups of Communists who made up what they lacked in numbers with the enormous prestige of the Soviet Union.

The Free Officers' unlikely success

Despite the importance of the extra-parliamentary challenge to the established order, the crisis in Egyptian politics was not resolved either by workers' revolution or by the setting up of an Islamic state. In fact it was a small group of junior officers in the army who dealt the final blow to the old rotten system, and who established the regime that followed. Nasser's Free Officers' movement was an unlikely candidate for success: the group only organized its first cells in the army in 1949, and had no support or roots outside the barracks. Not only were the Free Officers numerically weak, they were also ideologically confused, borrowing a mish-mash of ideas from both the Communists and the Brotherhood. In addition, their initial impetus for launching the coup was in response to the news that the army command was starting to move against them, rather than as part of a carefully timetabled plan of insurrection.

Yet the Free Officers and their political heirs have ruled Egypt for nearly half a century, and where they led the way dozens of others have followed. Syria, Sudan and Iraq all witnessed similar patterns of political development during the 1950s and 1960s. In Egypt, the success of the Free Officers meant the annihilation of the Communists as an independent political force as well as the co-option of the trade union movement by the state. In country after country around the Middle East, the same disastrous policies saw the left walk into the same dead-end as the Communists in Egypt. Nearly 50 years later, the heirs of the Free Officers still cling desperately to power. As the dreams of the 1940s finally unravel, we need to understand what led to their victory in the first place.

Uneven development

The political and social crisis of the 1940s had its roots deep in the uneven nature of economic development in Egypt. Throughout the nineteenth century, Egyptian development was distorted by the impact of European imperialism. As Charles Issawi describes, by the end of the century Egypt's main role was to produce primary goods for manufacture in Britain.[4] As a result, only those sectors concerned with the production, processing or distribution of Egypt's main primary goods advanced rapidly, while the rest stagnated.[5]

In addition to directly intervening in the Egyptian economy, European capitalists, following a pattern common to the whole of the Middle East, also encouraged the development of a native stratum of middlemen and agents, many of whom later began to invest in industry and land themselves.[6] Many of these entrepreneurs were Greek, Armenian, Syrian or Jewish, who kept themselves culturally distinct from the rest of the population. They spoke a different language, sent their children abroad to be educated and had little in common with the rest of the population.[7] The presence of this group of Egyptian-born 'foreign' capitalists left little room for the emergence of an Arabic-speaking native bourgeoisie because it had to compete with a well-rooted resident foreign bourgeoisie that shared cultural connections and political networks with European capital.

However, by the beginning of the twentieth century the earliest representatives of an Arabic-speaking Egyptian bourgeoisie had begun to emerge. They were chiefly wealthy through their vast landholdings, but had made some tentative steps towards investment in industry and, significantly, had played an important role in founding the first nationalist parties in Egypt. The 1920s and 1930s saw the beginnings of a growing economic independence for the nascent Egyptian bourgeoisie. Firms dominated by Egyptians rather than foreigners began to spring up and governments tried to encourage them with tariff protection from the ravages of the Great Depression.[8] In order to speed up the process of Egyptianization, the government purchased shares in key industries[9] and leading Egyptian industrialists began to shape the most important sectors of the economy with their own companies, such as the giant Misr complex that soon dominated the textile industry.

According to Jean and Simonne Lacouture, 'the First World War made Egypt a nation, the Second World War made her a power'.[10] The war led to a greater diversification of the economy, with whole new branches of industry being set up to fill the gaps in supplies as the normal mechanisms of international trade were interrupted. Production expanded in numerous industries: textiles, processed food, chemicals, glass, leather, cement and petroleum; often to meet the demands of the British army.[11] In addition, the British camps employed large numbers of Egyptians at relatively high rates of pay, who then had money to spend on Egyptian products without Egyptian employers having to pay a penny towards their wages.

The growing crisis

The buoyant fortunes of the native bourgeoisie were achieved at the cost of the impoverishment of the vast majority. The wholesale price index rose by 23 per cent in the six years of war, but the retail price index had soared to 300 per cent of its 1939 level by 1945.[12] Wages did not keep pace, and desperate poverty was the everyday experience of most Egyptians. High prices meant that 60–70 per cent of family income went on food, which did not provide an adequate diet.[13] In addition, rents had risen sharply, employment was precarious and working conditions were dangerous. Factory barracks in Mahalla al-Kubra were occupied by up to fifteen families sleeping in three shifts of four or five families at a time.[14]

The social problems were the most obvious warning signs that the long-term problems of the Egyptian economy had not been overcome by the growth spurt during the war. The war had damaged the rural economy. Productivity in agriculture declined by 28 per cent for wheat, 24 per cent for barley and onions, and 20 per cent for rice during the war years.[15] The war also disrupted the flow of public funds into the hydraulic system, leaving large irrigation projects unfinished.[16] Although the agricultural sector had begun to decline slightly in importance compared to the expanding industrial sector, it still formed the bedrock of the economy, and the damage done by the war was bound to hamper long-term industrial growth.

Finally, despite the rapid rate of Egyptianization, foreign capital, both resident and metropolitan, was still a very significant factor in the economy. For instance, in 1946 although the *Egyptian Stock Exchange Yearbook* listed 60 companies with Egyptian boards of directors, with a total capitalization of £E25,094,185, there were also 40 firms completely controlled by foreign metropolitan capital, and 57 controlled by foreign resident capital.[17]

The Second World War clearly showed both the potential for economic growth and the underlying economic weaknesses that had been the legacy of the past 60 years of economic development. The period between the end of the nineteenth century and 1945 had seen the emergence of a native bourgeoisie, but had also seen its growth stunted and its role limited by the pressure of imperialism. This native bourgeoisie had founded some of the institutions necessary for economic development, such as a system of tariff laws and the rudiments of a national financial system. Thus when the war forced the Egyptian economy into self-reliance, the suspension of foreign competition had proved a considerable stimulus to growth. Yet, it was clear that the process of industrialization itself was creating the conditions for a deep social crisis and widespread discontent with the unequal distribution of the wealth that growth provided.

Industrial workers were the first to show their anger. In numerical terms, the working class was still very small: estimates range from 1 million to 1.5 million. These workers were concentrated in the largest cities, especially Cairo, Alexandria and the factory towns of the delta such as Mahalla al-Kubra and Kafr al-Dawwar, while the rest of the country was relatively untouched by industrialization. The distribution of trade union membership in the early 1950s reflects this unevenness: 65 per cent of trade union members were in the main cities, 33 per cent in Cairo alone, 24 per cent in Alexandria and only 6 per cent in Upper Egypt.[18] However, this concentration is a crucial factor in explaining the disproportionate role played by the working class in the struggles of the post-war years. The concentrated structure of the working class meant that ideas of trade unionism and political struggle could spread extremely rapidly. The experience of the first political strikes exposed a very high proportion of workers to the arguments for organization and collective struggle.

Despite the growing importance of industry, Egyptian society in the 1940s was still predominantly a rural one. Three-quarters of the population lived in the countryside. The rural economy was dominated by the big landowners, who between them held 2 million feddans, or 32.2 per cent of agricultural land, although they represented only 0.5 per cent of the population.[19] The vast majority (94.3 per cent or 2.6 million owners) had to share 2.1 million feddans between them. The average size of smallholdings had dropped from 1.8 feddans in 1894 to 0.8 feddans in 1952,[20] representing a catastrophic fall in living standards for the fellahin. Since the minimum acreage sufficient to feed a family of four was calculated at 3 feddans, it is clear that the vast majority of the population was living on the verge of destitution. To compound the problem, land prices had skyrocketed during the 1940s: the average rent was £E25–50 per feddan, although the average yield was only £E17 per feddan. For many, the only hope of escape was migration to the towns. The desperate poverty in the countryside gave an added edge to the militancy of urban workers, who had no way back to their villages if they failed to find secure work in industry.

However, the first rumblings of discontent from the peasantry were far less politically influential than the active involvement of the petty bourgeoisie in the struggles after the war. Here the volatility of the political situation made itself most clear. The contradictory pressures of the period pushed some towards the organizations of the left, while others joined right-wing movements hoping to enforce social cohesion and stability by violence. In many cases the same individuals passed through dozens of different organizations representing all shades of political opinion.[21]

This political eclecticism was a reflection of the varying pressures on the petty bourgeoisie. This stratum consisted of the lower ranks of the government bureaucracy, small businesspeople and landowners, and the lower ranks of the army officer corps. Most were well educated, and students and graduates played a particularly significant role in the struggles after the war. They had many reasons for their frustration and resentment at the political system. The standard of living that put them above the masses of ordinary peasants and workers was constantly under threat. The precious gains they had made could always be wiped out by unemployment, sickness or rising prices, thrusting them back down into the poverty they had fought so long to escape. The pressure on living standards was, however, common to all but the very rich. The anger of the petty bourgeoisie was sharpened by the feeling that their aspirations were being cheated by the system.

Nation and class

The first signs of working-class militancy came during the war. In particular, the textile workers of Shubra al-Khayma in Cairo were active in building independent unions after the legalization of trade unions in 1942. There were huge numbers of strikes over pay, conditions and trade union recognition. The strikers became rapidly politicized through their experience of government repression and British wartime restrictions. The government's attempts to crush the trade union movement met with little success. In December, Shubra was under army occupation as wage disputes spiralled into a full-scale confrontation with the government. Anxious to contain the mounting agitation, Nuqrashi eventually requested the resumption of talks with the British over the implementation of the 1936 Anglo-Egyptian Treaty,[22] sparking off massive nationalist protests and strikes in January and February 1946.

The small Communist groups played an important role in shaping the emerging independent trade unions and the nascent nationalist movement. The 'New Dawn' group organized by Youssef Darwish and the Egyptian Movement for National Liberation (EMNL) led by Henri Curiel both sponsored representatives at the Congress of the World Federation of Trade Unions in September 1945. Youssef al-Mudarrik, the delegate sponsored by 'New Dawn' and the textile workers' union of Shubra, gained the endorsement of 102 unions representing 80,000 workers. The EMNL-backed delegate, Da'ud Nahum, was sponsored by 62 unions representing 60,000 workers.[23]

The Communists likewise began to gain real influence in the nationalist movement. This was a natural corollary of their work in the trade unions, since the working class was a fertile ground for nationalist ideas, especially given the impotence and timidity of the Wafd Party, which had led the struggles against imperialism in 1919, and which retained the political loyalty of the nationalist bourgeoisie. Firstly, the Communists' influence can be seen in the introduction of a distinctively left-wing nationalism into the working-class movement. The largest of the textile unions in Shubra stood a candidate in the elections of 1944. His manifesto called for social and political reforms in Egypt, such as the introduction of a minimum wage and distribution of land to the peasants. However, he also stood on a platform of militant nationalism, including the demand for 'Arab Union on a popular basis'.[24] Secondly, the Communists used their base in the trade unions to push for the inclusion of working-class demands in the aims of the nationalist movement. For instance, key members of the New Dawn group founded the first left nationalist organization, the Workers' Committee for National Liberation (WCNL), in late 1945. By February 1946 the presence of the trade unions at the head of the nationalist movement was well established. Delegates from the tramway unions and the textile workers were especially prominent among the 90 trade unions represented on the National Committee of Workers and Students (NCWS), which was set up in 1946.[25] Thus, at moments when the nationalist movement and the trade unions coalesced, the Communists found themselves at the head of both.

Challenge from below

The events of February 1946 turned the smouldering anger of workers and students into an explosive challenge to the established order. University students organized a demonstration to petition the king when the text of the Egyptian government's note on the treaty and the British reply were published. They were attacked by the British army and the Egyptian police force on the Abbas Bridge.[26] This massacre was the signal for a wide-scale radicalization of the nationalist movement. Student committees merged with working-class activists and formed the National Committee of Workers and Students, which quickly set up branches nationwide. This network of activists, which included a significant number of Communists, was able to mobilize huge numbers on demonstrations and near total general strikes on several occasions.[27] The student demonstration was followed up by a national day of action, known as Evacuation Day, on 21 February. The left Wafdist paper *al-Wafd al-Misry* published reports on demonstrations and strikes in every major town in the delta and as far south as Assyout.[28]

The radicalization of the nationalist movement gave a new impetus to the trade unions' own efforts to build a national trade union federation. The leaders of the most militant trade unions felt confident to organize a general strike by June, but at the last moment some of the more conservative transport unions pulled out under government pressure and the strike collapsed.[29] The nationalist demonstrations had also ground to a halt by this time, and the government was not slow to take advantage of the lull in the struggle to launch a frontal assault on the nationalist movement, the Communist groups and the trade unions.

The arrest of leading activists in the government clampdown of July 1946 was only a temporary setback. A wide-scale rash of strikes, this time directed at Egyptian-owned firms as well as foreign enterprises, was sparked off by an important dispute in the Misr Spinning mill in Mahalla al-Kubra in September 1947. Compared to the protests and strikes a year earlier, the confrontations with both the employers and the government were more intense. Firstly, the scope of the movement had broadened: originally the most radical and politicized workers had been the textile workers of Shubra, who were mostly employed directly by foreigners. The connection between their struggle for better wages and conditions and the nationalist struggle against foreign domination was clear to see. However, in September 1947 the strike movement spread to Misr Spinning in Mahalla, jewel-in-the-crown of Egyptian capitalism. Communist activists from the Democratic Movement for National Liberation (DMNL), which had been formed from the merger of the EMNL with the smaller Communist group Iskra, played a crucial role in organizing the strike. The DMNL's paper, *Al-Jamahir*, ran a centre-page spread on the Misr workers' struggles, then following a favourable reception at the factory gates, DMNL agitators signed on at the mill under false names to begin the work of organizing a secret factory cell which became the core of the strike committee.[30]

The strikers were originally protesting at an arbitrary system of fines imposed by management, and struck for the right to organize in an independent trade union.[31] Yet their cause became a rallying point for both the trade unions and the nationalist movement, proving that the wide network of solidarity built up over the past year had not been destroyed by government repression. The strike broke out on 6 September 1947; *Sawt al-Umma*, the left Wafdist daily, carried a report the next day, which already detailed messages of solidarity from all over the country and reported a stoppage by textile workers in Shubra in solidarity with their sacked colleagues.[32] In the days that followed, *Sawt al-Umma* reported that workers' organizations had sent a delegation of lawyers to Tanta in order to represent the arrested strikers, and published letters of support from various unions from the Port Workers' Union of Port Said to textile workers in Alexandria.[33]

Secondly, although the strike in Mahalla did not result in an outright victory, it opened the gates to a broadening tide of struggle throughout the winter and early spring.[34] The wave of strikes and protests showed not simply the depth of the nationalist movement's roots in particular sections of the working class, such as the textile workers, but also the breadth of the movement as new layers of workers were pulled into action. Male nurses at the Qasr al-Aini hospital were involved with a particularly violent strike in April, where police sent in to deal with them were showered with a hail of concrete slabs, boiling water and mattresses, which the nurses set on fire as they barricaded themselves in the hospital.[35] A national police strike took place at the same time, which was the result of mounting pressure from the lower ranks of the police force for a general amnesty for all their colleagues who had been disciplined for participating in the nationalist movement.[36] Troops were called in to direct the traffic and keep order, and in Alexandria a demonstration of police officers and men was joined by workers and students.[37] Tension was running high by the next day, as the policemen began to drift back to work and rioting broke out in some areas of the city.[38] According to the *Egyptian Gazette*, soldiers had been ordered to shoot looters on sight, and the city was under 'mob-rule'.[39]

A lull in the struggle

The outbreak of war in Palestine and the imposition of martial law, not to mention the crisis in the opposition groups, led to a lull in the nationalist struggles. However, a new wave of strikes broke out in 1950, culminating in a struggle over the implementation of the cost-of-living allowances in the Hawamidiyya sugar refinery. This strike neatly illustrated the dilemma of the Wafd, which had been returned to power in the general election of 1950, and underlined the ineffectiveness of the major parties in containing the working-class movement with promises of reform. Cost-of-living allowances to offset the effects of galloping inflation had been granted by the Wafd after a number of bitter strikes. The large employers, such as the owner of the Hawamidiyya plant, often refused to implement the law, provoking further strikes. However, because of its increasing dependency on the right wing of the Egyptian bourgeoisie, Wafd was powerless to insist that the employers comply with the law. After the strike had dragged on for weeks, the government promised to make up the difference between the old wage levels and the new.[40]

Revival of the nationalist movement

By autumn 1951 the nationalist movement had begun to revive, pushing the Wafd into taking the decisive step of abrogating the 1936 treaty with Britain on 8 October. This was the spark for further protests and strikes, which, as in 1948, showed an intensification of both the nationalist struggle and industrial militancy. Again, despite the setbacks caused by government repression, the strike movement was both deepening its influence within particular sections of the working class, such as the transport workers, and broadening out to involve wider sections of the population. There was a growing sense of coalescence between the demands of the nationalist movement and the trade unions, as before in 1946 and 1948. The Wafd was forced to support the radicalism of the nationalist movement, thus risking the confrontation with the British that it had hoped to avoid through negotiations.

Several linked developments point to the growing political crisis during the autumn and winter of 1951. Firstly, the abrogation of the treaty was the spark for the outbreak of a guerrilla war in the Canal Zone between bands of volunteer fighters, the fedayeen, and the British army. Various opposition groups from the Muslim Brotherhood to the Communists began to raise guerrilla units from among students and urban workers. They launched a series of attacks on British positions, to which the British responded by occupying the Canal Zone towns: Port Said, Ismailiyya and Suez. This only provoked a further radicalization in the nationalist movement, both in the Canal Zone itself and in the main cities.

Secondly, at the same time the strike wave gathered momentum. Workers from the Canal Zone quit their jobs in a general boycott of foreign companies and forced the Wafd into promising work for the unemployed in Cairo. In Ismailyya elementary schools went on strike as the school students organized their own protests against British occupation.[41] Transport workers in the major cities organized a wave of strikes demanding better pay and the nationalization of the public transport system. The DMNL continued to rebuild its influence in the trade union movement throughout 1951–2: prominent union officials representing Marconi workers, restaurant and hotel workers, bus workers, seamen, shoemakers, taxi drivers and other transport workers were all DMNL members. As in 1946, the upsurge in nationalist struggle took place against a background of radicalization in the trade union movement, which began again to coalesce at a national level.[42]

Thirdly, by New Year 1952 it was clear that the continuing unrest was sapping the strength of key organs of the state. Policemen had long been involved in the nationalist demonstrations, as the strike action of 1948 had shown. During the police strike, the government had been able to count on the army to keep order.[43] By 1952, however, the nationalist mood had infected large numbers of the troops and the junior officers. Nationalist cells flourished following the defeat in Palestine, but they had been contained by repression until late 1951. The Free Officers' group was in this period coming to real prominence in the army, through its leaflet campaigns, determined recruiting and particularly through the success of its candidates in the Officers' Club elections of December 1951. The DMNL played a significant role in shaping the politics and organizational structure of the Free Officers: it recruited a number of left-wing officers, such as Ahmad Hamroush, and drew others, such as Khaled Mohi al-Din, into its orbit as well as providing practical help for the fledging organization by printing the Free Officers' leaflets.[44]

The role of the Communists

The Communist organizations of the mid-1940s had none of the numerical strength of the right-wing opposition groups such as the Muslim Brotherhood, which claimed up to a million members during the 1940s. However, within the organized working class the Communists' ideas found a ready audience. In the nationalist movement as a whole, left-wing ideas also gained general acceptance as the sympathetic coverage of strikes in the left Wafdist press shows.[45] Communist organizations were far more influential than their numbers would suggest, because the rising tide of strikes and nationalist protests projected their voices on to the stage of national politics.[46] Yet despite this, the Communists found themselves in the same position as the Brotherhood when the Free Officers seized power: at first playing an enthusiastic supporting role in the coup, then finding themselves banned and driven underground by their former allies.

Despite the Communists' success in shaping the nationalist movement, they were always hampered by their small size. None of the Communist organizations of the 1940s was able to transform itself into a mass working-class party. The groups all remained extremely small, ranging in size from the New Dawn's five-member cell of 1945 to a high point of around 2,000 DMNL members in late 1951.[47] Even the largest of these organizations had a tendency to fracture into tiny competing splinter groups.[48] For instance, in 1947 the two largest groups, Iskra and the EMNL, merged to form a new organization, the Democratic Movement for National Liberation (DMNL). However, only a year later the merger began to unravel and the DMNL collapsed into a dozen different factions.

The small size of their organizations and their own disunity left the Communists vulnerable to repression and in constant danger of being completely swamped by the scale of the mass movement itself. Each time the nationalist protests and the strike wave provoked a political crisis that brought the old political order to the brink of collapse, the Communists were unable to take advantage of the situation. In 1946 the leaders of the National Committee of Workers and Students hesitated to push the movement on further after the successful general strikes in February. In 1948 the Communists were hampered both by factional infighting and by the Palestine problem – the Soviet Union's recognition of the new state of Israel tarnished the left's nationalist credentials. In 1952 they were eclipsed first by the rioting on 'Black Saturday' and then by the Free Officers' coup in July.

Promise and failure

The 'missed opportunities' of this period are a theme echoed by many left analyses of the nationalist movement.[49] Communist activists themselves also often volunteered explanations for the failures of the 1940s. Henri

Curiel, for instance, later attributed the political problems of the period to the inexperience of the leading members of the groups. 'At the time it could be said that the masses were still ready to follow us. But we no longer knew where to lead them: we were completely inexperienced. We were not the only ones to realise this. Sidqi Pasha was perfectly well aware of it.'[50] Even at the time, the Communist Party of Great Britain (CPGB) was concerned about the state of the Communist movement in Egypt: 'The Egyptian Communist movement is today composed of a few hundred isolated comrades, divided among themselves on theoretical questions . . . and while the comrades are wasting their efforts in such futile discussion they are neglecting their duty to participate in and try and lead the actual, concrete struggle going on in Egypt.'[51]

In addition to these problems, the dead weight of Stalinism hampered any attempts by the Egyptian Communists to respond to the rapidly shifting events of the 1940s. Following the common pattern of Stalinist parties from Spain to China, they argued that the goal of national liberation had to be achieved first, before the working class could mobilize for social revolution. An internal Communist Party document put it as follows: 'the people's democracy we want to establish in Egypt is not a form of the dictatorship of the Proletariat. We aim to establish a democratic dictatorship of all the classes struggling against imperialism and feudalism.'[52] The practical effect of this strategy was to force the Communists to look to the nationalist bourgeoisie, represented by the Wafd Party, as the genuine leadership of the nationalist movement. As the Wafd's bankruptcy became ever clearer, the Communists looked elsewhere to find an effective force to accomplish what the Wafd could not. This in the end pushed them to accept the agency of a small group of radical army officers, instead of the working class. Even when the Free Officers were consolidating their grip on power by attacking striking workers, the DMNL did not waver in its support. The DMNL paper *Al-Malayin* for 10 September 1952 ran a lead article entitled 'The road of the people and the army – a national front against imperialism and traitors'.[53]

More ideological contortions were expected of the Egyptian Communists later. By 1959, the CPGB had begun to argue that Communists should support Nasser as the anti-imperialist leader of a 'victorious national revolution'.[54] The persecuted Egyptian Communist movement was now supposed to support a regime that was imprisoning and torturing its members.

The echoes of the Communists' capitulation still have a resonance today. For a start, the disaster of the 1950s saw the destruction of Communism as an independent force in Egyptian society. This was not simply the result of the obliteration of the opposition to the Free Officers' regime; the Communist movement's impotence for the last 50 years is also a result of ideological and political bankruptcy. The ultimate failure of the project of national liberation not only undermined the Free Officers and their successors, but also discredited the claims of the Communists, who liquidated their organization into the new regime. The collapse of the Communist movement also had the effect of depriving the independent trade unions of political leadership in the crucial first few years after the Free Officers' seizure of power. The union leaders were co-opted and their organizations absorbed by the state.[55]

There was nothing inevitable in this process. Although the Communists faced massive objective difficulties, such as the small size of their organizations and their own inexperience, their ideas found as great an audience within the national movement as did the Muslim Brotherhood. In fact, the Brotherhood's awesome size and level of organization proved to be no guarantee of political leadership in a crisis. The depth of that crisis, and the weakness of the Free Officers' grip on power, was visible in the years after 1952. The struggle was not abruptly halted by the Free Officers' coup; on the contrary, as Joel Beinin has demonstrated, the number of strikes continued to rise, despite harsh repression.[56] The Free Officers were forced to make significant reforms in order to build a solid base of popular support: in particular, land redistribution, rent control and workers' rights. The crucial difference between before and after July 1952 was that the workers' movement lacked any kind of independent political leadership, and therefore failed to develop into a coherent challenge to the new regime.

The Free Officers' rule in its early stages was characterized by a combination of repression and reform. Today, their successors are engaged in dismantling what is left, relying on force to maintain their grip on power. There is now no limit on land ownership; the restrictions put in place by Nasser have been swept away. Rent controls have been all but abolished and the privatization of state industries is continuing apace. Growth in the Egyptian economy has benefited a tiny minority: government officials turned privateers, speculators and the elite employees of the multinationals. The rest of the population has seen living standards continue to fall, while unemployment is growing.

Without a coherent opposition to the government, discontent has not generalized beyond sudden outbreaks of militancy, such as strikes by textile and cement workers, and peasant protests in defence of Nasser's land laws. However, the conditions that produced the explosive mass movement of the 1940s are still present. Understanding that mass movement – both its promise and its ultimate failure – will be vital if future generations of revolutionary socialists in Egypt are to avoid repeating the mistakes of the past.

8

Northern Manufacturers and the Coming of the American Civil War

Andrew Dawson

From the 1830s a confident and expanding northern capitalism, promising 'free labour' to the American people, collided with southern slavery. On the eve of the civil war, the North far outweighed the South in every measure of strategic importance – especially population, industrial output, arms production and railroad mileage. Some Marxist historians who emphasize the centrality of material forces in historical explanation see the outcome of the war as inevitable. In this seemingly one-sided contest, a powerful and productive bourgeoisie took the revolutionary step of ending human bondage and dooming a less efficient planter class to extinction.[1]

Yet the outcome of the civil war was more problematical than this triumphalist interpretation suggests. The North was slow to end slavery: only in January 1863 did Lincoln introduce his Emancipation Proclamation. Indeed, until the end of 1864, the possibility of Confederate success on the battlefield or northern Democrat success at the polls placed the outcome of the war in jeopardy and might have forced Republicans to allow the South to go free or return under favourable conditions.[2] James McPherson, in his highly influential *Battle Cry of Freedom*, points to several key moments when the war could have gone against the North.[3] Marxists are, of course, well aware of the conservative side to America's revolution. Marx and Engels fulminated against cautious Union generals. Barrington Moore calls the war 'the last capitalist revolution', drawing attention to the fact that conditions favouring bourgeois revolution were fast disappearing; American industrialists' late arrival and the use of the state for revolutionary goals made conservatism more likely. Moore believes that only an alliance of manufacturers and small farmers prevented the civil war taking the same authoritarian path as the 1871 German unification and the Meiji restoration of 1868.[4]

I would argue that much of this hesitancy is the product of the social character of the class that led the revolution. Yet, few historians pay any attention to manufacturers and the civil war.[5] To explain the actions of industrial capital adequately, we need to explore the constituent elements of that class and lay bare the social forces it confronted. Easier said than done: while the American, English and French revolutions are subjects of intense historical inquiry, the American Civil War stands out for its lack of any sustained or explicit examination of the class that spearheaded the struggle. We still lack the kinds of detailed study that characterize our understanding of, for example, the English gentry or the French *sans culottes*.

Philadelphia workshop owners

In such a short space it is impossible to redress the deficiency. This is a study of engineering workshop proprietors in Philadelphia, the second largest city in the United States, from 1850 to the civil war. These workshop owners were a minority among the city's manufacturers. In 1850 they employed fewer than 5 per cent of the total workforce, compared with 18 per cent each for textiles and garments, the two largest branches.[6] Despite the size of their industry, however, these proprietors assumed the leadership of the new industrial class. Small masters in the city's textile and garment industries, many from immigrant backgrounds, were overawed by displays of mercantile wealth. They failed to participate in city politics and, later, fearful of offending southern suppliers, hung back in the sectional contest. In contrast, large-scale enterprises dominated machine building, with proprietors as familiar with exercising political power as they were with the management of their substantial foundries and machine shops. For the engineering workshop owners, the civil war was not only a battle against the planter class, it was also a clash with the existing rulers of the city, the mercantile class, and a contest for the loyalties of their employees.

By about 1840, Philadelphia's heavy engineering dominated the national market. Unable to compete against more powerful builders in Britain, workshop owners turned to tariff protection. In 1850, the average steam-engine maker invested $69,300 in their business, compared with $14,052 in textile manufacture and only $2,043 in boots and shoes.[7] Engine maker I. P. Morris, for example, employed 220 hands with capital of a quarter of a million dollars.[8] Businesses often needed large foundries, and proprietors, not able to accumulate sufficient savings, cultivated close ties with finance capital.[9] Owners of small commercial banks in the industrial suburbs and merchants and their sons joined mechanical partnerships.[10] Although the unequal relationship must have irked, proprietors benefited from the connection. Not until the economic boom of the 1850s and the political upheaval of the civil war did power swing decisively in favour of workshop owners. At the same time, as we shall see, the close connection had a conservative impact on the new class, for it blunted, though never destroyed, workshop owners' enthusiasm for the radicalism of the Republican Party. The urge to legitimate wage labour and to overthrow or displace existing classes, combined with a need for merchants' capital, explains the Janus face of Philadelphia machine building: on the one side, open, courageous and revolutionary while, on the other, cautious, authoritarian and secretive.

Internal division

The massive economic upswing of the 1840s and 1850s laid the foundation for workshop proprietors' fortunes and led to the triumph of manufacturing over mercantile capital. Yet, not until the civil war and the publication of federal income tax returns was the new situation visible. Old elite family names, such as Cadwalader, Biddle, Pepper and Ingersoll, appeared only in the lowest two income groups – $10,000–25,000 and $25,000–50,000 – well down the table.[11] In 1865, the 36 richest men in Philadelphia, with incomes over $100,000, were all manufacturers or bankers. Nine – Mathew Baird, Matthias Baldwin, Joseph Harrison, Richard F. Loper, Richard Norris, Robert Patterson, William Sellers, Thomas Tasker and John Towne[12] – were machine builders, iron founders or large investors in engineering.

The character of the mechanical elite took shape in the 1830s and 1840s as men of substance from artisan backgrounds and the city's scientific community turned to new forms of production. They were joined by a small number of proprietors from commercial backgrounds who rose to leadership positions. Men like Samuel Vaughan Merrick, John Towne and William and Richard Norris had family origins in commerce and finance, and most held conservative Democrat sympathies.[13] Although these men brought with them some of the cultural baggage and political assumptions of the old elite, a new and distinctive manufacturing class with its own political outlook was in the process of formation.

Merrick, who had the advantage of one foot in the world of mechanics and the other in the counting house, rose to dominate Philadelphia engineering in the ante-bellum period. His business produced municipal gas-lighting equipment in the 1830s, which encouraged him to enter local politics. Trusted by merchant and mechanic alike, he was the first president of the Pennsylvania Railroad and director of several financial institutions. Wealth enabled him to buy a house on fashionable Penn Square and affect the style of the country gentleman. Merrick was also an individual of profound ambiguity: keen to revolutionize the workshop, he was a firm supporter of existing social order. Like many, particularly in the older merchant class, he feared the abrasive message of anti-slavery.[14]

Most workshop owners were not like Merrick but had their feet firmly planted in mechanical culture. They were deeply suspicious of what they saw as the high living and immorality of the old merchant elite. 'As to father's [Coleman Sellers] social position in Phila.', recalled George Escol Sellers, 'it was all he wanted. Neither he nor mother made any pretensions to the St Peter's set or the Codfish aristocracy . . . Father's circle of acquaintances was large but it was among *producers* and *scientific* men he had some intimate and warm friends.'[15] Men such as locomotive builder Matthias Baldwin were suspicious of the paternalistic policies of the mercantile class. They favoured individual equality in the marketplace and civil rights for African-Americans, sympathized with anti-slavery and helped launch the Republican Party in Philadelphia. Differences between conservatives and radicals – merchant-mechanics and artisan-mechanics – were surmountable: owning large capitals, directing the labour of hundreds of mechanics and selling machinery against stiff competition brought both groups together in the halls of the Franklin Institute, the American Philosophical Society, the Board of Trade and, later, the Union League.

The marketplace and mechanics

Workshop owners debated among themselves the most effective way to control labour. Republican free labour promised all men a fair return on their labour and, for those languishing in wage labour, it also assured an easy exit to independent proprietorship. Underlying all of this was a belief that social justice was best served though unfettered individuals selling commodities and labour power in the marketplace. Most proprietors put their faith in free labour, but a small minority, doubting its ability to discipline labour, looked to more coercive methods. All were agreed, though, that in industry, flexible and productive wage labour held more advantage than slave labour. Nevertheless, wage labour brought its own problems as builders saw in the British industrial experience the frightening spectre of polarization and class conflict. Some proprietors turned to the ideas of the English utopian socialist Robert Owen, to help chart a way through the stormy waters of class conflict. His co-operative ideas so impressed the mechanic-scientific community that when he visited Philadelphia in 1824–5 some joined his communal experiment in New Harmony, Indiana.[16] On Owen's second visit in 1827, he stayed with Coleman Sellers. Sellers, troubled by English social conditions, sought a practical solution to problems of poverty. He held a party in Owen's honour, and the young George Escol Sellers vividly recalled the impression that Owen's 'silver tongue' made upon him.[17] Utopian socialism, paradoxically, was attractive to men of industry because it promised order in place of conflict and situated responsibility for directing society in the hands of the enlightened and intelligent.

Doubts about the market's ability to maintain order surfaced periodically among Philadelphia proprietors. During the early 1850s, the iron founder Stephen Colwell, a close friend of political economist Henry Carey, proposed an authoritarian alternative to Owen's tolerant paternalism. Colwell, just as much as Owen, rejected free-market capitalism as a means to regulate labour. To him, people were mutually dependent one upon the other but, due to different endowment of human capacities, inequality was a natural state of affairs. As *laissez-faire* capitalism offered only misery to the feckless dependent class, power needed vesting in the hands of wealthy 'intelligent and influential Christians'.[18] In 1851, Colwell anonymously published *New Themes for the Protestant Clergy*, which many thought attacked the churches for their materialism and lack of spiritual leadership from a socialist perspective.[19]

In the end, self-confident manufacturers had no need for repression. While this avoided Colwell's authoritarianism, at the same time the trumpeting of the North's system made conflict between planter and manufacturer more likely. The most visible and pressing contradiction to free labour was, clearly, southern slavery.

As large employers of labour, most machine builders – outside of a small group of wealthy proprietors with conservative mercantile connections – were hostile to slavery. George Hufty, Matthias Baldwin, John Sellers, William Sellers and Matthew Baird all opposed the system. Baldwin, particularly, in his fight against slavery and defence of the rights of free African-Americans, towered above them all. He encouraged black education. He was a member of the congregation of the First Presbyterian Church, whose evangelical pastor was Albert Barnes, the outspoken critic of slavery. In 1835, Baldwin defended black evangelist Pompey Hunt's right to preach in the city. At the 1837 Pennsylvania state constitutional convention, which Baldwin attended as a member of Philadelphia's Whig delegation, he unsuccessfully opposed a clause restricting the franchise to whites only.[20] Yet, while Baldwin supported civil rights, he opposed the extension of the franchise to newly arrived Irish-Catholic immigrants. Suspicious of the political judgement of the masses, Baldwin voted against increasing the number of state offices filled by popular election, and he defended the rights and privileges of corporations against the levelling aspirations of the agrarian Democrats.[21] In Baldwin's eyes, support for black enfranchisement and defence of the laws of supply and demand were of the same piece: freedom to buy and sell in the marketplace entitled everyone to political rights.

A handful of large workshop owners, persuaded by close association with the old elite, were indifferent to the moral and political objections to slavery, and when anti-slavery appeared on the national scene they reacted with alarm to its menacing implications. Affluent merchants, whether Whig or Democrat, believed firmly in the need for order, which encouraged many to accept slavery's legitimacy. Mercantile-mechanic

Samuel Merrick's workshop conducted an extensive business selling marine engines and sugar mills throughout the South. In contrast to Baldwin, who found the commercial connection uncomfortable (but profitable), Merrick welcomed the business and his family enjoyed the hospitality of gracious slave owners.[22] In 1834, when Merrick's pastor, William H. Furness, spoke out against slavery, Merrick quickly abandoned the wealthy First Unitarian Church, and a close friendship with the Furness family, for the more comfortable home of episcopalianism.[23]

Free labour's contested meaning

The expansion of northern manufacturing and the abrasive free-labour ideology not only put Philadelphia workshop owners on a collision course with planters, but also created tensions with both employees and merchants. These two conflicts, in very different ways, threatened to derail the revolutionary impulse that heightened sectional antagonism and led to the civil war.

As workshops increased in size, friction increased between employers and employees. In 1848, Baldwin mechanics declared that their employer 'does not, nor cannot, from his position in life form any adequate conception of the extremely embarrising [*sic*] (to say the least of it) and in many instances realy [*sic*] suffering condition of some of the men in his employ'.[24] Ten years later, Philadelphia mechanics formed the Machinists and Blacksmiths Union (MBU). While proprietors celebrated the freedom of the marketplace, mechanics intended to curtail its power. In early 1860, mechanics struck against the Baldwin Locomotive Works in a bid to redress a growing list of grievances. Republicanism recognized workers' rights to withdraw their labour, but was hostile to collective action. In the protracted and bitter dispute, the men were defeated.[25]

Despite increasing social distance, workshop owners and mechanics participated in the Republican Party and endorsed many aspects of free labour. As Protestants they shared an antipathy to Romanism, and they agreed that owning a business was good for the individual and the community. Job R. Barry and Milton Mendenhall – both Baldwin employees active in the labour movement since the 1840s – were founder members of the city's first Republican club.[26] According to Jonathan Fincher, another MBU member, Barry's 'manly opposition to imposition' led to his blacklisting by employers.[27] Owners and mechanics subscribed to different versions of the free-labour programme. Proprietors believed that freedom belonged to all men able to sign labour contracts. Slavery stood in stark contrast to such agreements, but so too, in a different way, did the collectivism of trade unions. Mechanics understood the wage system to be a one-sided affair; only the possession of productive wealth made them independent. Even Republicans sympathetic to labour, such as Horace

Greeley, doubted the efficacy of trade unionism. Greeley believed that the law of supply and demand determined wages. Job Barry, in a direct attack on Greeley in the mid-1860s, rejected the primacy of the marketplace by arguing that wages would increase once labour recognized its collective strength.[28]

Greeley, like Barry, Mendenhall and other Philadelphia mechanics, dismissed wage labour as a dependent status. 'The wage system is not natural,' declared Greeley, 'it is, in our view, but a step, a halting place, on the way from a bad system to a far better.' Workers should pool resources and establish co-operative ventures, or settle the free land of the West. There they would be free to fix their own hours of labour. 'Then why not either leave the capitalist, the employer, severely alone, or stop regarding him as an oppressor and robber?'[29] Barry – with direct experience of working for the massive Baldwin Locomotive Works – knew the unreality of avoiding employers. Greeley's call for mechanics to head west also went unheeded. Few mechanics, even Republicans like Barry, supported the demand for free land or the principle of free soil (no slavery in the Territories) – key elements in Republican free-labour ideology – and, as we shall see, during the secession crisis of 1860–1, they placated slave owners as a way to avoid bloodshed. The West was important to Republicanism and small farmers, but not to eastern labour.

Nevertheless, mechanic consciousness and Republicanism shared Greeley's belief that co-operatives were a means to elevate mechanics and foster cordial relations between capital and labour. 'By co-operation,' declared William Sylvis, leader of the Iron Molders Union, 'we will become a nation of employers – the employers of our own labor.'[30] Stimulated by wartime inflation, a small retail store opened in 1864 in the artisan district of Southwark. Co-operation offered the possibility of drawing skilled workers closer to their employers, as here was a movement that eschewed industrial action and pointed the finger of blame not at the boss but at the grasping corner shopkeeper. The senior partner in iron-founders Morris & Tasker joined the co-operative and, along with Merrick & Sons, they offered to buy stock in the co-operative if employees did the same.[31] While workshop owners and mechanics briefly came together in Southwark's settled community around Republican ideas of co-operation and social advancement, elsewhere proprietors had limited contact with employees and intended to rule their shops as they chose.

The old mercantile elite

Industrial expansion and the transformation of Philadelphia society in the 1840s and 1850s turned the old merchant class from a protector of infant manufactures into a stumbling block to future political progress.

Merchants, unlike manufacturers, had less desire to discipline directly the lower classes, alter existing political arrangements or centralize authority. At the national level, slave owners and merchants already had a satisfactory political settlement with the Constitution of 1787, and most Philadelphia merchants clung tenaciously to this compact until the South finally seceded.

For three decades before the civil war, workshop owners, along with other manufacturers, were minor partners with mercantile capital inside the Whig Party. Industrialists occupied a subaltern status, overshadowed both socially and politically by older interests in trade, commerce and banking. Born into a hostile world, manufacturing sought the protection of existing wealth and power. As we have seen, finance capital's loans to machine building aided social co-mingling. Also, through ventures such as the Pennsylvania Railroad, workshop owners allied themselves with merchants in securing a share of western markets. Yet, in the longer term, the interests of the two proved antithetical. Merchants organized the circulation of agricultural and manufacturing commodities, financed the supply of materials in the hands of small master craftsmen and lent to facilitate sale of the finished goods. They did not directly employ or control large numbers of workers.[32] Machine builders, in contrast, although they participated in the marketplace, devoted most attention to the workshop where, for their survival, they dreamed up new ways to revolutionize production and supervise their growing labour force. Machine builders recognized that their ascent to power was intimately linked to a change in class relations in the city. Remodelling the dark and private interiors of the city's workshops, paradoxically, encouraged builders like Merrick, Baldwin and I. P. Morris to refashion public life. In comparison, merchants, who had no direct interest in production, felt less compulsion to tinker with existing social arrangements. Manufacturers' urge to change social relations and to demand greater centralization of political power soon put machine builders on a collision course with merchants. The old, non-interventionist ways of controlling the city's affairs were a liability in the polarized mid-century industrial city.

In the turmoil following the depression of 1837–44, white mobs attacked African-Americans and Protestants attacked Irish Catholics. At the same time, youth gangs and volunteer fire companies in the townships beyond the city boundaries regularly confronted the ineffectual forces of order. Urban development, confined between the Schulykill and Delaware rivers, outgrew northern and southern boundaries. In both directions the city was a patchwork of industrial suburbs, with each borough, township and district jealously guarding its independence. Similarly fragmented were the forces of law and order. Yet, the older mercantile elite vacillated in the face of rising unrest. The anti-Irish-Catholic riots of 1844 assumed monstrous proportions partly as a result of the diffident response of the authorities.[33] They were reluctant to intervene so long as rioters stuck to the pre-industrial practice of settling scores among themselves. The scale of the riots failed to impress upon the mercantile elite the need to organize effective central control of the city, and some even expressed outrage at the actions of the militia in firing upon Protestant rioters. In autumn 1844, reformers called for the Pennsylvania legislature to extend the city boundaries to include the unruly industrial suburbs, but their demand was neutralized by prominent Whigs and Democrats.[34] The old rulers opposed centralization. Yet the deep anger of the mob and the length of the 1844 riots revealed to many manufacturers that the old ways of dealing with disorder were no longer sufficient.

The riots of 1844 exposed the weaknesses of the old elite, but until the manufacturing class could assert itself, a satisfactory remedy proved impossible. Manufacturers believed that existing methods of law enforcement were unsatisfactory in the modern city, where disturbance of whatever kind required crushing. Those alarmed by disorder insisted on a uniformed full-time police force under the control of a single municipal authority.

In 1853, prominent citizens proposed that the city annex the whole of adjoining Philadelphia county.[35] Among them were Stephen Colwell, I. P. Morris, Samuel Merrick, Matthias Baldwin and Horace Binney, while lawyer Eli K. Price had the backing of temperance reformers. Binney represented the old elite – he originally opposed consolidation but had changed his mind. The *North American*, voice of the city's manufacturers, also campaigned actively to secure consolidation.[36] Claiming that drink and corruption were the weapons of the fire companies, the reformers called for the creation of one municipal authority to check crime and lawlessness and promote prosperity. In the autumn, the city elected Price to the state Senate and William C. Patterson and Baldwin to the House on a cross-party platform, where they successfully passed a Consolidation Bill early the following year.[37]

The new industrial class remained subordinate to old wealth, but it had proved an effective force in changing the political landscape. In New York City, manufacturers were less capable of wresting power from merchants, and city authority remained divided and weak until the 1870s.[38]

Seizing power

In 1856, two years after the consolidation victory, Philadelphia's manufacturers created a Republican club – their basis of popular support in the city. Incensed by events in Kansas, the platform declared support for ending slavery in the Territories, as well as urging massive expenditure on internal improvements. William and John Sellers, partners in an expanding machine-tool firm, were early members. By 1860, their business was worth $280,000. At the other end of the scale was workshop owner

Stockton H. Evans, a member of the small firm of Charles Evans & Sons, worth $14,000.[39] Alongside them were large numbers of other manufacturers, small merchants, storekeepers and black-coated professionals. High tariffs, not anti-slavery, proved the best method to turn a small club representing manufacturers into a broad-based popular movement. In Pennsylvania, the tariff forged links with the disintegrating nativist American Party through a skilful blend of cultural and economic chauvinism: protectionism satisfied Republican manufacturers' desire for a united national market in the face of Democratic free-trade policies, while the nativists supported the tariff as a defence of American labour against cheap foreign labour.[40] At the same time, cautious Whig-Republicans were happy that the tariff obscured the party's radical anti-slavery credentials. In the May 1858 municipal elections the new organization, under the title of the People's Party, triumphed.[41] Victory in Philadelphia spread the party throughout Pennsylvania.

Rejecting the nativists' call for citizenship based on narrow religious and cultural characteristics, Republicans promised equal rights for all adult, native-born males, united in a national economy protected by the tariff. Following the financial panic of 1857 and the subsequent collapse, the tariff proposal enlisted support among those driven desperate by bankruptcy and unemployment.[42]

But further gains remained in doubt. John Brown's raid in late 1859 encouraged conservative Whig-Republicans to look for an alternative political vehicle. On 14 June 1860, a group of them, including Henry Carey, Morton McMichael, J. E. Thompson, president of the Pennsylvania Railroad, and Mayor Alexander Henry met non-Democratic southerners to discuss the possibility of resuscitating the Whig Party.[43]

The election of Lincoln in November 1860 turned threats of southern secession into reality. Workshop owners like Matthew Baird of the Baldwin Locomotive Works felt that this was a bluff as the South needed the North to suppress servile insurrection.[44] By January 1861, however, complacency had given way to alarm: Matthias Baldwin, Asa Whitney (former partner of Baldwin), along with prominent merchants, bankers and other manufacturers, wrote to a wavering President Buchanan urging him to 'pursue a conciliatory and thoroughly firm course . . . if an hour of need comes, you will have the support of the citizens of this and other commonwealths, therefore the Government is strong'.[45]

The secession crisis not only threatened to detach the conservative wing of the Republican Party, but also undermined the delicate links between skilled workers and employers built around Republican free-labour and tariff policies. In January 1861, mechanics from the city's machine shops and foundries, alarmed at the prospect of civil war, and refusing to make a blood sacrifice, organized their own independent peace movement. Neutral towards 'fanatical' northern abolitionists and 'treasonous' southern secessionist fire-eaters, they declared that, to save the Union, the

South needed reassuring. Mechanics endorsed the Crittenden Compromise, guaranteeing slavery where it existed, and conceded its right to expand in the Territories. Rejecting Republican ideas of free labour and free soil, and using the logic of 'an enemy of my enemy is my friend', many mechanics turned to Democrat-inspired ideas. As a party hostile to industrialism, it played upon workers' concerns by pointing to the spectre of freed slaves migrating northwards to flood an already glutted labour market. Although workers hated slavery, all the evidence points to their willingness to compromise with planters.

Alarmed by the distance between their own free-soil ideas and the pro-planter sentiment of their employees, workshop owners established links with the peace movement but could do nothing to change its direction. Unpalatable as it is to many, manufacturers constituted the revolutionary class and not their workforce. By February, the local peace movement, in alliance with mechanics from other border cities, acknowledged the South's right to peaceful withdrawal and looked forward to the creation of an association of the industrial classes. Independent politics was not to be, for soon afterwards Confederate guns fired on Fort Sumter and the armed conflict began.[46]

Industrialists threw themselves wholeheartedly into preserving the Union. They reserved jobs for volunteers, supported widows and orphans, sponsored the Great Sanitary Fair and organized factory militias in case of invasion.[47] Their finest political achievement, though, came in 1862 with the foundation of the Union League. The League represented the demise of the merchant class and the ascent of manufacturing. Tirelessly publicizing the northern cause, the League raised regiments of soldiers, called for the ending of slavery and supported black civil rights in Pennsylvania.[48]

Reassessing inevitability

Charles and Mary Beard believe that the outcome of the civil war was inevitable.[49] Marxists are tempted to offer a similar assessment. Yet this study of Philadelphia workshop owners encourages us to look at the process of revolution in a different light and to see its outcome as more problematical. Philadelphia workshop owners, because of the manner in which they matured, were cautious revolutionaries. The incubation of mechanical engineering within the folds of mercantile capital created powerful checks upon the revolutionary commitment of the new class. In addition, manufacturers needed to juggle a complex three-way relationship: firstly, in a bloody conflict with southern planters to end slavery; secondly, with a mercantile elite to wrest local political power; and, thirdly, with their own workforce to mobilize popular support to fight the slave power. Certainly, the contest with planters gives the war its

revolutionary character, but the outcomes of the subsidiary engagements
– which were also class struggles – made a powerful impact upon the pace
and direction of the revolutionary conflict.

While we might agree that the North's demographic and material supe-
riority made victory likely, nevertheless the precise resolution of each
encounter made the outcome less predictable. Here lies an explanation for
the slow adoption of a revolutionary programme on the part of the industrialists. Prominent members of the old mercantile elite continued a
rearguard opposition to the war throughout the conflict. In addition, proprietors were deeply worried about the political commitment of their
workforce. While labour joined in the contest to bring the rebels back into
the Union, unlike Republicanism it did not do so around a programme of
social revolution. Industrialists, torn between revolution and stability and
unable to rely absolutely on the urban working class, pursued a cautious
military strategy that, paradoxically, delayed victory. The civil war was a
triumph for liberal capital, but the multifaceted nature of the social contest made the revolution a hard-fought contest.

9

Industrial and Political Strategy in the 1972 British Strike Wave

Dave Lyddon and Ralph Darlington

The biggest strike wave in Britain since the early 1920s took place during 1968–74. One historian suggests that 'the labour unrest' in this period 'quite dwarfed its predecessor of 1910–14 in terms of its daring, its comprehensiveness and its success'.[1] The year 1972 particularly stands out.[2] Its high points were the miners' national official pay strike of January and February (with a siege of power stations and the symbolic closing of Saltley Gates) and the dockers' national unofficial campaign of 'blacking' and picketing of container bases in the spring and summer. The latter culminated in the imprisonment of five dockers and a developing strike movement for their release, including a call by the Trades Union Congress (TUC) General Council for a national one-day stoppage. A steadily escalating national building strike (with extensive use of flying pickets), and a wave of factory sit-ins in the Manchester area over the national engineering pay claim, were further demonstrations of the high levels of militancy that year. This chapter outlines the course of the four disputes, and discusses the tactics used. The solidarity given to the miners is then contrasted with the huge miners' lockouts of 1921 and 1926; this leads to some discussion of political strikes and the role of the TUC. The chapter concludes with brief comments on the contradictory role of the Communist Party (CP), in both leading and suppressing militancy.

The miners' strike

The miners' strike – the first national official strike in the industry since 1926 – lasted from 9 January to 27 February 1972, involved 308,500 workers directly and 'lost' 10,725,000 working days.[3] With the introduction of the National Power Loading Agreement in 1966, miners moving to new coalfaces transferred from piecework to an hourly rate; by the end of 1971 almost all faceworkers were on the same rate, irrespective of output. In 1971 all other underground workers were also put on to standard rates. The potential unity that these changes unleashed was fed by the material factor of many miners having their wages cut. As the official historian of post-war mining noted: 'It was the complicating changes in the wage structure that united the interests of mineworkers in aggressive national action.'[4]

The national strike threat was not taken particularly seriously and press comment suggested that the strike itself would have limited impact.[5] Matters turned out differently. Most miners' first concern was their own collieries. During the strike, 'The [TUC] General Council were concerned that . . . *in spite of instructions from the NUM* [National Union of Mineworkers], safety requirements were being met [two weeks into the strike] in only 36 pits' out of 289.[6] This totally unofficial action then led in many areas to mass pickets (often with arrests) to stop pit deputies doing the safety work, especially in early February.[7]

The miners in many areas started picketing other sites away from their collieries from the start of the strike, for example power stations in Scotland and coke plants in Yorkshire. This was an extension of the flying picket tactic that had been used to bring out miners in big unofficial strikes in 1969 and 1970.[8] The union's national office issued official instructions on picketing power stations but not until a few days into the strike. Non-mining regions of Britain were then allocated to different NUM areas: for example, the Barnsley panel of the Yorkshire miners was given East Anglia to picket, and Robert Taylor recounts how, when the tactic of spreading pickets thinly over too many locations there was failing, Yorkshire miner Arthur Scargill successfully pushed for mass picketing to be organized at each site in turn. Kent miners were allocated most of the London power stations to picket; independently, they too discovered the need for individual mass pickets to control fuel movements at docks and other coal users in the south-east of England.[9] As Prime Minister Edward Heath later admitted: 'The use of "flying pickets" . . . took us unawares.'[10]

It was estimated that 500 establishments across the country were picketed on a 24-hour basis.[11] This source also suggests that an average of 40,000 miners picketed each day, while others put it at 9,000[12] or 11,000[13] by early February, with perhaps 60,000 involved overall.[14] Whatever the exact figures, the scale of active participation probably dwarfed that of any other large strike. Allen summarizes the arguments about the miners' picketing: 'The complaint against it was not specifically its mass scale, or its mobility or . . . its legality, *but its effectiveness*.'[15]

Critical to this effectiveness was support from other workers. Following the railway unions' official recognition of any miners' picket lines,[16] the TUC General Council on the second day of the strike 'requested members of its affiliated unions not to cross picket lines', but this applied only to the movement of coal.[17] Support was not automatically forthcoming at local level and the picketing was often robust, but transport and railway union members fairly quickly respected the picket lines (which often had to be maintained 24 hours a day); the continuing problem, however, was non-union lorry drivers. In practice, union members tended to respect picket lines stopping not just coal. Several months after the strike *The Times* (2 August 1972) gave a graphic example:

> The driver and second man of a goods train of oil tankers . . . refused to take their train out of the yards. They said there were pickets on the line. Management could see no pickets . . . The driver rang . . . [ASLEF] headquarters and asked for a picket. A frantic telephone call to the NUM . . . led to the immediate dispatch of two 'flying pickets'. They unfurled a blanket bearing the slogan 'official NUM picket' from an overhead bridge and the train did not run.

The most affected organization was the Central Electricity Generating Board (CEGB), which reported in early February that it was 'in a state of siege', complained of the 'unrelenting blockade' of power stations, and considered itself to be 'conducting a guerilla war'.[18] The pickets' stranglehold on the supply of oil and essential gases to power stations was critical and accelerated the impact of the immobilization of coal supplies. The government declared a state of emergency on 9 February. A court of inquiry into the dispute was set up on 11 February and reported one week later. The miners did not call off their pickets during the court's hearings. On Thursday 17 February, the day before the inquiry's report was published, Industry Secretary John Davies read out the following dramatic statement to the House of Commons:

> Stocks of coal, lighting-up fuel and necessary chemicals . . . have diminished . . . with denial of available and necessary supplies still continuing as a result of unwillingness of other union members to cross picket lines . . . The combined effect [of the government's measures so far] . . . has been to reduce the consumption of coal at power stations by about 35 per cent . . . [D]irections for further restrictions . . . will allow supply to be maintained throughout next week at the still further reduced level, before reaching the point where we will be down to non-coal generated capacity – equal to 20–25 per cent of normal load – and sufficient to meet only the essential services . . . with very little left available for other users . . . If essential materials currently denied to the CEGB were made available, then the time by which this basic, essential services-only level would be reached would be extended by some seven to 10 days.[19]

The most remembered event in the years since the strike has been that of the police shutting the Saltley coke depot in east Birmingham on

Thursday, 10 February. CP member Arthur Harper, the Birmingham East AUEW district president, was pivotal in getting his union to support Scargill's plea for support on a mass picket. Tens of thousands of engineering and car workers from different unions struck, with sufficient thousands of them marching to the coke depot to seal it off.[20] But this was not the last dramatic moment in the strike. At Longannet power station in Scotland on 14 February, thirteen pickets were detained in custody, charged with 'mobbing and rioting'. A wave of protest forced their early release.[21] Strike pickets were eventually called off on 19 February following extra concessions beyond the court of inquiry report (see below).

The dockers and the Industrial Relations Act

In the early 1970s British dockers were experiencing a revolution in cargo-handling techniques. By an accident of history, the dockers' unofficial campaign against the effects of containerization on their job opportunities coincided with the full implementation of the 1971 Industrial Relations Act, which attempted to control tightly much trade union activity. Although the dockers' campaign was industrial, it unleashed a train of events that inevitably became increasingly political. Fred Lindop records in some detail the main developments and demonstrates that the continuing unofficial nature of the action not only put pressure on the dockers' main union, the Transport and General Workers' Union (TGWU), eventually to call an official national strike over the issue, but also inadvertently stiffened the resolve of the largest TUC-affiliated unions to maintain their policy of non-registration under the Act.[22]

The unofficial national port shop stewards' committee had agreed in December 1971 that all 'stuffing and stripping' of containers should be performed by registered dockworkers. A one-day unofficial national strike in January 1972 received widespread support. In Liverpool an unofficial joint TGWU committee of dockers and members of the union's commercial road transport trade group then drew up a document to be signed by hauliers using the docks on Merseyside. Most signed when their drivers were confronted at the dock gates. 'Blacking' was an 'unfair industrial practice' under the 1971 Act, and Heaton Transport of St Helens took a case to the National Industrial Relations Court (NIRC) in March. The TGWU was fined £5,000 when the blacking was not lifted; a £50,000 fine followed in April. The blacking of Heaton's lorries continued despite TGWU officers' pleas with the dockers. With the threat of sequestration of its assets hanging over the TGWU for its continuing contempt of court, the Finance and General Purposes Committee (F&GPC) of the TUC General Council voted in late April to advise the union to pay the fine (and hence to recognize the court). Even with its general secretary Jack Jones supporting the TUC decision, the TGWU general executive council only agreed to this by the chair's casting vote on 1 May.

The union took the case to the Court of Appeal in early May. By then the national stewards' committee had already extended the blacking to two firms in each port. This prompted a court case against the chair of the Hull port shop stewards, Walter Cunningham (who refused to attend the NIRC), and the TGWU. The case was eventually dropped by the company, Panalpina. In London, the dockers' inability to enforce the boycott sufficiently led to a picket of the depots of Dagenham Cold Storage and Midland Cold Storage and a decision to black all firms using them. As this was also not totally effective, a group of stewards from the Royal Docks picketed the Chobham Farm site in Stratford (east London) where lorries turned away from Dagenham were being diverted. When the chair and secretary of the London (and the Royal) docks stewards' committee argued against this move, their objections were overruled in practice and the site was picketed again.

On 13 June the Appeal Court (led by Lord Denning) reversed the NIRC judgment in the Heaton case, affirming that unions were not responsible for the actions of their stewards, thus crucially leaving the way open for imprisonment of individuals. This judgment caused Heath to fume: 'This was exactly what the union militants wanted.'[23] The NIRC had already made an interim order against three stewards picketing Chobham Farm. This was now altered to an order threatening them with imprisonment if they did not attend the court on Friday, 16 June and satisfactorily explain their conduct. Unofficial strikes broke out at most ports during Thursday and Friday. The union representing two of the men, the small National Amalgamated Stevedores and Dockers (NASD), was not persuaded by officers from the TGWU and the TUC to agree to their members being represented in court. A large picket assembled at Chobham Farm on the Friday but no arrests took place. Lord Denning had engineered a meeting between the Official Solicitor (who acted for those unable to represent themselves in legal matters) and Peter Pain QC (who normally acted for the TGWU). This enabled the Official Solicitor to instruct Pain to apply to the Appeal Court, which set aside the committals on a technicality.[24] Denning later claimed that 'We'd been told there was a danger of a general strike.'[25]

The picketing continued and Midland Cold Storage applied to the NIRC, naming seven dockers. Eventually warrants went out for the arrest of five of them on Friday, 21 July: four were found that day and lodged in Pentonville prison, while Vic Turner, the fifth, was arrested while picketing the prison the following day! Dockers around the country set in motion a wave of unofficial strikes across industry, culminating in the TUC General Council's call for a one-day stoppage just before the five were released after five days (see below).

The building workers' strike

The building workers' national pay strike, from 26 June to 22 September, was officially estimated to have involved 146,030 workers directly and 9,835 indirectly, and to have 'lost' 3,836,500 working days.[26] It consisted of selective stoppages for the first six weeks before it escalated into a much wider conflict, with the unions at its peak claiming 270,000 workers out at some 9,000 sites.[27]

The circumstances facing the building workers were very different from those confronting the miners and the dockers. First, about two-thirds of the industry's workforce was not unionized and huge numbers were scattered on small sites across the country: this presented a major obstacle to any national industrial action. Second, the main union, the Union of Construction and Allied Trades and Technicians (UCATT), had only just been created from the merger of three declining unions and its authority had yet to be established. Third, there had been an active rank-and-file organization since 1970, the Building Workers' Charter.

The build-up to the strike saw the emergence of centres of union organization in a number of towns, notably Birmingham and Liverpool, with campaigns against 'the lump' system of paying building workers.[28] Crane-top protests for days at a time in Birmingham and London further reflected the growing mood of militancy.[29] But the strike's beginnings were inauspicious. The plan was to escalate slowly though selective regional strikes, with six extra sites being brought out each week in every UCATT region. The numbers on strike at any particular time were a constant bone of contention, with the employers' estimates much lower than the unions'.[30] The first few weeks of the strike were also notable for the lack of coverage in the press, but by early August the newspapers were reporting about 20,000 workers on strike on some 300 sites.[31]

The period from the end of July to the middle of August was the turning point in the strike. Terry Austrin claims that at the end of July the regional action committee in Birmingham (where the Charter was particularly strong) moved for an all-out stoppage, first in Birmingham and then in the region, to be achieved by the use of flying pickets.[32] This local action reflected a wider mood, and a provisional settlement of the national strike, reported in the press on 1 August, was abandoned a week later as a number of area meetings also voted for all-out strikes. On 9 August the president of the National Federation of Building Trade Employers (NFBTE) was reported as claiming that 'militants were moving from site to site inciting workers into strike action' and that 'these militants have used strong-arm methods. They have called strikes official when they have not been.'[33] The NFTBE complained also that 'militant pickets . . ., in some areas, waited for operatives at pick-up points and public transport bus stops'.[34] While UCATT and two other unions – the

NUGMW and FTAT – were ready to settle, and an agreement was being drawn up from 4 August, the TGWU executive, under pressure from its members, rejected the terms on 7 August. As the Charter and the local action committees had by then persuaded most UCATT regions to oppose the offer, the UCATT executive found its authority rapidly waning and reversed its decision the next day.[35]

A week later, with 'intense pressure from militants for a total stoppage', the four unions agreed to strike against employers of between 60 and 200 workers.[36] But the momentum was with the rank-and-file local activists. The NFBTE sent out 15,000 letters to member firms to compile dossiers on flying pickets, claiming that 'the moderate elements . . . are being forced into intemperate action by travelling groups of militants which move from site to site'. By now UCATT's selective campaign had been 'wholly overtaken by militant action' and it was 'now busily declaring more and more official strikes to keep pace with the sites being unofficially pulled out by the militants'.[37] Austrin claims that all-out stoppages were eventually achieved in London, Bristol, Birmingham, Manchester, Liverpool, Glasgow, Edinburgh and Dundee before a settlement was reached.[38]

As with the miners, the building workers did not confine their activities to their own workplaces: pickets were arrested, for example, outside Rugby Portland Cement Company in Birmingham in late August as cement companies were targeted to cut off supplies to working sites.[39] But stopping the building sites was the overwhelming priority. This was behind what later became the most remembered aspect of the strike – the later arrest, trial and imprisonment of building workers for conspiracy.[40]

The engineering sit-ins

The Confederation of Shipbuilding and Engineering Unions (CSEU) had followed the lead given by its dominant constituent, the Amalgamated Union of Engineering Workers (AUEW), to fight that year's national engineering pay and conditions claim on a plant-by-plant basis. National industrial action, which had taken various forms since 1945,[41] was argued against by left-wing AUEW president Hugh Scanlon. The union had diverted most of its funds to secure them from any possible action under the Industrial Relations Act. With relatively high unemployment in the industry at the time, the executive was also reluctant to be forced into a national ballot in case it was lost. So the union's recalled National Committee (10 January 1972) agreed that individual plants should submit the full claim to their management and that the executive was 'authorised . . . to support any action which District Committees may recommend'. Scanlon added that it was hoped that district committees would be 'selective' about which firms to 'take on' and that district ballots should be held for levies to support those selected to take action.

In Greater Manchester, 'carbon copy' claims were agreed at a district-wide meeting of 700 shop stewards. Once these claims were rejected, another meeting decided on individual factory sanctions of an overtime ban and work-to-rule and a ban on piecework. A number of factories in Stockport did not wait until the agreed start of sanctions on 27 March and crucial features of the dispute were fixed before most factories had even started taking action. The local employers' association then announced that workers would be either suspended or only paid for work done. When management gave a few minutes' notice to suspend workers at one factory if they did not work normally, the workers voted to sit in.[42] After the AUEW executive made this action official, CSEU district secretary and CP member John Tocher announced: 'if there are widespread lockouts there will be widespread sit-ins'.[43] These became the dominant form of action in Greater Manchester, with up to 30 taking place, and perhaps 25,000 workers involved, at the height of the campaign.[44]

As important for the character of the dispute, however, was that when the local employers' association expelled a company for reducing the working week, the unions agreed that details of other settlements would be kept secret.[45] The Manchester factories were therefore not only isolated from other workforces within their own industry, they were isolated from each other. The two leading AUEW officials, who were also the popular leaders of the local engineering Broad Left, opposed attempts even to organize a joint occupation committee. Leading CP stewards continued to identify with Scanlon and the local officials and thus disarmed their supporters, unlike their counterparts in the docks and building industry.

Scanlon saw limited selective action as a means of forcing the employers back to the national bargaining table, mainly on the issue of raising the pitifully low basic rate, and had not envisaged such a district-wide campaign as in Manchester. The national Engineering Employers Federation (EEF) subsidized (through its Indemnity Fund) the Manchester employers' resistance to any hasty concessions on hours and holidays.[46] The employers in effect sat out the sit-ins. Given the heterogeneity of the engineering industry nationally, the Manchester factory sit-ins could hardly have been used to kick-start a broader wages movement, but once they had started in numbers they could have formed the rallying point for a serious national fight over the shorter working week. Yet in the middle of May, when the AUEW executive dropped the hours reduction from its claim, and the Manchester AUEW district committee followed suit, Tocher only described it at the time as a 'change of tactic'.[47] Even then a number of sit-ins carried on well into June (and some even later) before the unions eventually settled nationally with the employers in August on basic rates and holidays only. Tuckman estimates a national total of 49 occupations and that these and other actions on the claim cost the AUEW £2.5 million in strike benefit.[48] The AUEW Broad Left's relative failure in delivering results in 1972 marked a turning point in its fortunes.

Militant tactics

All four disputes displayed very militant tactics and high levels of rank-and-file participation. The coal strike was official, but was characterized by mass involvement (tens of thousands of pickets), with many activities going well beyond official guidelines. The momentum generated by the activists was articulated by leading left-wingers within the union, who mobilized a majority on the executive for a continuing militant position. Thus the union did not even call off the pickets, let alone the strike, while the court of inquiry was sitting. Further concessions were squeezed out of the National Coal Board while crisis talks were later held in Downing Street. As one Communist member, Jock Kane, put it: 'we have the government on the run so let us keep it running'.[49]

The building unions' early strategy of limited selective strikes was superseded after several weeks when rank-and-file activists around the country (many supporting the Building Workers' Charter) blocked a settlement in early August and escalated the action into an attempted all-out strike. While the NUM's eventual official strategy looked beyond miners' workplaces to strangle the movement of coal, building activists' most pressing concern was to shut down as many sites as possible, both union and non-union. This could only be done by picketing, which was the main similarity between the miners', dockers' and building workers' disputes.

The Economist argued that 'the rewarding of the miners' violent picketing . . . led directly to the picketing of the container depots this summer . . . [The] spectacular rewarding of this will make it easier to arrange tougher picketing in . . . [future] . . . strikes.'[50] This was not long in coming. At the end of the building strike, a correspondent on *The Times* (18 September 1972) noted that it had been 'the third major industrial dispute this year whose course was directed largely by the concerted action of pickets'; that the 'flying pickets' had had 'considerable success'; and that, while some had been prosecuted, 'the pickets had generally stopped a site and moved on before police arrived at the scene'.

Given that many lay union activists also hold official positions or sit on union committees, there has often been some confusion as to what is official and what is unofficial policy or action. The mass participation in the miners' strike and eventually in the building workers' strike blurred the distinction. Sometimes full-time officials were pulled along by rank-and-file initiatives though they might take credit for any successes.[51] By contrast, the dockers' activities were totally unofficial, except for the national strike from late July to mid-August that came after the release of the five from Pentonville. The blacking and picketing of certain container companies was consistently disowned by the official TGWU leadership because of the legal implications for the union; but this had little effect on the activists given the support of dockers (in both the TGWU and NASD). In fact, the unofficial campaign was a prelude to the official national strike and strengthened the officials' negotiating position. Jones himself argued that 'though the action in the docks . . . was unofficial, it was for the right purpose'.[52]

The engineering dispute was different in many ways from the other three. One AUEW convener referred to the sit-ins as 'an inside form of picketing'.[53] But there the resemblance ends. The other three disputes were characterized by activists looking beyond their own workplaces, while in engineering the unions' plant bargaining strategy constricted the potential of an otherwise almost unique movement in Manchester. After the summer of 1971, the 'work-in' tactic, which had been adopted by the Upper Clyde Shipbuilders shop stewards, popularized the idea of factory occupations throughout Britain. The most obvious defensive use was as a means to try to protect jobs in the short term by literally physically stopping plant closure and the removal of machinery; there were several examples of this throughout 1972.

Sit-ins had, however, been rarely used in Britain as an offensive tactic. Perhaps the biggest instance of this before 1972 had been in the little-known series of 'stay-down' strikes, to eradicate company unionism, in about a dozen South Wales collieries over a ten-day period in October 1935.[54] Even at the beginning of the Manchester engineering dispute in March 1972 it had initially been employed defensively, this time as a counter to management's suspension or threats of suspension of workers taking limited industrial action. But the simplicity of the tactic caught on, and when the AUEW executive gave official support to the first factory sitting in, it became the dominant form of action rather than the strike in Manchester. 'Inside picketing' on its own, however, did not generate a wider response within the industry let alone outside it.

Solidarity action, political strikes and the TUC

Comparisons with their 1921 and 1926 lockouts can only emphasize the scale of the miners' success in 1972. In both the earlier cases the miners were dependent on other unions either threatening or taking strike action in support. From the beginning of the 1921 dispute, the miners had officially pulled out safety men and had picketed the collieries to stop replacements, with some success. After nine days the miners agreed to allow safety work to be carried out after persuasion by the other unions in the Triple Alliance (the miners, the railwaymen and the transport workers being prepared to strike in each other's support, given that action by one group would lead to mass layoffs in the others). As Cole argued, this 'eliminate[d] the chief factor which would have necessitated a speedy settlement of the dispute'.[55] It also meant the use of outside labour, and this was to have serious repercussions. Many safety workers failed to get their jobs back after 1921 and the various enginemen's unions left the Miners' Federation of Great Britain (MFGB). When, five months into the miners' lockout in 1926, the MFGB desperately attempted to stop safety work, it had only limited impact.[56] By contrast, in 1972 the union's official policy was to keep safety men at work, yet there occurred the most sustained withdrawal of them ever – on an unofficial basis – increasingly backed up in many areas by mass picketing to stop deputies and officials doing the work.

The Economist claimed that Midlands miners, among others, 'had believed that the damage to underground equipment would prove to be their biggest bargaining counter'. To their surprise – and the government's – they were 'frankly amazed at the havoc they appear to have caused [by picketing]. None of them expected the strike to bite so deeply.'[57] While the ban on safety work was unofficial, the picketing strategy adopted away from the collieries could not have been as extensive as it was without being officially sanctioned.

This 'secondary' picketing was unprecedented in its audacity. Efforts to stop coal entering, or being moved between, power stations complemented the NUM's decision to block coal imports at the docks and most other movements of coal inside the country, but it had never been done before. Once initiated, it led rapidly and almost inevitably to three further developments: picketing outside the immediate area of the coalfields, with large numbers of miners having to be away from home for days at a time; targeting other essential materials required in coal-fired stations; and stopping oil entering oil-fired stations. Success in these endeavours required co-operation from workers in other unions, especially as many power stations were supplied with coal or oil directly by rail links or sea transport, both being difficult to picket.

There had been an attempted embargo on the movement of coal in the 1921 lockout, but it was fraught with difficulty coming in the wake of 'Black Friday' when the transport and railway unions pulled away at the last moment from striking in support of the miners. Following a big increase in imported coal, 'sporadic local refusals' to handle it quickly led to the executives of the National Union of Railwaymen (NUR) and the Transport Workers' Federation putting an embargo on such 'tainted' imported coal and on any British coal destined for other than domestic use. However, some transport unions did not enforce it and employers also dismissed or suspended many of the workers operating the embargo. For example, the suspension of dockers led to a month-long total strike by the Scottish Union of Dock Labourers on the Clyde; but they were replaced by non-union labour. On the railways, local NUR officials had the difficult task of deciding which coal was blacked and which not; many members were reluctant to obey merely local instructions; and 300 were dismissed for carrying out the embargo. While there were sporadic stoppages, such as at Bristol docks and at Greenwich power station, it was very difficult to make the embargo effective under such conditions and the unions lifted it after five or six weeks, while the miners fought on for another month before accepting defeat.[58]

Days after the TUC called off the 1926 general strike in support of the miners, the MFGB approached the transport unions for an embargo on coal. They were turned down. The NUR and the train drivers' union ASLEF replied jointly that 'we have carried out our obligations' by joining the general strike and that they were 'now engaged in a tremendous fight for the re-employment of all our members'.[59] Ernest Bevin of the TGWU invoked the experience of 1921 'when men came out . . . and never got back': 'to pick out small sections of men and tell them to carry the weight of the embargo means leaving them on the stones or putting the docks out in support'.[60]

The solidarity exhibited by other workers in the 1972 miners' strike was therefore very different from 1921 and 1926. The 1926 general strike in support of the miners was an extension of the tactic of the 'Triple Alliance'. Under the agreed control of the TUC General Council, it was more clearly a political challenge to government policy than even 1921 had been – and this was an important factor in the TUC leadership calling it off. By contrast, the 1972 strike took place within a framework of limited official support for the miners from affected unions, but in practice the picket lines, and unionized workers' general willingness to recognize them, meant a very quick and almost totally effective blockade of the electricity power stations. The NUM in 1972 was able to escalate the strike outside the normal constraints of Congress House and it was the militancy of its own members that dictated its agenda, rather than involvement in a formal pact with other unions or the TUC.

A wider movement was nearly precipitated at the time, but this has been overlooked by subsequent commentators. During the miners' strike, unions representing electricity supply workers threatened official industrial action over their own pay claim, and there was some unofficial action. An overtime ban was due to come into force at midnight on 7 February 1972 (four weeks into the miners' strike) and this forced government ministers to delay imposing restrictions on the supply of electricity (thus making cuts, when they came, much more drastic).[61] On that same day, 'Just how close the country came to chaos may be judged from the fact that there was an argument on the trade union side about the possibility of joint action with the miners.' The electricity union negotiators split 6–6 over the increased offer. Frank Chapple of the Electricians used his casting vote as chair for acceptance, arguing that 'to bring down the Government by industrial action would only lead to a general election in which the Conservatives would be returned with a landslide majority'.[62] Chapple later elaborated on this: 'such dual action would be seen as a challenge to the state, tantamount to a general strike . . . Industrial action for political ends is not for me and, so far, it is also alien to the TUC.'[63]

However, the TUC's opposition to the Industrial Relations Act always had the potential of drawing it into some form of political strike against its use. The Labour government in 1969 had prefigured parts of the Conservative legislation in its White Paper, *In Place of Strife*. Serious opposition to this was instigated by the Liaison Committee for the Defence of Trade Unions (LCDTU), a Communist Party front organization. There was near unanimous opposition at national union level to the strike action advocated by the LCDTU in February and May 1969. But McIlroy and Campbell argue that the May strike particularly 'broke the post-1926 *omerta* on political strikes'.[64] The immediate result was a recalled TUC and official opposition to the government's proposals that saw them eventually dropped.

An important precedent had been set. The LCDTU organized another (and bigger) unofficial one-day strike, in December 1970, against the Conservatives' Industrial Relations Bill. By this stage the AUEW and the TGWU (the two largest unions, with avowedly left-wing leaders and organizing some of the most militant groups of workers) had opposed all three strikes against anti-union proposals. But both these and other unions warned the TUC General Council that it could lose control of the opposition to the Bill. The General Council therefore called for local demonstrations on 12 January 1971 (which inevitably included strikes), while its huge national 'Kill the Bill' demonstration on Sunday, 21 February indicated the potential scale of the opposition. This groundswell culminated in the AUEW and some smaller unions calling their members out on two one-day strikes in March 1971, the second on the day of a TUC Special Congress.[65] At this, the TUC advised unions not to register under the new legislation or to co-operate with bodies set up under it, while at the September 1971 annual TUC the AUEW won a motion instructing unions not to register under the Industrial Relations Act.

Once the Act had come into full force, the official movement (apart from the AUEW) tended, however reluctantly, to comply with it, as with the ballot and the cooling-off period in the official railway dispute of spring 1972.[66] But the dockers' cases proved less tractable. As noted earlier, the TUC F&GPC had advised the TGWU to pay its fines rather than face sequestration. This was challenged at the next General Council meeting on 4 May, where Scanlon argued that 'the General Council had now put the Movement on a slippery slope which would lead to co-operation with NIRC'. He argued that 'a fresh strategy was called for'. Other union leaders suggested that 'if some unions wanted a head-on clash with the government, a general strike or a token general strike, they should say so, because that was where the policy being advocated from some quarters would lead'. Very early on in the docks dispute, therefore, the spectre of a general strike was being raised.

Following the threatened imprisonment of three dockers, the TUC F&GPC (26 June) considered the document 'Industrial Relations Act – Review of the Situation'. This argued that 'a policy of using industrial action to compel the present government to repeal the Act would not be effective'. It noted that 'there will be outbursts of industrial action and other hostile demonstrations, which neither unions themselves nor the TUC will be able to restrain'. However, there was 'no evidence that the affiliated unions have reached the point where they would be prepared to hand over to the General Council the authority to use the strike weapon for what would in fact be a political purpose'.

When five dockers were jailed on 21 July, Jones made it clear that they were to be given no assistance by the TGWU and its officials were not to visit them.[67] The dockers' own actions in calling for secondary action in the form of strikes for the release of the Pentonville Five and the growing support for such action forced the TUC General Council to confront its own role. As well as an unofficial national docks strike, delegations from the dockers had persuaded key groups in Fleet Street to stop the national newspapers, and other groups were gradually coming out or responding to pickets or appeals for solidarity. While these still numbered, at most, in the low hundreds of thousands (partly because of summer holidays for many industrial workers), there was a momentum developing.[68] The Communist Party was particularly prominent in arguing for a one-day strike by the TUC.[69]

The TUC F&GPC met in the afternoon of Monday, 24 July. Some members argued for a 'national one-day stoppage of work', particularly because 'if the General Council did not themselves take action of this kind unofficial bodies would assume leadership'. On Wednesday 26 July, it was reported at the beginning of the General Council meeting that 'the House of Lords would, that morning, give their decision on the appeal, and following that the Official Solicitor would probably go to the NIRC', leading to the dockers' release. The following debate has to be judged in that context.

Scanlon moved that the General Council 'call on all affiliated unions to organise a one-day stoppage of work and demonstrations on Monday next July 31' for the dockers' release. Roy Grantham of the Clerical Workers countered that for 'the General Secretary to call a one-day official stoppage of the whole of the movement could lead to the possibility of a general strike'. Thus, 'the action proposed would be regarded by any Government as a challenge to its authority, and as a challenge to the right of Parliament to create legislation and to ensure that it was carried out'. Chapple was more forceful: 'No doubt some people thought that, if a crisis was created by a one-day general strike and a complete general strike, the General Council would win. They might however lose. He would not wish the democratic form of Government changed as a result of strike action.'

TUC general secretary Vic Feather responded disingenuously that 'any suggestion that the one-day stoppage could be construed as a political general strike could be dismissed quickly. To organise a political or general strike would certainly take more than five days.' Replying to the debate, Scanlon pointed out that 'the motion was *not seeking a confrontation with Government, or a revolution, or a general strike*' (emphasis added). Unions 'would be able to differentiate between a strike and a one-day stoppage of protest. A strike and a protest stoppage were not the same.' He concluded: 'He was sure that the carrying of the motion would in itself ensure speedy action by the Official Solicitor towards getting the dockers released.' Thus even Scanlon, who had taken up the most uncompromising opposition to co-operation with the Act, distanced himself from an openly political stance. The motion was passed and the TUC circulars calling for, and (with the dockers' release later that day) cancelling, action were headed 'Protest Stoppage of Work'.[70]

Conclusion

In 1972 the miners' aggressive strategy was successful in gaining widespread support at relatively little cost to other unions and workers; within a few weeks their growing success silenced any critics within the movement. But while receiving support from the movement, the miners were never subservient to the TUC and were able to dictate their own fate. Perhaps memories of 1926 were too strong on both sides.

In the campaign against the Industrial Relations Act, the TUC leadership and most national union leaders were reluctant to move beyond verbal opposition, for fear of coming into conflict with the law, and the early operation of the Act saw one gradual concession after another, orchestrated by the TUC General Council majority. The dockers' unofficial campaign against containerization became entangled with the Act, but the traditions of unofficial activity in the docks were strong enough to resist the TGWU's attempts to get their action called off. The Appeal Court judgment, leaving the way open for imprisonment of shop stewards, could not have been predicted. The dockers' determination that theirs was an industrial struggle (which had to be won), and not a political one (in which case the blandishments of the TGWU and TUC leaders might have worked to defuse the situation), led to the jailings. But the campaign of secondary strikes to get the dockers released was clearly political, whatever TUC leaders on both right and left might argue.

The broad opposition to the Industrial Relations Act owed much to the earlier work of the CP-controlled LCDTU. Its mission was 'to activate the official machinery of the unions and TUC, not to replace it',[71] and on the Act it had been fairly successful. This position was an extension of the CP's own line that 'rank and file action was the forward moment in the mobilization of the official machinery, not an alternative to it'.[72] Yet the events of 1972 revealed the flaw in the CP's industrial strategy. Its implantation in the AUEW's official structure, and its support for the union's leader Scanlon, demobilized its membership and supporters in that year's engineering dispute. CP officials and leading stewards in Manchester engineering, after having started a militant district-wide campaign, accepted the restrictions of the AUEW's national official strategy of plant bargaining over a reduced claim, and thus became a brake on development of the district campaign, which ended in demoralization.

In the other three disputes covered in this chapter, the role of CP members was oppositional to the incumbent union leadership to varying degrees. In the dockers' case, the CP was a significant part of the unofficial leadership, which acted, for most of the year, independently of the TGWU officials. In the building dispute, the CP was again an important component in the local leadership of the activists who wrested the initiative away from the national officials by dramatically extending the official strike. The CP on the miners' executive effectively became the voice of the activists against the established right-wing leadership, and pursued a particularly intransigent line.

But these actions were not seen by the CP as providing an alternative to the disastrous national policy pursued in engineering. In the mines and the building industry, emphasis on getting left officials elected took precedence over sustaining rank-and-file activity in the years after 1972; in the London docks, the independence of the activists soon drove most away from the CP line.[73] Yet independence from the official movement, both from individual unions and the TUC, had been critical in putting workers in a much stronger bargaining position at key moments in 1972. But the main left-wing grouping in British trade unions in the early 1970s saw the election of, and support for, left-wing union leaders as its central strategy. Rank-and-file action was secondary. The traditional sectionalist trade union agenda, while briefly challenged by the dramatic upsurge of militant working-class struggles in 1972, was left intact.

10

Class Consciousness and National Consciousness in the Scottish General Strike of 1820

Neil Davidson

On the morning of Sunday, 2 April 1820, inhabitants of the south-western Lowlands of Scotland awoke to find an Address flyposted on the walls of Glasgow and the nearby industrial towns. Signed 'By order of the Committee of Organisation for Forming a Provisional Government', it demanded action to secure manhood suffrage and annual parliaments:

> In this present state of affairs we earnestly request of all to desist from their Labours, from and after this day, the First of April; and attend wholly to the recovery of their Rights, and consider it as the duty of every man not to recommence until he is in possession of those rights [*sic*] which distinguishes the FREEMAN from the SLAVE; viz: That of giving consent to the laws by which he is governed.

The Address appealed to soldiers not to fight against the 'citizens' but to join with them in the struggle against 'despotism', as sections of the army had done during the Spanish revolution earlier that year.[1]

The response to the demand was spectacular. The Lord Provost of Glasgow wrote to the Home Office that 'Almost the whole population of the working classes have obeyed the orders contained in the treasonable proclamation by striking work.'[2] He was not exaggerating. By 9 April, when the strike was abandoned, around 60,000 workers along the Clyde valley – a significant if unquantifiable proportion of the world industrial proletariat at that time – had struck in support of the demands contained in the proclamation. And support had grown as the strike continued: mill workers were successfully picketed out in Glasgow on 3 April, while on the same day in Paisley 300 armed men shut the mills down completely.

Alongside the industrial action, however, were several attempts at military risings which had less success. On 4 April a small group of Glasgow radicals attempted to capture cannon stored at the Carron Iron Works by Falkirk. At Bonnymuir about 40 of them were surprised by a cavalry troop of roughly the same size and, after a skirmish which resulted in deaths on both sides, 18 were captured. The other main attempt took place two days later in Strathaven, where a few dozen radicals began to march towards Rutherglen but dispersed before even encountering the military. The risings that accompanied the strike were therefore abortive, largely because they were intended to occur simultaneously with insurrections in the north of England, which the Scottish insurgents believed – not entirely accurately – to have been called off.[3]

Attempts were made to victimize striking workers on the return to work, but these were by no means all successful, itself an indication that the strike had been abandoned rather than defeated. Barr and Co. in Greenhead, for example, attempted to reduce wages by 8 per cent after the return to work, but the men staged a further stoppage of six or seven weeks – seven times the length of the original strike – until they were accepted back on their original wages.[4] The aftermath of the insurrectionary movement was less happy. The bourgeoisie took their revenge with the juridical execution of Andrew Hardie and John Baird, two leaders of the Bonnymuir rising, and John Wilson, an old Jacobin who had led the Strathaven affair. What is noticeable, however, is the relative restraint with which repression was applied. Dozens of arrested rebels could have faced the same fate as the three martyrs, which suggests either that state officials feared they would be unable to secure convictions in all cases, or that they were unwilling to risk possible further unrest by continuing with the executions.

The first general strike in history is usually thought to have taken place in August 1842, following the second rejection of the Charter by the British Parliament.[5] Three crucial elements have to be in place for a general strike to have occurred, regardless of the extent to which the strike in question is run by the bureaucracy or the rank and file: first, that it occurs across a contiguous area (city, region or nation-state); second, that it involves different groups of workers, not only those with the same employer; third, that these workers are striking for the same objective, and not simply participating simultaneously in a series of separate actions with different aims. On these criteria, the working class of south-west Scotland were the first to conduct a regional general strike in the history of capitalism, a strike which, furthermore, was as directed at securing political objectives as its successor in 1842. It is rarely remembered as such, not least in Scotland itself, where 1820 is largely commemorated for the abortive insurrections, which are themselves interpreted as nationalist risings against English domination.[6] Even the fact that the general strike took place in south-west Scotland, rather than the comparable area of north-west England, has been interpreted in a nationalist way, as demonstrating the greater militancy of Scottish workers. There are two issues requiring exploration here.

The first is the different course of events in Scotland and England. In Mirfield in Yorkshire, the one area where the call for a general strike was issued, it went unheeded. Yet the subsequent history of the labour movement in Britain does not suggest that Scottish workers are intrinsically more militant than their English or Welsh brothers and sisters. The second is the extent to which the activities of Scottish workers were influenced by a (Scottish) nationalist agenda. The Strathaven radicals did indeed carry a banner saying 'Scotland Free or a Desert', but this is scarcely conclusive. The very fact joint risings had been planned for both sides of the border suggests that they were designed to secure British objectives. The character of both the Scottish working-class militancy of 1820 (class consciousness) and the national context within which it was expressed (national consciousness) were produced by a combination of specific material conditions under which Scotland entered the process of capitalist industrialization, and the responses that it generated. Both were the outcome of an intensive process of combined and uneven development.

Combined and uneven development

The process was identified by Leon Trotsky in an attempt to explain what he called 'the peculiarities of Russian development' in the early twentieth century, but his theorization can be applied to other nations in other historical periods. Trotsky argued that in relation to the advanced countries, the backward are condemned neither to repeat their experience, nor to find their progress towards development blocked by them, but under certain conditions could adopt their technological, organizational and intellectual achievements as a prelude to overtaking them. Combined and uneven development is indeterminate in its results. In the period of the transition from feudalism to capitalism, societies where the transition was at an early stage often assimilated the achievements of those which had completed it – not to speed up the process, but the better to preserve the existing form of society. In the case of Russia itself, a feudal absolutist state initiated the process of capitalist industrialization during the 1860s, principally in order to compete militarily in a European state system where mass-produced armaments were indispensable. As a result, the most backward society in Europe also contained the largest factories with the most up-to-date technologies. Naturally this had implications for the class consciousness of the working class produced by the process of industrialization. That class was originally drawn not, as it had been in England, from members of the existing urban craft guilds, but mainly from the peasantry, who were plunged into urban life and the discipline of factory labour, and who were denied political expression for their grievances by the same autocratic regime that had called them into being for its own ends. These developments were central to the way in which the Russian revolutions of 1905 and 1917 developed in the cities.[7] The socioeconomic transformation that took place in Scotland between 1746 and 1820 was unprecedented in European history, and would not be seen again on such a scale until the industrialization of the Soviet Union after 1929. Indeed, the experience of Scotland was far closer to that of the Soviet Union than England in terms of the speed and intensity with which it occurred. No direct parallels are possible because of the different historical periods in which the respective births of the Scottish and Russian working classes took place, but four key similarities can be identified. It is not merely that Scotland experienced industrialization and urbanization far more quickly and intensively than England; it also 'skipped the intervening stages' between peasant self-sufficiency and wage labour which England had experienced. The resulting clash between an undisciplined working class of immediate rural origin and a state apparatus inherited from the transitional period would exercise a profound influence over the initial formation of the working-class movement.

Industrialization

Industrialization is not simply the dominance of the capitalist mode of production within an economy. Most countries went through a stage where capitalist relations of production prevailed, but in which the agricultural sector was still dominant, a position Scotland was in when Adam Smith published *The Wealth of Nations* in 1776. Nor does industrialization necessarily involve the dominance of large-scale or heavy industry, although in later, more consciously planned industrialization such as that of the Soviet Union, it has done so. In fact, heavy industry – pig-iron production, and consequently steamship building, railway construction and the increased demand for coal – became central to the Scottish economy only in the 1840s. Nevertheless, industrialization was complete by 1820.

Before the mid-nineteenth century, industrialization generally fell between the advent of a capitalist economy *per se* and the shift to heavy industry, and provided the link between these processes. It involved two key stages. The first was the transition from artisanal manufacture – which had existed under all previous modes of production – to what Marx calls 'the manufacturing period proper', where 'manufacture is the predominant form taken by capitalist production'. As Marx points out, this can happen in two ways: either the capitalist assembles craftsmen together under one roof to perform their different handicrafts in the production of a commodity (e.g. cloth manufacture); or the capitalist assembles craftsmen under one roof all of whom are skilled in the same handicraft. The end result in either case is 'a productive mechanism whose organs are human beings'. The second stage was the replacement of labour power by the instruments of labour themselves, which now become the starting point for production. The transition from manufacture to machinofacture involves a shift from a process where the organization of labour has changed to one where the instruments of labour have changed.[8]

The first industry to see these changes was textiles and, more specifically, cotton. It was in this industry in particular that, between 1730 and 1780, capitalist industrialization was first established in the form of factories of skilled spinners and weavers, with the latter beginning to base their loom shops in proximity to the merchant warehouses and to be employed as wage-labourers, reliant on the merchants for access to the means of production, the loom. Yet within the ten years from 1780 to 1790 the technology and the skills of the employees were redirected towards cotton. Between 1770, when James Hargreaves took out the patent on his jenny, which transformed cotton spinning operations, and 1822, when the stampmaster of linen cloth made his last records, the amount produced in the west of Scotland fell from 40 per cent of the Scottish total output to less than 0.5 per cent. In 1780 there were precisely two cotton spinning mills in Scotland, but by 1787 there were seventeen and by 1834 there were 134, the majority of which were within a 25-mile radius of Glasgow. The way in which the Scottish cotton industry borrowed from the English is a classic example of combined and uneven development at work. Even the areas into which the Scottish industry did not follow the English, such as the production of cheaper cotton goods, were influenced by the need to find markets outside those already captured by the Lancashire pioneers, in this case fine cotton yarn.[9]

The number of handloom weavers in Scotland increased from 25,000 in 1780 to 58,000 in 1800 and to 78,000 in 1820, and the figure continued to grow, although at a slower rate, until decline began around 1840. Approximately two-thirds of these operatives worked for houses in the Glasgow and Paisley area. The people who became weavers came from three different sources: in ascending order of numerical importance, the Highlands, Ireland and the rural Lowlands, migration from which, unlike similar areas in England, was not blocked by the operation of the Poor Law. In Paisley during 1821, for example, only 7 per cent of the inhabitants were originally from the Highlands, and these do not appear to have been primarily involved in weaving.[10] By 1816, however, we find around 600 Highlanders employed as farm servants or labourers, and 800 in the printfields and bleachfields. One report claimed that, with their backgrounds in agriculture and fishing, Highlanders were 'not suited' for employment in such alien activity as factory work.[11] The role of the Irish was more significant, with perhaps as many as 25 per cent of weavers in Scotland being native Irish by 1820, of which the number employed in Glasgow and its environs was greater, reaching perhaps a third of those employed in the occupation.[12]

Urbanization

Industrialization was at the centre of a wider process of transformation. In 1755 the Scottish population was calculated by Alexander Webster as being 1,265,380.[13] This was only a 2.5 per cent increase on the 1691 figure of 1,234,575.[14] By the first reliable census of 1801 it had risen to 1,608,420 and by 1831 to 2,364,368. Between 1755 and 1801, the population of the west of Scotland grew by 82.7 per cent, or three times that for Scotland as a whole, while Lanarkshire grew by 80.7 per cent and Renfrewshire by 194.6 per cent.[15]

Most of the new population lived in towns. In 1700 Scotland was only the tenth most urbanized country in western Europe, but by 1750 it was seventh, by 1800 fourth and by 1850 second only to England and Wales. By the latter date fully 35.9 per cent of the population lived in towns of over 5,000 and the rate of urban expansion was the highest anywhere.[16]

Take, for example, cities with more than 100,000 inhabitants. In 1800, 959,300 people, or 10.5 per cent of the total population of England and Wales, lived in cities of that size; no one in Scotland did. By 1850, the figures for England and Wales were 3,992,100 people, or 21.7 per cent of the total population, but for Scotland they had leapt to 490,700 people or 16.8 per cent of the total population.[17] Across the eighteenth century, the percentage of the English population living in towns of over 1,000 rose from 13.3 per cent to 20.3 per cent; the percentage of the Scottish population rose from 5.3 per cent to 17.3 per cent – more than a threefold increase.[18]

Given the way in which population and industry had shifted to the south-west, the experience of Glasgow is central. It grew more rapidly than any other town, expanding by 270 per cent between 1755 and 1801. As many as 50 new streets and squares may have been built in the city in the three years between 1788 and 1791.[19] And who lived in these streets and squares? On the eve of 1820, 15,208 out of 129,917 Glaswegians were of Irish birth (although only 8,254 of these were Roman Catholic).[20] Nor was Glasgow unique in the west in this respect. Between 1755 and 1801 the population of Paisley grew from 2,509 to 31,179 and it has been estimated that between 15,000 and 20,000 of these were immigrants, the majority either from the surrounding Ayrshire countryside or from the Highlands and the Western Isles.[21]

The conditions in which these migrants were expected to live and work were inhuman. Again, the experience of Glasgow is central. The population rose from 7,385 in 1801 to 274,533 in 1841, the biggest increase of 45.9 per cent taking place between 1811 and 1821, the very decade that saw average real wages begin a twenty-year fall, or rather, collapse, across the range of occupations. Of the other major British cities only Manchester, with an increase of 40.4 per cent, experienced comparable growth. The infrastructure of the city was unable to cope with increases of this magnitude, especially in the provision of basic amenities like housing and sanitation. One outcome was that mortality per 1,000 of the population, which had fallen from 32.2 to 17.1 between 1791 and 1801, now began to rise again, reaching 21.2 in 1811 and averaging 24.8 between 1821 and 1824. From 1818, and contributing to these figures, were recurrent epidemics of infectious diseases, of which typhus proved the biggest killer. Yet the growing urban crisis coincided with the dominance of the very ideology that was least prepared to countenance public intervention to deal with it. The funds available through the Scottish Poor Law were inadequate and fell throughout the period: totalling £14,487 in 1813, they temporarily rose in 1815 at the beginning of the post-war slump, but declined thereafter, reaching a low of £11,413 in 1822.[22] As social need increased, the funding necessary to meet it decreased, as the bourgeoisie abandoned the paternalist attitudes that had softened inequalities in the old, fundamentally rural Scotland where social power had also carried personal obligation.

Proletarianization

The new working class did not consist solely of migrants from the rural Lowlands, the Highlands and Ireland. Some were members of the urban guilds, or their descendants. Unlike their equivalents elsewhere in western Europe, or the merchants in their own country, Scottish craftsmen did not begin to organize themselves into artisan guilds until the fifteenth and sixteenth centuries. Once they had taken this step, however, the 'incorporations' provided them with effective economic control over the various crafts, most importantly by controlling the number of entrants into the profession and the nature of the training that apprentices had to undergo in order to become time-served. In England, where the organization of the artisan guilds was in any case more fluid, reflecting an economy where capitalist relations of production had already made far more inroads than across the border, guild privileges came under increasing legal attack from the end of the seventeenth century in particular. It was not until the latter half of the eighteenth century that equivalent moves were made in Scotland. Partly this was a result of the expansion of the market. On the one hand, skilled journeymen chose to set up on their own account, either within the burgh (thus risking a fine) or outside, where the incorporation had no authority. On the other hand, because of the increase in legitimate numbers, the master might began to treat ap prentices as workers, to be trained by the journeymen, not as people who were effectively part of the household for the five or seven years of their training. In some cases, masters hired skilled labour from the country who had no formal training at all. The result, in the case of the first, was to weaken the guilds externally, by placing masters outside their powers of regulation, and in the case of the second, to begin the process of class differentiation within the craft. Increasingly, as the eighteenth century drew to a revolutionary close, those working in the various trades – most importantly the handloom weavers – began to be, and to perceive themselves to be, wage-earners who would never rise to become masters themselves.[23]

The situation of these workers was still relatively privileged, however, compared to that which the majority of the new working class found in the slums of Glasgow and its satellite towns. The social explosion that this combustible human material threatened was widely recognized by the ruling class and its ideologues, and this was generated not only by the workplace where they laboured, but also by the environment in which they lived. It would be wrong, however, to imagine that working-class organization was simply propelled by inchoate rage; in many cases it embodied a political response that drew on the previous experience of migrants to the industrial towns. This was particularly the case for those who came from the Highlands and Ireland, although we know far more about the attitudes of the latter. For the Catholics in particular, there were additional reasons for political radicalism which were not solely connected with the situation in Ireland itself, but also with their position within Scottish society. The Catholic Irish were also under less direct ideological control than they would have been in Ireland: there were no Catholic schools in the west of Scotland until 1816 and as late as 1836 there was only one priest in Glasgow for every 9,000–11,000 Catholics.[24]

What was the level of Irish involvement in the events between 1815 and 1820? The point to note is that the Irish presence in Scotland was simply much greater than in England, with only 2.9 per cent of the population of England and Wales Irish in 1851, compared to 7.2 per cent in Scotland.[25] The Irish presence among the radicals was at least proportionate to their presence in the workforce, if not to the population as a whole. Around 30 leaders of the underground radical organization were arrested in February 1817. Of the thirteen whose nationality or occupation has been established, five were Irish and four of them were weavers. The events of 1820 reveal a similar picture. Two of the sixteen men sentenced to transportation for their part in the Battle of Bonnymuir were originally from County Down; one was a stocking-maker, the other a weaver. Two of the seven men arrested for their part in the riot in Greenock were Irish, both labourers.[26]

What were the religious backgrounds of the Irish who were involved in the movement? Here we encounter two disabling assumptions. The first is that the Protestant Irish in Scotland were invariably Loyalist defenders of British imperialism and the Ascendancy in Ireland, and were able to fuse with the native Scottish working class through a shared Protestantism, these religious and social solidarities leading not only to differentiation from the Catholic Irish immigrants, but also to opposition to them in a way that prevented solidarity as workers.[27] The second is that the Catholic Irish in Scotland were invariably concerned with nationalist politics in Ireland and withdrew from Scottish or British working-class political life, allowing employers to use them as blacklegs or cheap labour and thus legitimizing the opposition of Protestant workers.[28] Neither of these assumptions stands up to examination of what happened between 1815 and 1820.

First, although Irish participation in the secret societies was limited to Protestants, they did not aim to exclude Catholics from their organizations and indeed consciously sought to involve them in activity. These Protestants, part of the anti-sectarian Presbyterian United Irish tradition, must be distinguished from those who were involved in the anti-Catholic Orange Lodges being established in Scotland at this time.[29] Second, even if Irish Catholics played only a limited role in the secret societies, there is strong evidence to suggest that they, alongside the Protestant Irish, were heavily involved in the general strike of April 1820. Aside from evidence concerning particular individuals, the unanimity of the response to the strike call among weavers and spinners – given the extent to which the Irish had filled the latter occupation in particular – makes it difficult to avoid the conclusion that Irish spinners, in addition to Irish weavers, struck in support of the radicals.[30] Third, and finally, we must ask whether involvement on the part of both the Protestant and Catholic Irish principally aimed to aid the movement for a republic in Ireland, rather than in Britain. There is evidence that Irish membership of the United Scotsmen or participation in their activities during the 1790s was conducted on this basis. By the second wave of radicalism, immigration had taken on a permanent character and motivations correspondingly shifted.[31]

The unreformed state

It is possible that the pressures building up on the side of the working class might have been less had the British state in Scotland been more responsive to its demands. But this quasi-independent apparatus retained all the most reactionary attributes of the Scottish state that merged with England in 1707.

Feudalism was destroyed in Scotland after 1746 more thoroughly and consciously than it had been in England, but the superstructure that had grown up during the feudal epoch remained in place and provides the second parallel with the Russian situation of a hundred years later. At the end of the eighteenth century, around 0.2 per cent of Scotland's population were enfranchised, the lowest of all of the three kingdoms.[32] The county franchise in 1790 was 2,655, equal to Preston in England (2,800), less than half that of Bristol (6,000), one-fifth that of the City of London

(12,000) and one-seventh that of Westminster. In individual counties the number of voters could be as few as three, as was the case in Bute.[33] The burghal electorate was even smaller. Only 33 people were enfranchised in the Scottish capital of Edinburgh. In 1790 only nine county and burgh elections were even contested.[34] It was not merely that the franchise was restricted: before 1832 Scotland was virtually a one-party state in a way that England had ceased to be. And that party was the Tory Party.

The protections enjoyed by the English – a functioning jury system, an active parliamentary opposition, a history of constitutional safeguards against arbitrary power – provided real limits to the activities of the state which did not exist in Scotland. The only aspect of the state in Scotland which met the needs of workers with anything approaching regularity – the juridical apparatus that regulated the wages and conditions of workers in the guilds – was also the only aspect under threat from the bourgeoisie. The new employers opposed the use that the guilds could make of the courts to increase their wages. For the former it offended against the doctrines of market supremacy that increasingly characterized bourgeois ideology (and which, as we have seen, was also leading them to oppose municipal taxation as a means of solving the urban crisis). The ferocity with which members of the Scottish legal establishment responded to the radical movement of the 1790s was not inconsistent with a degree of paternalism towards the guilds, as long as they kept their place. The same attitude that informed Lord Braxfield and his colleagues in sentencing Thomas Muir and his comrades for stirring up the lower orders against the system itself, also lay behind his support for the arrangement by which workers could find some redress, and which consequently gave at least partial legitimacy to society in their eyes. If industry had remained in the traditional forms long established in the burghs along the Scottish east coast, the use of the courts might have been tolerated, but in the hands of an industrialized and volatile workforce it no longer played the same stabilizing role. For the new employers and their ideologues, educated in a version of Adam Smith's ideas which emphasized the free market at the expense of his mistrust of employer organization, the system of regulated order typical of the feudal and transitional economy was an obstacle to accumulation and had to be destroyed. The judges, magistrates and justices who had operated the existing system rapidly adapted to that which was replacing it.

The transformation from a 'social' economy (perhaps based on a deeper 'moral' economy) to a 'market' economy within the law occurred between 1808 and 1813, when trade union organization in itself became a criminal offence after the defeat of the Handloom Weavers' Association and the trial of its leading members. Even as late as 1808 Lord Meadowbank was in a minority when he rhetorically asked 'what it is that fixes the rate of reasonable wages, except a free market'. Only six years later, the statutes on wage regulation, which had existed since the sixteenth century, were abolished in both England and Scotland, removing the last remaining defence offered by pre-industrial Scottish society to the new capitalist order.[35]

Class consciousness

The precipitants of the general strike came in the immediate aftermath of the Napoleonic Wars. The Battle of Waterloo in 1815 saw the end of nearly twenty years of war against France, and the decline of war demand brought widespread unemployment, exacerbated by the return of demobilized soldiers and emigration from the north of Ireland. Adding further to working-class distress was the abolition of income tax and the consequent shifting of taxation on to essential consumer goods like salt and soap.[36] A radical tradition had existed in Scotland since the formation of the Friends of the People in 1792. However, it was the post-war crisis that brought for the first time the mass of artisans and workers into the movement for political reform, which had previously been dominated by the petty bourgeoisie and dissident members of the bourgeoisie themselves. By the beginning of 1820 an underground committee had been established to build for action, and both workers and the yeomanry were drilling with weapons in anticipation of the conflict to come. On 22 February a congress of delegates met in Paisley to make the final plans. Their leadership was dominated by handloom weavers.

There seem to be three reasons why weavers played this role: first, the defeat of their attempts to unionize in 1812 and the consequent blocking of any road to improved conditions through workplace organization; second, the decline in living standards (their wages may have halved between 1815 and 1818), partly as a result of the wage cuts imposed after the defeat of 1812, partly as a result of a cyclical downturn in demand; and third, the compatibility of political doctrines associated with the movement after 1815, such as male suffrage and the secret ballot, with those traditionally supported by them since the 1790s. The question of why they tended to belong to the physical force wing of the movement is less clear, although it may be explained by the peculiar intensity of economic hardship in the 1810s, combined with the realization, at least among a minority of weavers, that their difficulties stemmed from the beginnings of long-term decline of the industry, rather than short-term cyclical fluctuations.[37] Even though the leadership of the movement between 1815 and 1820 came from an established occupation in decline, the greater level of industrial militancy in Scotland at this time was a reaction of an unprepared population to the speed and intensity of the industrialization process.

The general strike of 1820 clearly demonstrated a qualitative shift in the emergence of working-class consciousness, although the separation between reformist and revolutionary consciousness was not – and could not be – clear at this date, if only because the nature of the state meant that reforms themselves required insurrectionary activity. The shift was, however, also evident in much smaller ways. The rules of the Edinburgh Society of Bookbinders originally allowed both masters and journeymen to be members, but in 1822 they were amended to allow only the latter to do so.[38]

The result of industrialization and urbanization in Scotland was therefore to remove the unevenness between Lowland Scotland and England and, with it, the special conditions that had produced the militancy of the Scottish response. Indeed, the apparent lack of success of both industrial militancy and insurrection, combined with an upswing in the economic cycle, produced a turn towards constitutional reform among the labour movement which benefited the Whig Party rather than any working-class organization. From being in advance of the working class in England, the working class in Scotland fell behind it in terms of organization and militancy until the rise of the Shop Stewards Movement during the First World War.

Dual national consciousness

From some point between 1746 and 1820, all classes in Scotland began, for different reasons, to treat the British aspect of their national identity as politically decisive. Although Scottish workers were aware that different conditions pertained on either side of the border (since their demands were intended to remove these differences), they do not appear to have considered themselves as either being 'led' by their English brothers and sisters, or acting in opposition to them, but seem to have realized that the British state was not susceptible to overthrow (or even reform) on one side of the border alone.

These attitudes go back to the very beginning of Scottish radicalism. At no time in the history of the radical movement between 1792 and 1820 was Scottish nationalism the predominant political ideology. The United Scotsmen's oath called upon prospective members to swear that they would persevere in endeavouring 'to form a brotherhood of affection amongst Britons of every description' and 'to obtain an equal, full and adequate Representation of all the People of Great Britain'.[39] Virtually the same form of words reappears in the oath that one of the secret societies which emerged in 1815 required its members to swear:

> In the awful presence of God, I, A.B., do voluntarily swear that I will persevere in my endeavours to form a brotherhood of affection amongst Britons of every description who are considered worthy of confidence; and that I will persevere in my endeavours to obtain for all

the people of Great Britain and Ireland not disqualified by crimes or insanity the elective franchise at the age of 21 with free and equal representation and annual parliaments.[40]

At demonstrations in Paisley during 1819 the banners not only bore the names of William Wallace and Robert the Bruce, but also invoked the Magna Carta and the rights of Britons. One resolution passed by a meeting of reformers at Rutherglen on 23 October 1819 stated their opposition to government 'subversion of the British constitution', while another called for 'Universal Suffrage and Annual Parliaments: without which, and election by Ballot, it is impossible to save this country [Britain] from Military despotism'.[41] Those attending the Rutherglen meeting sang 'God Save the King' and 'Rule, Britannia' – surely expressions of a reformist attitude to the British state. Nor is it the case that Scottish radicals were unconcerned with contemporary events in England. On 11 September 1819 the second meeting in that year to demand reform was held on Meikleriggs Muir near Paisley, specifically to protest against the Peterloo Massacre and the outrage against Britishness that the actions of the magistrates and yeomen represented.[42] The clearest example of the predominance of Britishness is, however, given by the general strike of April 1820 itself.

The proclamation that detonated the strike was addressed to 'the Inhabitants of Great Britain and Ireland', whom it calls 'Britons', evoking 'those rights consecrated to them, by MAGNA CARTA and the BILL OF RIGHTS'.[43] For some modern Scottish nationalists, such an assumption of the primacy of British identity combined with a reliance on the symbols of English radicalism can only mean one thing – the proclamation must be the product of English *agents provocateurs*.[44] In fact the text was most probably a collaborative effort between four Glaswegian weavers and an English radical called Joseph Brayshaw, who might have introduced the references to Magna Carta.[45] This is of twofold significance. First, none of his Scottish colleagues felt it necessary to remove this or other references to the English historical tradition. Second, saturated with the imagery of English radicalism as the proclamation is, the workers who read it took it as their cue to begin strike action in support of the radical demands.

The adoption of English radical imagery in Scotland was reciprocated by the adoption of Scottish radical imagery in England. Indeed, the appropriation of one song – Burn's 'Scots Wha Ha'e' – by English radicals is a perfect illustration of this process. One demonstration in Sheffield during 1820 marched to the Brocco behind bands playing the '"Dead March in Saul" and "Scots Wha Ha'e Wi' Wallace Bled".'[46] 'Scots Wha Ha'e' was still being sung in the Lancashire cotton mills in the 1830s as a rallying song for liberty.[47] And in his history of the Chartist movement R. G. Gammage records a meeting of 'several thousand persons' at Sunderland in 1838: 'Before the business of the meeting commenced the united bands struck up with the fine old martial and patriotic air of "Scots Wha Ha'e Wi' Wallace Bled".'[48]

The point is perhaps best illustrated by another, less famous song:

> What land has not seen Britain's crimson flag flying,
> The *meteor of murder, but justice the plea,*
> Has the blood of her sons, in her ruthless wars dying,
> Been the warm showers! to nourish fair liberty's tree.
> Yes! if placemen and paupers in myriads unceasing,
> If nations degraded, white slave trade increasing,
> if scorn with oppression be reckon'd a blessing,
> Then Britain has nourish'd fair liberty's tree.

Here Britain features both as the leadership of the alliance that crushed the revolutionary hopes of 1789 ('For kings have resolved that in Europe for ever/The tocsin of freedom shall sound never again'), and as one source of the power that will eventually overthrow them:

> May the time soon arrive when the tyrant and minion
> Shall be heard of no more save in tales of the evening,
> When freemen from labour in circle conveying,
> Tell them o'er, in the shade of liberty's tree.[49]

The site of action for the singer is Britain, but the subject is the international upheaval between 1789 and 1820. What nationality was the author? In fact, this is an anonymous Scottish piece, first performed in Paisley at the Saracen's Head Inn to celebrate the release from prison of the English radical Henry 'Orator' Hunt on 22 October 1822. Yet without this knowledge, there is no way of saying whether the author is Scottish or English.

There are four reasons for the dominance of 'British' over 'Scottish' consciousness in working-class politics. First, there were no material obstacles in the way of this merging of classes. The key contrast here is with relations between Protestant and Catholic workers in pre-partition Ireland. If Scottish workers had suffered racial or national oppression at the hands of the English, similar to that which Catholic Irish workers suffered at the hands of the British, then joint British industrial and political organization would have been impossible. They did not.

Second, earlier notions of what it meant to be Scottish, including those which defined Scottishness in relation to not being from the Highlands, Ireland or England, were being completely restructured. When the population centre of gravity switched from rural to urban, all the existing towns increased in size to some extent, and this changed perceptions of Scottishness. None of these towns, not even Edinburgh, expanded to the same degree as Glasgow. As we have seen, the social effects of industrialization were immense. Not only had the economic centre of the nation moved to the west, but the very conception of what it meant to be Scottish had moved with it. In part these changes were geographic and occupational. The industrial west increasingly became identified with Scotland, and for many of the people who lived and worked there, it was the only Scotland they had ever known. Many of these people were Irish. The period of industrialization, to which the Irish immigration contributed so much, involved the most intensive social change Scotland had yet experienced, and a Scottishness that included not only Highland immigrants but Catholic Irish would have been unrecognizable before 1746.

Third, the state against which both Scottish and English workers were ranged was a British state. The significance of this is often overlooked in effusions concerning the wonders of Scotland's supposed civic nationalism. No nation – at least among the 'historic' nations of Europe – has ever been just the creation of a state apparatus, but neither was Scotland just the creation of civil society. In short, nationhood in Scotland, at the stage of both Scottish proto-national consciousness before 1707 and dual Scottish-British national consciousness after, was always conditioned by the state. What has confused the issue, of course, is that after 1707 it was a British state which undertook the conditioning, including that relating to the Scottish aspects of British identity.

Fourth, and finally, there was no 'useable' Scottish history embodying the values that the organized section of the class wished to assert. Naturally the Scottish radicals continued to look to their own national history for inspiration. On 13 June 1815, a crowd of perhaps 10,000 marched from Strathaven to Drumclog, where the Covenanters defeated Claverhouse, then to Allanton, where they believed Sir William Wallace once defeated the English.[50] But Wallace and the later Covenanters were not enough to construct an entire radical tradition. And so although the early labour movement in Scotland incorporated radical symbolism from earlier periods of Scottish history into its traditions and iconography, it was equally open to English influences.

Let us conclude with the figure whose letters and diaries provide the richest source of information on bourgeois fears during this period: Walter Scott. Scott was concerned to mobilize his version of Scottish national identity precisely to stop class consciousness becoming dominant, and the spectacle of the royal visit in 1822, which Scott did so much to organize and direct, was an at least partially successful attempt to do so. The irony here, surely, is that the major contribution made by Scottishness to the events of the radical years was a component not, as is so often claimed, of working-class militancy, but of the ideology of counter-revolution. In a letter written in 1826, Scott suggested that only the retention of the Scottish identity prevented Scottish people, or at least their lower orders, from becoming 'damned mischievous Englishmen': 'The restless and yet laborious and constantly watchful character of the people, their desire for speculation in politics or anything else, only restrained by some proud feelings about their own country, now become antiquated and which late measures will tend to destroy, will make them under a wrong direction the most formidable revolutionists who ever took the field of innovation.'[51] We may be grateful that Scottish workers ignored his advice, and overcame 'proud feelings about their own country' to become 'formidable revolutionists' in 1820.

Notes

Introduction: Socialist History beyond the Millennium

1. H. Kaye, *The British Marxist Historians* (London: Macmillan, 1995 edn).
2. E. Hobsbawm, 'The History Group of the Communist Party', in M. Cornforth (ed.), *Rebels and their Causes: Essays in Honour of A. L. Morton* (London, 1978), pp. 21–48; V. Kiernan, 'Making Histories', *Our History Journal*, 8 (1984), pp. 7–10; D. Parker, 'The Communist Party and its Historians 1946–89', *Socialist History*, 12 (1997), pp. 33–58; and B. Schwarz, '"The People" in History: The Communist Party Historians Group', in R. Johnson et al. (eds), *Making Histories: Studies in History-Writing and Politics* (London: Hutchinson, 1982), pp. 44–95. The minutes of the party historians are held among the Communist Party files (CP) in the National Museum of Labour History, in Manchester, at CP/CENT/CULT/5/11.
3. R. Samuel, *History Workshop 1967–1991: Collectanea and Souvenir Volume* (Oxford: History Workshop, 1991), p. i.
4. F. Wheen, *Karl Marx* (London: Fourth Estate, 1999).
5. A key text is R. Samuel, *Theatres of Memory*, Vol. 1: *Past and Present in Contemporary Culture* (London: Verso, 1994).
6. S. Ashman, 'The Communist Party Historians Group', in J. Rees (ed.), *Essays on Historical Materialism* (London: Bookmarks, 1998), pp. 145–60.
7. *Independent on Sunday*, 26 December 1999.
8. C. Harman, in D. Renton and K. Flett (eds), *The Twentieth Century: A Century of Wars and Revolutions?* (London: Rivers Oram, 2000), pp. 220–32.
9. J. Belchem, 'A Language of Classlessness', *Labour History Review*, 57/2 (1992), pp. 43–4; N. Kirk, 'The Continuing Relevance and Engagements of Class', *Labour History Review*, 60/3 (1995), pp. 2–15; M. Chase, S. Fielding and K. Flett, 'Debate: The Current and Future Position of Labour History', *Labour History Review*, 60/3 (1995), pp. 46–53.
10. K. Flett, 'Where is Labour History Going?', *Labour History Review*, 58/1 (1993), pp. 35–6.
11. P. Joyce, 'The Return of History: Postmodernism and the Politics of Academic History in Britain', *Past and Present*, 158 (1998), pp. 207–35.
12. There is a summary of the relevant American literature in J. Stein, 'Where's the Beef?', *International Labor and Working-Class History*, 57 (2000), pp. 40–7.
13. Samuel, *History Workshop*, p. xiii.

Chapter 1   The Pre-history of Social Movements: From Newport to Seattle

1. J. Charlton, *The Chartists: The First National Workers' Movement* (London: Bookmarks, 1997); J. Charlton, *'It just went like tinder': The Mass Movement and New Unionism in Britain, 1889* (London: Bookmarks, 1999).
2. J. Charlton, 'Talking Seattle', *International Socialism*, 86 (2000), pp. 3–18.

3. R. W. Postgate, *The Builders History* (London: NFBTO, 1923), p. 343.

4. T. Wright, *Our New Masters* (London: Strahan and Co., 1873), for a discussion of the state of the working classes, pp. 1–61, 359–82. Booth's *London* is a monumental work. His view of workers' attitudes pervades it. Beatrice Webb's account of dockers' lives written before the Great Dock Strike in 1887 is a good example. 'The Dockers', in C. Booth, *Life and Labour of the People in London* (London: Macmillan, 1904).

5. J. Saville, *1848: The British State and the Chartist Movement* (Cambridge: Cambridge University Press, 1987), 'prolegomena'.

6. *Seattle Times*, 24 November to 8 December 1999.

7. Charlton, 'Talking Seattle', pp. 8–9.

8. D. Jones, *The Last Rising: The Newport Insurrection of 1839* (Oxford: Clarendon, 1985); M. Jenkins, *The General Strike of 1842* (London: Lawrence and Wishart, 1980); Saville, *1848*.

9. By 'subjective' factors I mean the actions of actors, while the term 'objective' refers to economic, political and social/cultural factors.

10. Jones, *Last Rising*, ch. 5.

11. Charlton, *Tinder*, pp. 20–2.

12. Ibid., pp. 22–4.

13. Charlton, 'Talking Seattle'.

Chapter 2   The Strange Death of Liberal Bradford

1. G. Dangerfield, *The Strange Death of Liberal England* (London: Serif, 1997).

2. L. Trotsky, *Trotsky's Writings on Britain* (London: New Park, 1974, 3 volumes), Vol. 2, p. 14.

3. H. J. Schultz, *English Liberalism and the State* (Lexington, Mass.: Heath, 1971), p. 3.

4. Ibid.

5. W. D. Ross, 'Bradford Politics 1880–1906', Bradford University PhD thesis.

6. Ibid., p. 27.

7. P. Morgan, 'From Tea to Toyota', *Socialist Review*, no. 218, April 1998.

8. V. I. Lenin, *Imperialism: The Highest Stage of Capitalism* (New York: International Publishers, 1939).

9. Morgan, 'From Tea to Toyota'.

10. Ross, *Bradford Politics*.

11. Ibid., p. 19.

12. C. Peace, *The Manningham Mill Strike* (Hull: University of Hull, 1975).

13. Ibid., p. 15.

14. Ibid., p. 26.

15. Ibid., p. 68.

16. K. Laybourn, *The Rise of Socialism in Britain* (Stroud: Sutton, 1997); also C. Bambery, 'Labour's History of Hope and Betrayal', *International Socialism Journal*, 76 (1997), pp. 139–54.

17. From Tony Jowett's notes.

18. E. Halevy, *Imperialism and the Rise of Labour* (London: Ernest Benn, 1929), p. 246.

19. Ibid., pp. 246–81.

20. T. Cliff and D. Gluckstein, *The Labour Party: A Marxist History* (London: Bookmarks, 1988), p. 25.

21. Ibid.

22. Ibid.

23. Ibid.

24. Ibid.

25. Ibid., p. 17.
26. Halevy, *Imperialism*, p. 275.
27. Ibid.
28. *Yorkshire Factory Times*, 10 March 1910.
29. J. Newsinger, 'Jim Larkin, Syndicalism and the Dublin Lockout', *International Socialism Journal*, 25 (1984), pp. 3–37, 14.
30. Newsinger, 'Jim Larkin'.
31. Bradford Trades Council minutes, September 1913.
32. Dangerfield, *The Strange Death of Liberal England*, p. 178.
33. Bradford Trades Council minutes, 1912.

Chapter 3   Palmiro Togliatti, Loyal Servant of Stalin

1. Donald Sassoon, 'Togliatti, Stalin, Hungary and the Tasks of Historians', and Tobias Abse, 'Togliatti and 1956: A Response to Sassoon', both in *Journal of Southern Europe and the Balkans*, 1/1 (1999), pp. 33–8 and 39–48.
2. This subtext is made explicit in L. Canfora, *Togliatti e i dilemmi della politica* (Bari: Laterza, 1989), especially pp. 11–19.
3. E. Aga-Rossi and V. Zaslavsky, *Togliatti e Stalin: Il Pci e la politica estera staliniana negli archivi di Mosca* (Milan: Il Mulino, 1997).
4. Ibid., pp. 275–80, especially the claim on p. 275 that 'in the last half century the advance of democracy at the world level . . . has been the result of the leadership of the United States, of its economic, technological and military force'.
5. *Revolutionary History*, 7/2 (1999), pp. 285–98, especially her claim that 'Aga-Rossi and Zaslavsky's offering, however, belongs to an historiographical school that has long been discredited, and this greatly reduces its value for the historian' (p. 298).
6. A. Agosti, *Palmiro Togliatti* (Turin: Unione Tipografico Editrice Torinese, 1996).
7. G. Bocca, *Palmiro Togliatti* (Bari: Laterza, 1977 edn).
8. T. Behan, *The Long Awaited Moment: The Working Class and the Italian Communist Party in Milan, 1943–1948* (New York: Peter Lang, 1997).
9. See Abse, 'Togliatti and 1956', especially pp. 40–5.
10. Bocca, *Palmiro Togliatti*, Vol. I, p. 78.
11. Togliatti had completed his original, law, degree.
12. Bocca, *Palmiro Togliatti*, Vol. I, p. 80.
13. Ibid., p.81.
14. For Secchia's combination of Stalinism and revolutionary hopes, see M. Mafai, *L'uomo che sognava la lotta armata* (Milan: Rizzoli, 1984). Aga-Rossi and Zaslavsky, *Togliatti e Stalin*, pp. 296–300, contains a fascinating transcript of a discussion between Stalin and Secchia on 14 December 1947 in which Stalin agrees with Togliatti's assessment of the Italian situation and advises Secchia against an insurrection.
15. Bocca, *Palmiro Togliatti*, Vol. I, pp. 17–18, 29. Some believe that he was not even a member in 1914, despite his repeated claims to have been one. The fascists burnt the records of the Turin Socialist section on 18 December 1922, so the question is not amenable to documentary proof.
16. B. Bolloten, *The Spanish Civil War: Revolution and Counter-revolution* (London: University of North Carolina Press, 1991 edn), p. 133.
17. Ibid., p. 788.
18. Ibid., p. 810.
19. Ibid., p. 133.
20. Ibid., p. 133.
21. Ibid., p. 134.

22. F. Claudin, *The Communist Movement: From Comintern to Cominform* (Harmondsworth: Penguin, 1975; English translation of 1970 Spanish text), pp. 697–8.

23. Bolloten, *Spanish Civil War*, p. 134.

24. T. Rees, 'The Highpoint of Comintern Influence? The Communist Party and the Civil War in Spain', in Tim Rees and Andrew Thorpe (eds), *International Communism and the Communist International 1919–43* (Manchester: Manchester University Press, 1998), pp. 143–67. One assumes this author is motivated by the usual wearisome apolitical academic penchant for revisionism for its own sake rather than any hidden pro-PCI agenda of the Sassoon–Hobsbawm–Agosti– Spriano variety, but he appears singularly devoid of any inkling about how Stalinist parties functioned; a particularly priceless example of the surreal world Rees inhabits is the risible claim that 'In particular, decision-making in the Central Committee became more open and collective in nature encouraged by the sympathetic attitude that Togliatti took towards the Spanish leaders following the injunction of Dimitrov "neither to limit nor suffocate in any way the initiative or personality of the Spanish leaders"' (Rees and Thorpe, p. 157). Given the way in which Togliatti only very reluctantly accepted any collective decision making in the PCI in the last couple of years of his life, the very notion of such an egalitarian approach to his Spanish comrades beggars belief. I will give specific examples of Spanish Communist speeches and documents drafted by Togliatti later in the chapter which should serve to refute Rees's bizarre theory.

25. M. and M. Ferrara, *Conversando con Togliatti* (Rome: Edizioni di Cultura Sociale, 1953).

26. Bocca, *Palmiro Togliatti*.

27. J. Hernandez, *Yo fui un ministro de Stalin* (Mexico City: Editorial America, 1953).

28. Bolloten, *Spanish Civil War*, p. 365.

29. Bocca, *Palmiro Togliatti*, Vol. I, p. 286.

30. Ibid..

31. Ibid., p.285.

32. P. Spriano, *Togliatti: Segretario dell'Internazionale* (Roma: Ed. Riuniti, 1988), p.216.

33. Bocca says that Vidali, who lent him Hernandez's books, said: 'It is better to read them, even if he went over to the other side' (Bocca, *Palmiro Togliatti*, Vol. 2, p. 706. This hardly adds weight to Vidali's denials. Vidali, like Scoccimarro, eventually regarded Togliatti as betraying Stalin's legacy, so he may have been deliberately sowing doubts in Bocca's mind.

34. Bocca, *Palmiro Togliatti*, Vol. I, pp. 282, 287.

35. Ibid., p. 286.

36. Hugh Thomas may indeed describe the book as 'This unpleasant work of the leading Communist renegade from Spain' (H. Thomas, *The Spanish Civil War* (Harmondsworth: Penguin, 1968), p. 285), but he makes frequent use of it as Spriano grudgingly acknowledges, without indicating that Thomas accepts Hernandez's account of Togliatti's early arrival.

37. Spriano, *Togliatti: Segretario dell'Internazionale*, p. 95; Bolloten, *Spanish Civil War*, p. 785.

38. Bolloten, *Spanish Civil War*, p. 786.

39. Agosti, *Palmiro Togliatti*, p. 590. This nugget is tucked away in the source notes; the academic historian Agosti, unlike the journalist Bocca, does not use proper footnotes.

40. Bocca, *Palmiro Togliatti*, Vol. I, p. 285.

41. Bolloten, *Spanish Civil War*, p. 364.

42. Ibid.

43. London: Macmillan, 1984.

44. B. Bolloten, *The Grand Camouflage: The Spanish Civil War and Revolution*

1936–39 (London: Hollis, 1961); B. Bolloten, *The Spanish Revolution: The Left and the Struggle for Power during the Civil War* (London and Chapel Hill: University of North Carolina Press, 1979).

45. Carr's certainty about the date of Togliatti's arrival in Spain is based on Togliatti and Spriano alone, for to quote Carr, *The Comintern* (p. 39): 'Hernandez names Togliatti among those present. But Togliatti, on his own showing, did not come to Spain till July 1937, and other evidence conclusively supports him'; the only reference given for other evidence is 'P. Spriano, *Storia del Partito Comunista Italiano*, iii (Torino: Einaudi, 1970), 215'. Therefore, one can legitimately criticize both Carr and his research assistant Tamara Deutscher for a very inconsistent approach to these sources, given that when it came to a document issued in the name of the PCE Central Committee bearing the date 10 March 1939 and calling for an end to resistance, they accepted the testimony of Claudin's 6 March 1983 letter to Tamara Deutscher, to the effect that this document was indeed written by Togliatti, in preference to that of Togliatti and Spriano, who were anxious to disclaim it. Carr's comment in the text that '*The tortuous argument* was characteristic of Togliatti's pen' or his barbed footnote in which he says 'direct attribution of it to Togliatti comes from hostile and unreliable sources. Spriano *coyly remarks* that Togliatti and Checca issued an appeal on March 10 "to gain a few days' time"' (p. 78, my italics) does not tally with his earlier presentation of this duo as impeccable paragons of honesty when it was their word against Hernandez's.

46. Rees adopts the circular argument that Hernandez's testimony on one occasion is 'clearly suspect' and on another occasion 'suspect' because he lists Togliatti as a participant in meetings (Rees, 'The Highpoint', pp. 165, 166). Rees cites Carr's *The Comintern and the Spanish Civil War* as convincing supplementary authority on the issue and loftily proclaims 'For an excellent recent overview of Togliatti's relationship with the PCE during the war, see A. Agosti, *Togliatti* (Turin: UTET, 1996), pp. 225–43' (Rees, p. 166). In short, Rees does not seem to have looked at Bocca's biography with its testimony from Scoccimarro or to have noticed that Bolloten's sources for his belief in Togliatti's early arrival in Spain include Martinez Amutio and Sanchez Vazquez, the validity of whose claims is in no way linked to the question of Hernandez's veracity or lack of it.

47. Claudin, *The Communist Movement*, p. 712, his italics.

48. Ibid., p. 710. The more usual approach is to see José Diaz's speech at a public meeting on 9 May 1937 as the signal of the Spanish Communists' murderous intentions. This speech included the following bloodcurdling words: 'Is it not perfectly clear that the Trotskyists are not a political or social organisation of a definite tendency like the Anarchists, Socialists or Republicans, but a gang of spies and provocateurs in the service of international fascism? The Trotskyist provocateurs must be swept away. This is why I stated in my speech at the recent plenary session of the central committee not only that this organisation should be dissolved in Spain and its press suspended, but that Trotskyism should be swept out of all civilised countries, that is, if we really want to get rid of the vermin ... In Spain itself, who but the Trotskyists inspired the criminal putsch in Catalonia?' (Bolloten, *Spanish Civil War*, p. 463).

49. Claudin, *The Communist Movement*, p. 711.

50. Bolloten, *Spanish Civil War*, p. 511; translation of quotation from Juan-Simeon Vidarte, *Todos fuimos culpables* (Mexico City: Fondo de Cultura Economica, 1973), pp. 732–3. Moron's own account in his earlier *Politica de ayer y politica de manana* (Mexico City: Oasis, 1942), while not so explicit, tallied in general terms and included the statement: 'Señor Irujo, the entire cabinet, the public prosecutor and I knew perfectly well where to find the only person responsible for the abduction of Nin' (translation in Bolloten, *Spanish Civil War*, p. 511).

51. Bolloten, *Spanish Civil War*, p. 506.

52. Ibid., pp. 506–7.

53. Translation taken from Bolloten, *Spanish Civil War*, p. 889; Bolloten took it from a Spanish text that quoted Bocca. The original text is in Bocca, *Palmiro Togliatti*, Vol. I, p. 301. This is Bolloten's only reference to Bocca's work, which he never read, despite the centrality of Togliatti to Bolloten's account of Communist actions in the civil war.

54. Bocca, *Palmiro Togliatti*, Vol. I, p. 301.

55. Bolloten, *The Spanish Revolution*, 1979, p. 430, had already raised the possibility that Berneri might have been assassinated by 'Franquist Fifth Columnists in the service of the OVRA' rather than the Communists.

56. Bolloten, *Spanish Civil War*, pp. 875–7, which contains a very detailed statement on the subject written by Bolloten's research assistant George Esenwein.

57. For a full English text, see Carr, *The Comintern and the Spanish Civil War*, pp. 86–7.

58. Here Claudin cites a Soviet work published in 1960 as confirming the account given by Caballero's Socialist friend Araquistain (Claudin, *The Communist Movement*, pp. 707–8).

59. Ibid., p. 708.

60. Bolloten, *Spanish Civil War*, p. 363, quoting Togliatti's words as given by Hernandez.

61. Bolloten, *Spanish Civil War*, p. 133. In a footnote he explains 'For this information I am grateful to a number of Spanish Communist refugees, whom I met in Mexico in the 1940s' (p. 788).

62. After Caballero passionately denounced his opponents at a public meeting in Madrid on 17 October 1937, he was stopped at gunpoint on his way to Alicante for the first of a series of public meetings elsewhere in republican Spain. For details, see Bolloten, *Spanish Civil War*, p. 562.

63. Ibid., p. 561.

64. Carr, *The Spanish Civil War and the Comintern*, p. 68. Carr based this account on a Soviet work published in 1981. Whilst both Bolloten and Bocca suspected Communist influence, they gave garbled versions that under-estimated the degree of direct Comintern and PCE involvement. Bolloten quoted the pro-Communist American journalist Louis Fischer as attributing the idea of the thirteen war aims to the British Communist film producer Ivor Montagu, who allegedly had a conversation with the pro-Communist but nominally socialist Vayo, who then put the idea to Negrin; Bolloten wrongly believed that the PCE 'had not been directly involved in the elaboration of the thirteen war aims'. Bocca believed the thirteen war aims were the product of a correspondence between Togliatti and Negrin via the prime minister's secretary, who was an old friend of Vidali – Bocca based this story on Vidali's testimony. More significantly, Bocca shrewdly remarked on the similarity of the thirteen points to Togliatti's programme for the Italian Resistance in 1944–5. See Bolloten, *Spanish Civil War*, pp. 645–6, and Bocca, *Palmiro Togliatti*, Vol. 2, p. 303.

65. Bolloten, *Spanish Civil War*, p. 924.

66. Ibid., p. 680.

67. Aga-Rossi and Zaslavsky, *Togliatti e Stalin*, pp. 58 and 64.

68. Giorgio Bocca, *Palmiro Togliatti*, Vol. I, p. 352; Ian Birchall, *Workers against the Monolith: The Communist Parties since 1943* (London: Pluto, 1974), p. 23.

69. Aga-Rossi and Zaslavsky, *Togliatti e Stalin*, p. 59.

70. Ibid., p. 60.

71. Ibid., p. 61.

72. Ibid.

73. Ibid., p. 62.

74. A transcript in Italian translation is reproduced in Aga-Rossi and Zaslavsky, *Togliatti e Stalin*, pp. 287–95.

75. Ibid., pp. 62–3.

76. Ibid., p. 63.
77. Ibid., p. 72.
78. M. Gilbert, *The Italian Revolution: The End of Politics, Italian Style?* (Boulder, Colo., and Oxford: Westview Press, 1995), p. 72.
79. G. Vacca, *Togliatti Sconosciuto* (Rome: Edizioni l'Unità, 1994), pp. 69–70, cited in Aga-Rossi and Zaslavsky, *Togliatti e Stalin*, pp. 59 and 70.
80. Agosti, *Palmiro Togliatti*, pp. 274–5.
81. Ibid., p. 274.
82. Ibid., p. 275.
83. The most blatant and polemical statement of this view, undiluted by much empirical evidence, can be found in Canfora, *Togliatti e i dilemmi della politica*, pp. 101–15 – a section entitled 'La guerra è finita: Togliatti 1944–64'. Canfora's Togliatti seems to leap free from Stalin's influence in a single bound on his return to Italy; Agosti's apologetics are much more nuanced.
84. Bolloten, *Spanish Civil War*, p. 134.

Chapter 4 Terence Powderly, the Knights of Labor and the Great Upheaval

1. Sophus Nelson to TVP, 26 August 1885; L. P. Custer to TVP, 16 July 1886, Terence Vincent Powderly Papers (hereafter cited as PP).
2. TVP, 'The Army of the Discontented,' *North American Review* (April 1885), pp. 369–77.
3. Kim Voss, *The Making of American Exceptionalism: The Knights of Labor and Class Formation in the Nineteenth Century* (Ithaca: Cornell University Press, 1993), p. 232.
4. Gregory S. Kealey and Bryan D. Palmer, *Dreaming of What Might Be: The Knights of Labor in Ontario, 1880–1900* (New York and Cambridge: Cambridge University Press, 1982), p. 394.
5. Harry J. Carman, Henry David and Paul N. Guthrie (eds), *The Path I Trod: The Autobiography of Terence V. Powderly* (New York: Columbia Studies in American Culture, 1940), p. 42; TVP, *An Address Delivered in Music Hall, Providence, RI* (Boston, 1886), p. 13.
6. TVP 'to the officers and members of LA 222', 26 April 1877, PP; TVP, *Powderly at Priceburg* (Philadelphia, 1890), p. 8.
7. TVP to Joseph Buchanan, 13 August 1886, PP; 1891 Toledo GA, 'Report of the General Master Workman', p. 1.
8. For a recent appreciation of horizontal unionism, see Staughton Lynd (ed.), *'We Are All Leaders': The Alternative Unionism in the Early 1930s* (Urbana and Chicago: Chicago University Press, 1996). See also the fascinating discussion of this book by Robert Zieger, Roger Horowitz, Ronald Edsforth, Cecilia Bucki and Staughton Lynd in ' *"We Are All Leaders"*: A Symposium on a Collection of Essays Dealing with Alternative Unionism in the Early 1930s,' *Labor History*, 38 (spring–summer 1997), pp. 165–201.
9. B. Laurie, *Artisans Into Workers* (New York: Hill and Wang, 1989), p. 167; Judith Goldberg, 'Strikes, Organizing, and Change: The Knights of Labor in Philadelphia, 1869–1890,' unpublished PhD diss., New York University, 1985, pp. 283–4.
10. For Troy, see M. H. Davies to Peter Catanooch, 8 February; on the AT&SF, see Alden Huling to TVP, 8 February; on Lynn, see Nellie Hardison and Maggie Phillips to TVP, 8 February, Peter McGeough to TVP, 5 March and TVP to McGeough, 9 March; on Lewiston, see H. E. Yeaton to TVP, 8 February and O. C. Phillips to TVP, 8 February 1886. A successful lockout of cigar makers at Homer, New York in December 1885 had emboldened other employers in town, including the Homer Wagon

156 *New Approaches to Socialist History*

Works, to pursue the same strategy, despite the fact that Powderly had visited the town's employers on New Year's day on a mission of peace. See Ray Bliss to TVP, 22 and 26 December 1885; TVP to Bliss, 26 and 28 December 1885; Alex Patterson to TVP, 29 December 1885; TVP to W. N. Brockway, 29 December 1885 and 2 January 1886; Brockway to TVP, 29 December 1885; TVP to Turner, 29 December 1885; TVP to Gage, Hitchcok and Gage, 30 December 1885; TVP to Homer Wagon Company, 2 January 1886; Henry Mente to TVP, 28 February 1886. On Toronto, see D. J. O'Donoghue to TVP, 8 February; on Amsterdam, see P. H. Cummins to TVP, 10 February; on St Louis, see Martin Witter to TVP, 8 February; for New York railroad workers, see Officers and Members of LA 3240 to TVP, 9 February; on Danville, see Louis Eberly to TVP, 9 February; on Little Rock, see Dan Frazier Tomson to TVP, 14 February; on Des Moines, see John Sally to TVP, 13 February, 1 March and 8 March, and TVP to Sally, 8 March; on Earlington, see William Smith to TVP, 25 February and TVP to Smith, 22 March; on Springfield, see J. T. McDonald to TVP, 3 March; on Gloversville, see P. H. Cummins to TVP, 1 March 1886, PP.

11. George Clarke to TVP, 8 February; Joseph G. O'Kelly to TVP, 9 and 22 January, 12 February; *Chicago Evening Mail*, 18 January; Richard Griffiths to TVP, 8 and 27 January, 22 February; Maxwell Brothers to TVP, 30 January; 'A working man' to TVP, 11 March 1886, PP.

12. Laurie, *Artisans*, p. 167; Richard Oestreicher, 'Terence V. Powderly, the Knights of Labor, and Artisanal Republicanism', in Melvyn Dubovsky and Warren Van Tine (eds), *Labor Leaders in America* (Illinois: University of Illinois Press, 1987), pp. 30–61, 52; P. Foner, *History of the Labor Movement* (New York: International Publishers, 10 volumes), Vol. 2, pp. 82–3.

13. Oestreicher, 'Artisinal Republicanism,' p. 52.

14. Compare Powderly's attitudes in Carman et al., *The Path I Trod*, pp. 104–5 with Mitchell's in his *Organized Labor: Its Problems, Purposes and Ideals* (Philadelphia: American Book and Bible, 1903).

15. TVP to Tom O'Reilly, 25 October 1886, PP.

16. Oestreicher, 'Artisinal Republicanism', p. 53.

17. In addition to TVP's correspondence, see the litany of troubles and appeals granted by the General Executive Board in its report, *Proceedings*, 1886 Richmond GA, pp. 94–138; GEB, 'Appeal for Aid', 10 September 1886.

18. *Proceedings*, 1886 Richmond General Assembly, pp. 45–6; TVP, 'to all subordinate Assemblies of the Order', 19 November 1886, PP.

19. Rubber workers in New Brunswick, New Jersey were typical. After the board denied their request for support during an 1887 lockout, they hung an obituary notice on the door of their sanctuary: 'On Friday Evening April 29, Local Assembly No. 3,354 K. of L., killed by the General Executive Board'. Quoted in Foner, *History of the Labor Movement*, Vol. 2, p. 160.

20. J. Simmons Meynardie to TVP, 12 December 1886; TVP to Meynardie, 23 December 1886; M. M. Connor to TVP, 27 January and 24 February 1887; TVP to Connor, 19 February 1887; Mullen to TVP, 22 and 29 January, 18 February 1887; TVP to Mullen, 18 and 26 January 1887, PP. Typical, too, was the historical assessment; the authority on the Knights in the South argued that the national office supplied so little 'because Powderly, in his opposition to strikes, believed the struggle was doomed and wished it to end quickly' (Melton McLaurin, *The Knights of Labor in the South* (Westport, Conn.: Greenwood Press, 1978), p. 72).

21. Eric Hobsbawm, *Labouring Men: Studies in the History of Labour* (London: Weidenfeld and Nicolson, 1964), p. 144.

22. See, among others, Foner, *History of the Labor Movement*, Vol. 2, pp. 162–6; N. Kirk, *Labour and Society* (Aldershot: Ashgate, 1994), Vol. 2, p. 124; Laurie, *Artisans*, p. 170; and especially the extended discussion in Oestreicher, *Solidarity and Fragmentation*, pp. 187–211.

23. TVP, *Thirty Years of Labor, 1859–1889* (New York: Augustus M. Kelley, 1967 edn), pp. 534–5.

24. On the mechanisms of power wielded by trade union presidents, see Warren Van Tine, *The Making of the Labor Bureaucrat: Union Leadership in the United States, 1870–1920* (Amherst: University of Massachusetts Press, 1973), chapter 5.

25. Robert Zieger, *The CIO, 1935–1955* (Chapel Hill: University of North Carolina Press, 1995); Steve Fraser, *Labor Will Rule: Sidney Hillman and the Rise of American Labor* (New York: Free Press, 1991); Nelson Lichtenstein, *The Most Dangerous Man in Detroit: Walter Reuther and the Fate of American Labor* (New York: Basic Books, 1995).

26. TVP, *The Path I Trod*, p. 105.

27. David Montgomery, 'Strikes in Nineteenth-century America', *Social Science History*, 1 (winter 1980), p. 98.

28. Daniel Nelson is one of the few recent historians prepared to blame 'lack of preparation' and 'inadequate resources' for the setbacks. 'Historians have emphasized Powderly's mismanagement of KOL strikes', he argues, 'but Powderly's role is hard to distinguish from . . . other union executives. What was different was the Knights' lax control of the strike power and meager provisions for strike relief' (*Shifting Fortunes: The Rise and Decline of American Labor* (Chicago: Ivan R. Dee, 1997), p. 64).

29. Montgomery, 'Strikes in Nineteenth-century America,' p. 99.

Chapter 5   Socialism as Sacrifice: The Life and Politics of Stafford Cripps

Thanks to Tobias Abse, Anne Alexander, Ian Birchall, Lawrence Black, Keith Flett and Roger Spalding for comments on drafts of this chapter.

1. Many of these figures already have their biographers, including B. Pimlott, *Harold Wilson* (London: HarperCollins, 1992); T. Burridge, *Clement Attlee: A Political Biography* (London: Jonathan Cape, 1987); M. Foot, *Aneurin Bevan 1897–1960* (London: Indigo, 1999); and D. Marquand, *Ramsay MacDonald* (London: Richard Cohen, 1997).

2. G. Brown, *Maxton* (London: Mainstream, 1986), pp. 19–21.

3. It should be noted that in Gabriel Gorodetsky's account, Cripps appears a much more exemplary figure than he does here. See G. Gorodetsky, *Stafford Cripps' Mission to Moscow 1940–1942* (Cambridge: Cambridge University Press, 1984).

4. C. Bryant, *Stafford Cripps: The First Modern Chancellor* (London: Hodder and Stoughton, 1997).

5. S. Burgess, *Stafford Cripps: A Political Life* (London: Gollancz, 1999).

6. P. Clarke, *The Cripps Version: The Life of Sir Stafford Cripps 1889–1952* (London: Penguin, 2002).

7. This point is argued at length in a superb short book: A. Davies, *Where Did the Forties Go? A Popular History* (London: Pluto, 1984). I try to make a similar case, more briefly, in D. Renton, *Fascists, Anti-Fascists and Britain in the 1940s* (London: Macmillan, 2000), pp. 130–44.

8. E. Estorick, *Stafford Cripps* (London: Heinemann, 1949), p. 44.

9. Bryant, *Stafford Cripps*, p. 75.

10. Burgess, *Stafford Cripps*, p. 48.

11. P. Foot, 'Labour's Fantastic Idea – Socialism', *Guardian*, 27 November 1999.

12. J. Davies, *To Build a New Jerusalem. The Labour Movement from the 1880s to the 1990s* (London: Michael Joseph, 1992), pp. 77–96.

13. N. Branson and B. Moore, 'Labour–Communist Relations, 1920–1951. Part 1: 1920–1935', *Our History*, 82 (1990), p. 56; F. Copeman, *Reason in Revolt* (London: Blandford Press, 1948), pp. 43–53.

14. T. Cliff and D. Gluckstein, *The Labour Party: A Marxist History* (London: Bookmarks, 1988), pp. 166–7.

15. S. Cripps, *Can Socialism Come Through Constitutional Means?* (London: Socialist League, 1932).

16. Debate on the Supply Committee. Board of Trade, 14 April 1932, 264 H. C. Deb 5s. Letter from Roger Spalding to the author, 20 July 2001.

17. Cliff and Gluckstein, *The Labour Party*, p. 170.

18. W. Hannington, *Unemployed Struggles* (London: Lawrence and Wishart, 1936); P. Strauss, *Cripps: Advocate and Rebel* (London: 1943). I am grateful to Roger Spalding, author of a forthcoming book comparing Cripps and Michael Foot, for these references.

19. J. Eaden and D. Renton, *History of the Communist Party since 1920* (London: Palgrave, 2002), pp. 54–5.

20. Again thanks to Roger Spalding for this reference.

21. Cliff and Gluckstein, *The Labour Party*, pp. 186–9.

22. Cited in P. Hennessy, *Never Again: Britain 1945–1951* (London: Vintage, 1993 edn), p. 382.

23. *Daily Herald*, 20 October 1950.

24. Hennessy, *Never Again*, pp. 376–7.

25. Davies, *To Build a New Jerusalem*, p. 120.

26. Peter Clarke points out that the latter habit was short-lived. Clarke, *The Cripps Version*, p. 68.

27. Burgess, *Stafford Cripps*, p. 260.

28. Davies, *Where Did the Forties Go?*, p. 74.

29. Clarke, *The Cripps Version*, pp. 26, 65.

30. Burgess, *Stafford Cripps*, p. 78.

31. Bryant, *Stafford Cripps*, pp. 143–4; Burgess, *Stafford Cripps*, pp. 111, 123.

32. Foot, 'Labour's Fantastic Idea'.

33. Burgess, *Stafford Cripps*, pp. 159–60.

34. 'Rocking Against Racism', in D. Widgery, *Preserving Disorder* (London: Pluto, 1990), pp. 115–21, 116.

Chapter 6   Alfred Rosmer and the Red International of Labour Unions

1. At present Rosmer is known to English readers almost exclusively through his memoirs of the Comintern period, *Lenin's Moscow*. A selection of writings covering the whole of Rosmer's career was published in *Revolutionary History*, 7/4 (2000).

2. A. Rosmer, *Lenin's Moscow* (London: Bookmarks 1987, first published Paris: Pierre Horay, 1953), p. 15.

3. Amédée Dunois wrote of him in the *Bulletin communiste* in 1921:

> If he does not shine in the front rank, it is because his modesty is unparalleled and because he will always prefer positions of devotion and work to those of honour . . . French workers should learn Rosmer's name: it is that of a man who, having emerged from their class, has loyally come back to them. (P Broué: 'Léon Trotsky, Alfred Rosmer', *Le Mouvement social*, 47 (1964), p. 138)

4. This remark was quoted by veteran syndicalist Roger Hagnauer in his obituary of Rosmer (*La Révolution prolétarienne*, May 1964, p. 99; *Revolutionary History*, 7/4, p. 9); Rosmer's name does not appear in the index to Lenin's *Collected Works* (Moscow: Progress, 1978).

5. See A. Rosmer, 'Il y a quarante ans . . .', *La Révolution prolétarienne*, January 1951, pp. 1–3; *Revolutionary History*, 7/4, pp. 14–20.

6. For anarchists and syndicalists the main division in modern society was not

economic exploitation, as it was for the Marxists, but the exercise of authority. Since they did not see the cause of capitalism's destruction in economic forces, their politics tended to be voluntaristic and hence moralistic. (See Victor Serge's pamphlet, 'The Anarchists and the Experience of the Russian Revolution', in *Revolution in Danger* (London: Redwords, 1997), pp. 81–120.)

7. C. Gras, *Alfred Rosmer (1877–1964) et le mouvement révolutionnaire international* (Paris: Maspero, 1971), p. 20.

8. 2, 5, 7, 9, 28 September 1913; the final article appears in *Revolutionary History*, 7/4, pp. 26–8.

9. 'On the day when the factory needed women and children, the family was done for. It may serve as a theme for academic dissertations; it may serve as a basis for still-born social systems. The bourgeoisie, who celebrate its virtues, have crushed and demolished it. And they don't want it for themselves any more, since they don't have children and they live in hotels' (*La Bataille syndicaliste*, 28 September 1913, p. 1; *Revolutionary History* 7/4, p. 27).

10. *Lenin's Moscow*, p. 53.

11. James Klugmann's *History of the Communist Party of Great Britain*, Vol. I (London: Lawrence and Wishart, 1968), names Rosmer as signatory of a 'Manifesto to the Organised Workers of Britain' (p. 109), but scrupulously excludes him from the index for fear that any reader might imagine him to be a figure of significance. (J. T. Murphy, his fellow-signatory, is duly indexed.)

12. L. Trotsky, A. and M. Rosmer, *Correspondance 1929–1939* (Paris: Gallimard, 1982), p. 131.

13. Ibid., p.163.

14. *La Révolution prolétarienne*, September 1951, p. 288. *Revolutionary History*, 7/4, pp. 158–9.

15. M. Nadeau, *Grâces leur soient rendues* (Paris: Albin Michel, 1990), pp. 266–76.

16. Gras, *Alfred Rosmer*, pp. 416–26. In a letter to Stan Newens of the Socialist Review group he wrote on 2 November 1954:

> The R.P. [*La Révolution prolétarienne*] is still published but I have personally ceased to work for it. There was a serious crisis among the men who constitute the redaction committee, some of them asserting the opinion that the proletarian internationalism must be put aside for a time, the only issue being to enter one of the 2 big blocs, of course the American. The same history as in 1914.

I am extremely grateful to Stan Newens for making available two hitherto unknown letters by Rosmer. They appear in full in *Revolutionary History*, 7/4, pp. 159–61.

17. W. Kendall, *The Labour Movement in Europe* (London: Allen Lane, 1975), p. 283.

18. The misrepresentation is surprising, since Kendall interviewed Rosmer when preparing his earlier *The Revolutionary Movement in Britain 1900–21* (London: Weidenfeld and Nicolson, 1969). See p. vi.

19. T. Cliff and D. Gluckstein, *Marxism and Trade Union Struggle: The General Strike of 1926* (London: Bookmarks, 1986), pp. 44, 48–50, 55.

20. R. Darlington, *The Political Trajectory of J. T. Murphy* (Liverpool: Liverpool University Press, 1998), p. 95.

21. There is an exhaustive discussion of the foundation of the RILU in Reiner Tosstorff's post-doctoral thesis; there is a summary of this in *Communist History Network Newsletter*, no. 8, July 2000, and an extract appears in *Revolutionary History*, 7/4, pp. 60–6. I am extremely grateful to Herr Tosstorff for allowing me to read sections of this important and valuable thesis.

22. See E. Goldmann, *Living my Life* (New York: A. A. Knopf, 1931), Vol. II, p. 765; A Berkman, *The Bolshevik Myth* (London: Hutchinson, 1925), p. 143; Makhno's *Memoirs*, cited in *Ni Dieu ni maître* (Lausanne: La Cité, 1969), p. 461.

23. See Tosstorff thesis.

24. *Lenin's Moscow*, p. 72.

25. The majority voted to affiliate to the Comintern at the Tours Congress in December 1920.

26. Kendall, *The Labour Movement in Europe*, pp. 339, 380.

27. J. Maitron, *Le Mouvement anarchiste en France* (Paris: Maspero, 1975), Vol. II, p. 42.

28. A simplified scenario is often presented whereby the mass parties of the Communist International were created by splits in the Social Democratic parties. In fact such a process took place in, at best, half a dozen countries. Even in what appears to be the classic case of the French Communist Party, the syndicalists, never members of the SFIO, played a key role in creating the circumstances in which a mass Communist Party could be established. Writing the syndicalists out of history can lead to some serious strategic misunderstandings.

29. J Riddell (ed.), *Workers of the World and Oppressed Peoples, Unite!* (Proceedings and Documents of the Second Congress 1920, New York: Pathfinder, 1991), Vol. I, p. 323.

30. *Lenin's Moscow*, p. 48.

31. L. Trotsky, 'Marcel Martinet', *Revolutionary History*, 7/2, pp. 191–3.

32. See A. Resis, 'Comintern Policy towards the World Trade-Union Movement: the First Year', in J. S. Curtiss (ed.), *Essays in Russian and Soviet History* (Leiden: E. J. Brill, 1963), pp. 237–52.

33. L. Trotsky, *The First Five Years of the Communist International* (New York: Pioneer, 1945), Vol. I, pp. 26–7.

34. As Rosmer points out, the delegates, including the highly moralistic syndicalists, were not shocked by this; they understood only too well the context of right-wing repression and purge in the unions which Lenin was referring to (*Lenin's Moscow*, p. 61).

35. Syndicalism was not a homogeneous doctrine; it took very different forms in different countries. See R. Tosstorff's thesis and W. Thorpe, *'The Workers Themselves': Revolutionary Syndicalism and International Labour 1913–1923* (Dordrecht: Kluwer, 1989).

36. Various attempts have recently been made to 'rehabilitate' Levi: P. Broué, *Histoire de l'internationale communiste* (Paris: Fayard, 1997), pp. 222–8; D. Fernbach, 'Rosa Luxemburg's Political Heir: An Appreciation of Paul Levi', *New Left Review*, no. 238 (1999), pp. 3–25. Rosmer's comments on Levi in *Lenin's Moscow* are almost invariably negative; we are told that 'he loathed all anarchists and syndicalist *en bloc*' (p. 95). This particular speech seems to confirm the view that Levi, while undoubtedly gifted (and certainly correct in principle in his criticism of the March Action), did not have the patience to convince ultra-lefts and lacked the qualities required in a workers' leader.

37. *Workers of the World and Oppressed Peoples, Unite!*, p. 166.

38. Ibid., p. 85.

39. Tosstorff thesis.

40. *Workers of the World and Oppressed Peoples, Unite!*, pp. 144, 146.

41. Pestaña broke with the Comintern shortly after the Congress; this anti-parliamentarian died a deputy.

42. *Workers of the World and Oppressed Peoples, Unite!*, pp. 150–1.

43. See T. Cliff, *Lenin*, Vol. 1 (London: Pluto, 1975) and Vol. 2 (London: Pluto, 1976).

44. *Workers of the World and Oppressed Peoples, Unite!*, p. 156.

45. Ibid., pp. 168–71.

46. *The First Five Years of the Communist International*, Vol. I, p. 90 (*Workers of the World and Oppressed Peoples, Unite!*, pp. 171–5). It is only necessary to read the

speeches of Lenin and Trotsky alongside those of Zinoviev and Levi to abandon for ever the notion of a monolithic phenomenon called 'Bolshevism'.

47. *La Vie ouvrière,* 26 November 1920; reprinted in L. Trotsky, *Le Mouvement communiste en France (1919–1939)* (Paris: Editions de Minuit, 1967), pp. 87–95.

48. See I. Birchall, 'Success and Failure of the Comintern', in D. Renton and K. Flett (eds), *A Century of Wars and Revolutions? Essays in Twentieth Century History* (London: Rivers Oram, 2000).

49. Darlington, *The Political Trajectory*, pp. 41–2.

50. A. Rosmer, *Le Mouvement ouvrier pendant la guerre* (Paris: Librairie du Travail, 1936), pp. 254–8.

51. Kendall, *The Labour Movement in Europe*, pp. 339, 344.

52. As Pataud and Pouget put it in their classic fictional account of the syndicalist revolution: 'Hitherto, the unions had, with rare exceptions, merely brought together the working-class elite, which fought for general improvement and enabled the passive beings, the non-unionised, to benefit from its efforts' (E. Pataud and E. Pouget, *Comment nous ferons la révolution*, Paris: Editions de la guerre sociale, 1909, p. 77). This tradition of minority unionism has persisted in France; in 1968, out of ten million strikers at best three million were unionized.

53. Darlington, *The Political Trajectory*, p. 95.

54. Tosstorff thesis.

55. Tosstorff thesis.

56. *Lenin's Moscow*, pp. 109–10.

57. Ibid., pp. 118–19.

58. G. P. Maximoff, *The Guillotine at Work* (Chicago: Chicago Section of the Alexander Berkman Fund, 1940), pp. 440–3. In *Lenin's Moscow* (pp. 115–16) Rosmer records only one meeting, whereas Maximoff claims four took place. See Thorpe, *'The Workers Themselves'*, p. 302.

59. *Lenin's Moscow*, p. 97. The actual text is quite as bad as Rosmer's parody:
> You are the chief bulwark of capitalism, now living out its last days – you are the watchdogs of capital, barking furiously at all those who approach your master's lair. You are the last bourgeois barricade which the revolutionary working class must storm to clear the road to a new life, to happiness and to true freedom . . . [etc. etc.] (J. Degras (ed.), *The Communist International 1919–1943*, London: Frank Cass, 1971, Vol. I, pp. 204–5)

60. J. T. Murphy, *The 'Reds' in Congress* (London: British Bureau, Red International of Trade and Industrial Unions, 1921), pp. 7–8.

61. Ibid., p. 12.

62. *Lenin's Moscow*, p. 157.

63. In her brief life of *Tom Mann* (London: Lawrence and Wishart, 1936) Dona Torr makes no reference to the manoeuvrings of the Congress, but merely records that Mann, after discussions with Lenin, threw in his lot with the RILU and the Comintern. She also, bizarrely, claims that 'Lenin took an active role in the RILU Congress' (p. 45). In fact Lenin was on holiday on medical orders, and his only role was to send a letter (*Collected Works*, Vol. XXXII, Moscow: Progress, 1965, p. 501); since this was read immediately before the final singing of the 'Internationale', it cannot have influenced any of the decisions (*The 'Reds' in Congress*, p. 28.) Ms Torr, as a religious Stalinist, doubtless felt that Lenin, like the Holy Ghost, must be omnipresent. And in 1936 any mention of Zinoviev's role would have been, to say the least, tactless.

64. The theses adopted by the Third Congress of the Comintern had defined the position:
> The party must learn to exercise decisive influence in the unions without subjecting them to petty control. It is the union cell, not the union as such, which is under the authority of the party. It is only by patient, devoted, and intelligent work by the cells in the unions that the party will be able to bring about a state of

affairs in which the unions as a whole will readily and joyfully follow party advice. (J. Degras (ed.), *The Communist International 1919–1943*, Vol. I, p. 277)
65. This statement, adopted by the CGT Amiens Congress, laid down that 'The CGT brings together, independently of any political school, all workers who are aware of the struggle that must be waged for the disappearance of wage-labour and of the employers.' It declared that all trade unionists were free to participate in any struggle they saw fit, but enjoined them not to bring their political or philosophical ideas into the union.
66. 'Rede des Genossen Rosmer', *Bibliothek der Roten Gewerkschafts-internationale*, Vol. III (Berlin, 1921), pp. 5–20; *Revolutionary History*, 7/4, pp. 67–80.
67. The rejection of formalism was an important theme in Rosmer's thinking. Compare his comments on post-Leninist Russia, in which he condemned the fetishism of the party and contrasted this to a Leninist flexibility in matters of organizational form:
A few years ago, when these questions could be discussed in the International, when the respective roles of the party, the unions and the soviets were considered, we generally came to the conclusion that the Party seemed to be the most temporary organism, and that it was either the soviets or the unions which would take on the dominant role in the building of Communist society.
With Lenin, who was so attentive to reality and to revolutionary necessities, a balance was established between these different forces.
Now the Party men have come out on top and their day-to-day policies have triumphed. (A. Rosmer, 'La Légende du trotskysme', *La Révolution prolétarienne*, February 1925, p. 4; *Revolutionary History*, 7/4, p. 100)
68. Thorpe, *'The Workers Themselves'*, p. 181.
69. Ibid., pp. 187, 192.
70. As Trotsky wrote to Rosmer on 22 May 1922:
Some comrades assure us with the greatest gravity that the failure of the party in the trade union movement can be explained by the mistake of the last Congress which established an organic link between the two Internationals. It would seem that the mass of workers are up in arms because they have learnt that permanent reciprocal representation has been established between the Comintern and the Profintern. In fact, this is great naivety. The masses who are attracted by the Profintern are not interested in such organizational subtleties. What attracts them is the flag of the proletarian revolution, of communism, of the Soviet Republic, of workers' and peasants' Russia. To imagine that a rank-and-file worker who prefers Moscow to Amsterdam will be scared off because an exchange of representatives is established between the two Internationals is to fail to distinguish the masses from the trade union bureaucracy. (Trotsky, *Le Mouvement communiste en France*, p. 179)
71. Thorpe, *'The Workers Themselves'*, p. 233.
72. Ibid., p. 194.
73. *Lenin's Moscow*, p. 251.
74. *Correspondance internationale*, no. 72, 23 September 1922; translated in V. Serge, *Witness to the German Revolution* (London: Redwords, 2000), pp. 5–6.
75. *Lenin's Moscow*, p. 238.
76. In January 1920 Zinoviev addressed an 'Appeal to the IWW'. Here he argued:
The word *politics* is to many members of the IWW like a red flag to a bull – or a capitalist . . .
This is using the word *politics* in too narrow a sense. One of the principles upon which the IWW was founded is expressed in the saying of Karl Marx, 'Every class struggle is a political struggle.' That is to say, every struggle of the workers against the capitalists is a struggle of the workers for the *political*

power – the state. (*Workers of the World and Oppressed Peoples, Unite!*, p. 930)

The fact that this is so much more intelligent and better written than Zinoviev's usual efforts supports the presumption that it was co-authored by John Reed.

Chapter 7   From National Liberation to Social Revolution: Egypt 1945–53

1. J. and S. Lacouture, *Egypt in Transition* (London: Methuen, 1958), pp. 107–9.
2. Ibid.
3. Ibid.
4. Charles Issawi, *An Economic History of the Middle East and North Africa* (London: Methuen, 1982), p. 8.
5. Issawi, *An Economic History*, p. 155, notes that there was 'practically no industry in Egypt until the turn of the century'; see also chapter 3 on the development of the transport infrastructure.
6. Ibid., p. 8.
7. See G. Perrault, *A Man Apart: A Life of Henri Curiel* (London: Zed Books, 1987) ,W. Ghali, *Beer in the Snooker Club*, (London: Serpent's Tail, 1987) and A. Aciman, *Out of Egypt* (London: Random House, 1996) for descriptions of these communities in biography, fiction and memoirs.
8. C. Issawi, *Egypt at Mid-century* (Oxford: Oxford University Press, 1954), p. 140.
9. R. Tignor, *The State, Private Enterprise and Economic Change in Egypt* (Princeton: Princeton University Press, 1984), p. 191.
10. Lacouture and Lacouture, *Egypt in Transition*, p. 97.
11. S. Radwan, *Capital Formation in Egyptian Industry and Agriculture 1882–1967* (Ithaca: Ithaca Press, 1986), p. 193.
12. *Egyptian Gazette*, 25 January 1946.
13. Tignor, *The State*, p. 216.
14. Ibid., p. 223.
15. Radwan, *Capital Formation*, p. 315.
16. Ibid., p. 135.
17. Tignor, *The State*, p. 193.
18. 'The Present Class Alignment in Egypt', n.d., in the archives of the Communist Party of Great Britain (CP) at the National Museum of Labour History, Manchester, CP/CENT/INT/56/03.
19. H. Ansari, *Egypt: The Stalled Society* (New York: State University of New York Press, 1986), p. 73.
20. Ibid., pp. 73–4. See also G. Baer, *A History of Landownership in Modern Egypt* (London: Oxford University Press, 1962), pp. 71–146, for a more detailed account.
21. For instance, Nasser joined the Muslim Brotherhood, went to Misr al-Fatat meetings, co-operated with the Communists and flirted with Wafdist politics. See K. Mohi al-Din, *Memories of a Revolution* (Cairo: American University in Cairo Press, 1995 edn).
22. The Anglo-Egyptian Treaty formally ended British control of Egypt and gave the country independence, but maintained British occupation of the Canal Zone.
23. J. Beinin and Z. Lockman, *Workers on the Nile* (Princeton: Princeton University Press, 1987), p. 333.
24. 'Election Programme of the Worker Candidate, Abdel Gayed Abdel Gawad, Shubra al-Khayma', November 1944, CP/CENT/INT/56/03.
25. 'The Egyptian Independence Movement Today', 23 April 1946, CP/CENT/INT/56/03.
26. *Wafd al-Misry*, 10 February 1946.

27. 'Untitled Report from Cairo', 22 February 1946, CP/CENT/INT/56/03.
28. *Wafd al-Misry*, 22 February 1946.
29. Beinin and Lockman, *Workers on the Nile*, p. 348.
30. Ibid., pp. 353–4.
31. *Sawt al-Umma*, 7 September 1947.
32. *Sawt al-Umma*, 7 September 1947.
33. *Sawt al-Umma*, 7 and 8 September 1947.
34. Beinin and Lockman, *Workers on the Nile*, pp. 356–7.
35. *Egyptian Gazette*, 8 April 1948.
36. *Egyptian Gazette*, 5 April 1948.
37. *Egyptian Gazette*, 5 April 1948.
38. *Egyptian Gazette*, 6 April 1948.
39. *Egyptian Gazette*, 6 and 7 April 1948.
40. Beinin and Lockman, *Workers on the Nile*, p. 399.
41. *Egyptian Gazette*, 23 January 1952.
42. Beinin and Lockman, *Workers on the Nile*, pp. 403–7.
43. *Ikhwan al-Muslimeen*, 6 April 1948.
44. Interview with Ahmad Hamroush, 8–9 September 1996.
45. See *Wafd al-Misry* on the strikes of February and March 1946, *Sawt al-Umma* had a column written by Mahmoud al-Askari, from the Shubra textile workers' union. *Sawt al-Umma*, 2 September 1947.
46. *Sawt al-Umma* ran articles about police repression (29 July 1946), an advert for a book on Communism (20 August 1946), articles about the Communist Party of Great Britain's involvement in a campaign of occupying council houses in London (11 September 1946), coverage of the miners' strike in Britain (1 September 1947), a report on the conference of the Trades Union Congress in Britain (6 September 1947) as well as extensive coverage of local strikes.
47. Beinin and Lockman, *Workers on the Nile,* p. 405.
48. S. Botman, 'Oppositional Politics in Egypt: The Communist Movement 1936–1954', PhD thesis, Harvard University, 1984, p. 266.
49. M. Hussein, *Class Conflict in Egypt* (New York: Monthly Review Press, 1973), p. 84; A. A. al-Malek, *Egypt: Military Society* (London: Random House, 1968).
50. Henri Curiel, quoted in Perrault, *A Man Apart*, p. 120.
51. 'Short Commentary on the Draft Programme for the ECP', n.d., CP/CENT/INT/56/03.
52. 'Note on Communist Policy for Egypt', n.d., CP/CENT/INT/56/03.
53. 'Summary of Articles from Al-Malayin', 10 September 1952, CP/CENT/INT/56/04.
54. 'Report Made by a Representative of the Co-ordination Committee', n.d., CP/CENT/INT/56/04.
55. See R. Bianchi, 'The Corporatization of the Egyptian Labour Movement', *Middle East Journal*, 40 (1986), pp. 41–2.
56. J. Benin, 'Labor, Capital and the State in Nasserist Egypt 1952–61', *International Journal of Middle Eastern Studies*, 21 (1989), p. 77.

Chapter 8 Northern Manufacturers and the Coming of the American Civil War

My thanks to Fred Lindop for commenting on this paper.

1. Early Marxist history often suffered from a crude economic determinism. See especially A. M. Simons, *Social Forces in American History* (New York: Macmillan, 1911); and L. M. Hacker, *The Triumph of American Capitalism* (New York: Columbia University Press, 1940). Neither believed that slavery lay at the heart of the dispute.

2. For an examination of the possible consequences of a Confederate victory, see R. L. Ransom 'Fact and Counterfact: The Second American Revolution', *Civil War History*, 45 (March 1999), pp. 37–60.

3. J. M. McPherson, *Battle Cry of Freedom* (New York: Oxford University Press, 1988). Chris Harman berates McPherson for suggesting that at various moments during the war the South might have succeeded ('Clash of Two Systems', *Socialist Review*, 131 (May 1990), p. 26).

4. K. Marx and F. Engels, *The Civil War in the US* (New York: International Publishers, 1961), p. 203; B. Moore Jr, *Social Origins of Dictatorship and Democracy* (Harmondsworth: Penguin, 1969), chapter 3. See also A. Callinicos, 'Bourgeois Revolutions and Historical Materialism', *Socialist Review*, 43 (June 1989), pp. 151–9. For a stimulating Marxist account of slavery and industrial capitalism's difficult coexistence up to 1850 see J. Ashworth, *Slavery, Capitalism and Politics in the Antebellum Republic* (Cambridge: Cambridge University Press, 1995).

5. An exception is P. S. Foner, *Business and Slavery: The New York Merchants and the Irrepressible Conflict* (Chapel Hill: University of North Carolina Press, 1941).

6. B. Laurie and M. Schmitz, 'Manufacture and Productivity', in T. Hershberg (ed.), *Philadelphia: Work, Space, Family and Group Experience in the Nineteenth Century* (New York: Oxford University Press, 1981), pp. 45, 49, 66.

7. Ibid.

8. '1850 Manuscript Census of Manufactures', Philadelphia Social History Project 0179 (hereafter MCM, PSHP).

9. In the textile and garment industries, in contrast, social barriers restricted contact between rich merchants and small immigrant manufacturers (P. Scranton, *Proprietary Capitalism: The Textile Manufacture at Philadelphia, 1800–1885* (Cambridge: Cambridge University Press, 1983), pp. 132–3).

10. C. Robson, *The Manufactories and Manufacturers of Pennsylvania of the Nineteenth Century* (Philadelphia: Galaxy Publishing Co., 1875), p. 26.

11. E. D. Baltzell, *Philadelphia Gentlemen* (Glencoe, Ill.: Free Press, 1958), pp. 108–9. A comfortable middle-class income was approximately $4,000–5,000 per annum.

12. *The Rich Men of Philadelphia: Income Tax of the Residents of Philadelphia and Bucks County for the Year Ending April 30, 1865* (Philadelphia: n.p., 1865), p. 5.

13. Eighty-seven workshop owners enumerated in the 1850 Manuscript Census of Manufactures were linked to the Manuscript Population Census. This, supplemented by traditional biographical sources, provides information about the social character of workshop owners.

14. T. Coulson, 'Some Prominent Members of the Franklin Institute: Samuel Vaughan Merrick, 1801–1870', *Journal of the Franklin Institute*, 258 (November 1854), pp. 336–46; C. Penrose, *Samuel Vaughan Merrick* (New York: Newcomen Society of England American Branch, 1946), pp. 10–11, 14; D. R. Goodwin, 'Obituary Notice of Samuel Vaughan Merrick', *Proceedings of the American Philosophical Society*, 11 (1869–70), pp. 586–97.

15. 'Recollections of Coleman Sellers by his Son George Escol Sellers', pp. 48–9, Peale-Sellers Papers, American Philosophical Society.

16. A. F. C. Wallace, *Rockdale: The Growth of an American Village in the Early Industrial Revolution* (New York: Norton, 1972), p. 78.

17. 'Recollections of Coleman Sellers', p. 46.

18. S. Colwell, *The Claims of Labor, and their Precedence to the Claims of Free Trade* (Philadelphia: C. Sherman, 1861), pp. 7, 9, 16–20, 27; the quotation is from p. 17.

19. E. M. Geffen, 'Philadelphia Protestantism Reacts to Social Reform Movements before the Civil War', *Pennsylvania History*, 30 (April 1963), p. 210.

20. *Proceedings and Debates of the Convention of the Commonwealth of Pennsylvania to Propose Amendments to the Constitution*, 10 (Harrisburg: Packer, Barrett and Parke, 1838), pp. 106, 125–6, 130.

21. H. R. Mueller, *The Whig Party in Pennsylvania* (New York: Columbia University Press, 1922), p. 36.

22. M. W. Brinton, *Their Lives and Mine* (Philadelphia: the author, 1972), pp. 33–7.

23. Ibid., pp. 21–2.

24. Petition signed by M. Mendenhall and J. H. Johnson, 15 November 1848, Incoming Correspondence, Baldwin Locomotive Works Papers, Historical Society of Pennsylvania. For an excellent history of the works see J. K. Brown, *The Baldwin Locomotive Works, 1831–1915* (Baltimore: Johns Hopkins University Press, 1995).

25. J. Fincher, 'Early History of Our Organization', *Machinists and Blacksmiths' International Journal*, 9 (March 1972), p. 564.

26. 'The Original Constitution and List of Members of the First Republican Club, Formed in the City of Philadelphia, 1856' (Philadelphia, 1856), Union League Archive, Philadelphia.

27. Fincher, 'Early History of Our Organization', p. 565.

28. 'The Tribune on Eight Hours,' *Fincher's Trade's Review*, 22 July 1865, p. 64; 'Our Correspondents', ibid., 2 September 1865, pp. 106–7; ibid., 9 September 1865, p. 116.

29. 'Eight Hours a Day', *Tribune*, 11 November 1865; *Fincher's Trade's Review*, 2 December 1865, p. 8.

30. J. C. Sylvis, *The Life, Speeches, Labors and Essays of William H. Sylvis* (Philadelphia: Claxton, Remsen and Haffelfinger, 1872), p. 168.

31. *National Trades Review*, 28 April 1866, p. 1. Two years later the Keystone Co-operative Machine Shop was founded on South Fifteenth Street.

32. Capitalism was deeply embedded within American society from the beginning, but it initially relied upon earlier systems of production. Merchant capital traded with small producers who, at least nominally, retained their independence. Only with the arrival of modern factories did capitalists finally control the labour process. In Marx's terminology, the 'formal subsumption' of labour to capital gave way to 'real subsumption' (Karl Marx, *Capital* (Harmondsworth: Penguin, 1976), pp. 1019–25). The contrasting economic ties between merchant and small producer and industrial capitalist and wage worker account for the different political behaviour. For other suggestive remarks, see E. Fox-Genovese and Eugene D. Genovese, *Fruits of Merchant Capital* (Oxford: Oxford University Press, 1983), pp. 4–6.

33. For the riots, see M. Feldberg, *The Philadelphia Riots: A Study of Ethnic Conflict* (Westport: Greenwood Press, 1975).

34. S. B. Warner, *The Private City: Philadelphia in Three Periods of Its Growth* (Philadelphia: University of Pennsylvania Press, 1968), p. 152.

35. E. K. Price, *The History of the Consolidation of the City of Philadelphia* (Philadelphia: J. B. Lippincott, 1873), pp. 14–37, 90, 111–19.

36. R. L. Bloom, 'Morton McMichael's North American', *Pennsylvania Magazine of History and Biography*, 77 (April 1953), p. 177.

37. Mueller, *Whig Party*, 205; J. T. Scharf and T. Westcott, *History of Philadelphia*, Vol. 1 (Philadelphia: L. H. Everts, 1884), p. 715.

38. I. Bernstein, *The New York Draft Riots: Their Significance for American Society and Politics in the Age of the Civil War* (New York: Oxford University Press, 1990).

39. 'The Original Constitution and List of Members'; 1860 MCM, PSHP, 0359; ibid., 0156.

40. W. Dusinberre, *Civil War Issues in Philadelphia, 1856–1865* (Philadelphia: University of Pennsylvania Press, 1965), pp. 77–8. E. Foner, *Free Soil, Free Labor, Free Men* (New York: Oxford University Press, 1970), pp. 202, 255, stresses the importance of free labour in bringing the two parties together.

41. *Public Ledger*, 5 May 1858, p. 2; Scharf and Westcott, *History of Philadelphia*, Vol. 1, p. 728.

42. Dusinberre, *Civil War Issues*, pp. 77–8.

43. Ibid., pp. 93–4.
44. M. Baird to E. F. Raworth, 8 December 1860, Letter Copy Book, Baldwin Locomotive Works Papers.
45. J. F. Fisher et al. to J. Buchanan, 28 January 1861, Buchanan Papers, Historical Society of Pennsylvania.
46. The peace movement can be followed in the pages of the *Public Ledger*, January–February 1861.
47. For the Sanitary Fair, see J. Matthew Gallman, *Mastering Wartime* (Cambridge: Cambridge University Press, 1990), chapter 6.
48. M. Whiteman, *Gentlemen in Crisis* (Philadelphia: Union League, 1975).
49. C. and M. Beard, *The Rise of American Civilization*, Vol. II (New York: Macmillan, 1927), chapter 18.

Chapter 9   Industrial and Political Strategy in the 1972 British Strike Wave

Research for this chapter was financially assisted by grants provided by the Economic and Social Research Council (R000222876) and the British Academy (SS-1821/APN8398).
    1. R. Harrison, in E. Hobsbawm et al., *The Forward March of Labour Halted?* (London: Verso, 1981), p. 55.
    2. D. Lyddon, ' "Glorious Summer", 1972: The High Tide of Rank and File Militancy', in J. McIlroy, N. Fishman and A. Campbell (eds), *British Trade Unionism and Industrial Politics*, Vol. 2: *The High Tide of Trade Unionism, 1964–79* (Aldershot: Ashgate, 1999); R. Darlington and D. Lyddon, *Glorious Summer: Class Struggle in Britain 1972* (London: Bookmarks, 2001).
    3. 'Stoppages of Work due to Industrial Disputes in 1972', *Department of Employment Gazette*, June 1973.
    4. W. Ashworth, *The History of the British Coal Industry*, Vol. 5: *1946–1982: The Nationalized Industry* (Oxford: Clarendon Press, 1986), p. 305.
    5. *New Statesman*, 18 February 1972, pp. 200–1.
    6. Trades Union Congress, *Annual Report* (London: TUC, 1972), p. 98; emphasis added.
    7. B. McCormick, *Industrial Relations in the Coal Industry* (London: Macmillan, 1979), pp. 222–3.
    8. V. L. Allen, *The Militancy of British Miners* (Shipley: The Moor Press, 1981), pp. 155–9, 163–5.
    9. R. Taylor, *The Fifth Estate: Britain's Unions in the Seventies* (London: Routledge and Kegan Paul, 1978), pp. 260–5; Allen, *Militancy of British Miners*, pp. 181–206; M. Pitt, *The World on our Backs: The Kent Miners and the 1972 Miners' Strikes* (London: Lawrence and Wishart, 1979), pp. 122–66.
    10. E. Heath, *The Course of My Life: My Autobiography* (London: Hodder and Stoughton, 1998), p. 350.
    11. 'The Miners' Strike', *Labour Research*, April 1972, pp. 74–5.
    12. E. G. Varley, in *Parliamentary Debates*, 5th Series, Vol. 830, 8 February 1972, col. 1209, which also suggests 1,000 picket lines.
    13. R. Taylor, *The Fifth Estate: Britain's Unions in the Seventies* (London: Routledge and Kegan Paul, 1978), p. 263.
    14 J. Gormley, *Battered Cherub: The Autobiography of Joe Gormley* (London: Hamish Hamilton, 1982), p. 103.
    15. Allen, *Militancy of British Miners*, p. 200 (emphasis added).
    16. *Financial Times*, 7, 10 January 1972.
    17. TUC, *Annual Report*, 1972, pp. 97–8.

18. *The Times*, 2, 5, 15 February 1972.
19. J. Davies, in *Parliamentary Debates*, 5th Series, Vol. 831, 17 February 1972, cols 623–4.
20. R. Geary, *Policing Industrial Disputes: 1893 to 1985* (London: Methuen, 1986), pp. 73–8; F. Watters, *Being Frank: The Memoirs of Frank Watters* (Barnsley: Monkspring, 1992), p. 63.
21. P. Wallington, 'The Case of the Longannet Miners and the Criminal Liability of Pickets', *Industrial Law Journal*, 1/4 (1972), pp. 219–23.
22. F. Lindop, 'The Dockers and the Industrial Relations Act, Part 1: Shop Stewards and Containerization', *Historical Studies in Industrial Relations*, 5 (1998), pp. 33–72; F. Lindop, 'The Dockers and the Industrial Relations Act, Part 2: The Arrest and Release of the Pentonville Five', *Historical Studies in Industrial Relations*, 6 (1998), pp. 65–100.
23. Heath, *Course of My Life*, p. 406.
24. G. Lewis, *Lord Hailsham: A Life* (London: Jonathan Cape, 1997), pp. 348–9; Lord Denning, *The Closing Chapter* (London: Butterworths, 1983), pp. 169–73.
25. Lindop, 'Arrest and Release of the Pentonville Five', p. 74.
26. 'Stoppages of Work due to Industrial Disputes in 1972', *Department of Employment Gazette*, June 1973.
27. *The Times*, 31 August 1972.
28. T. Austrin, 'The "Lump" in the UK Construction Industry', in T. Nichols (ed.), *Capital and Labour: Studies in the Capitalist Labour Process* (Glasgow: Fontana, 1980).
29. *Guardian*, 1, 3 June 1972.
30. T. Austrin, 'Industrial Relations in the Construction Industry', unpublished PhD thesis, University of Bristol, pp. 288–91, 296.
31. K. Sim, 'What Building Strike?', *New Statesman*, 11 February 1972.
32. Austrin, 'Industrial Relations in the Construction Industry', p. 297.
33. *The Times*, 1, 7, 8, 9 August 1972.
34. National Federation of Building Trade Employers, *Annual Report* (NFBTE, 1972).
35. NFBTE Council document, 17 August 1972.
36. *The Times*, 15, 16 August 1972.
37. *The Times*, 21, 22 August 1972.
38. Austrin, 'Industrial Relations in the Construction Industry', p. 309.
39. *Financial Times*, 24 August 1972.
40. J. Arnison, *The Shrewsbury Three: Strikes, Pickets and 'Conspiracy'* (London: Lawrence and Wishart, 1974).
41. D. Lyddon, 'Rediscovering the Past: Recent British Strike Tactics in Historical Perspective', *Historical Studies in Industrial Relations*, 5 (1998), pp. 107–51.
42. *Guardian*, 17 March 1972; *The Times*, 20 March 1972.
43. *Guardian*, 23 March 1972.
44. T. Bishop, 'When Workers Take Control', *Personnel Management* (March 1973), p. 26.
45. J. Gretton, 'To Sit or not to Sit?', *New Society*, 15 June 1972, p. 565.
46. *The Economist*, 20 May 1972, p. 106.
47. *Guardian*, 16 May 1972.
48. A. Tuckman, 'Industrial Action and Hegemony: Workplace Occupation in Britain 1971 to 1981', unpublished PhD thesis, University of Hull, 1985.
49. Allen, *Militancy of British Miners*, p. 217.
50. *The Economist*, 5 August 1972, p. 13.
51. Gormley, *Battered Cherub*, pp. 95–118; L. Wood, *A Union to Build: The Story of UCATT* (London: Lawrence and Wishart, 1979), p. 18.
52. TUC General Council, 4 May 1972.
53. *Guardian*, 8 April 1972.

54. H. Francis and D. Smith, *The Fed: A History of South Wales Miners in the Twentieth Century* (London: Lawrence and Wishart, 1980), pp. 277–94.

55. G. D. H. Cole, *Labour in the Coal-mining Industry (1914–1921)* (Oxford: Clarendon Press, 1923), p. 207.

56. H. A. Clegg, *A History of British Trade Unions since 1889*, Vol. 2: *1911–1933* (Oxford: Clarendon Press, 1985), pp. 416–17.

57. *The Economist*, 19 February 1972, p. 68.

58. Clegg, *History of British Trade Unions*, pp. 315–16; K. Coates and T. Topham, *The Making of the Transport and General Workers' Union: The Emergence of the Labour Movement 1870–1922*, Vol. 1, Part 2 (Oxford: Blackwell, 1991), pp. 786–8; A. Bullock, *The Life and Times of Ernest Bevin*, Vol. 1: *Trade Union Leader*, 1881–1940 (London: Heinemann, 1960), pp. 182–3; P. Bagwell, *The Railwaymen: The History of the National Union of Railwaymen* (London: George Allen and Unwin, 1963), pp. 464–5; Cole, *Labour in the Coal-mining Industry*, pp. 222–8.

59. R. Page Arnot, *The Miners: Years of Struggle – A History of the Miners' Federation of Great Britain (from 1910 onwards)* (London: George Allen and Unwin, 1953), p. 466.

60. Bullock, *Life and Times of Ernest Bevin*, p. 352.

61. J. Torode, 'Miners: A "Special Case"?', *New Statesman*, 11 February 1972, p. 173.

62. *The Times*, 8, 9 February 1972.

63. F. Chapple, *Sparks Fly! A Trade Union Life* (London: Michael Joseph, 1984), p. 126.

64. J. McIlroy and A. Campbell, 'Organizing the Militants: The Liaison Committee for the Defence of Trade Unions, 1966–1979', *British Journal of Industrial Relations*, 37/1 (1999), p. 11.

65. J. E. Mortimer, *History of the Boilermakers' Society*, Vol. 3: *1940–1989* (London: Verso, 1994), p. 245.

66. P. Bagwell, *The Railwaymen*, Vol. 2: *The Beeching Era and After* (London: George Allen and Unwin, 1982), pp. 245–68.

67. Lindop, 'Arrest and Release of the Pentonville Five', p. 82.

68. Ibid., pp. 84–5.

69. McIlroy and Campbell, 'Organizing the Militants', pp. 18–20.

70. TUC Circulars 206 and 208, 1971–2.

71. McIlroy and Campbell, 'Organizing the Militants', pp. 24–5.

72. J. McIlroy, 'Notes on the Communist Party and Industrial Politics', in J. McIlroy, N. Fishman and A. Campbell (eds), *British Trade Unionism and Industrial Politics*, Vol. 2: *The High Tide of Trade Unionism, 1964–79* (Aldershot: Ashgate, 1999), p. 219.

73. Ibid., pp. 227, 237–41.

Chapter 10   Class Consciousness and National Consciousness in the Scottish General Strike of 1820

1. 'Address to the Inhabitants of Great Britain and Ireland', reproduced in I. MacDougall (ed.), *Labour in Scotland: A Pictorial History from the Eighteenth Century to the Present* (Edinburgh: Mainstream, 1985), plate 29, p. 44.

2. Montieth to Sidmouth, 3 and 4 April 1820, Public Records Office, Home Office Series, 102/32.

3. Several local risings did in fact take place in England, involving 300–500 people in Barnsley and 200 in an abandoned attack on Attercliffe barracks. See, for example, J. Stevenson, *Popular Disturbances in England, 1700–1870* (New York: Longman, 1979), pp. 216–17.

4. W. H. Fraser, *Conflict and Class* (Edinburgh: John Donald, 1988), p. 111.

5. Rosa Luxemburg quotes Engels to this effect in 'The Mass Strike, the Political Party and the Trade Unions', *Rosa Luxemburg Speaks*, edited with an introduction by M.-A. Walters (New York, London and Sydney: Pathfinder, 1970), p. 155. See also T. Cliff and D. Gluckstein, *Marxism and the Trade Union Struggle: The General Strike of 1926* (London: Bookmarks, 1986), p. 22.

6. See, for example, P. Berresford Ellis and S. Mac a' Ghobhainn, *The Scottish Insurrection of 1820* (London: Pluto, 1970), p. 296 and J. D. Young, *The Rousing of the Scottish Working Class* (London: Croom Helm, 1979), p. 45. A disproportionate emphasis on the insurrections occurs even in the work of the few non-Scottish historians who have noticed that the strike took place. Mick Jenkins, for example, writes that 'a general strike was seen as an integral part of the insurrection'. See *The General Strike of 1842* (London: Lawrence and Wishart, 1982), p. 32.

7. L. D. Trotsky, *The History of the Russian Revolution* (London: Pluto, 1977), p. 27. See also Luxemburg, 'The Mass Strike, the Political Party and the Trade Unions', pp. 155–81.

8. K. Marx, *Capital* (Harmondsworth: Penguin, 1976), Vol. 1, pp. 457, 489, 493, 497, 508.

9. A. Slaven, *The Economic Development of the West of Scotland* (London: Economic and Social Research Council, 1975), pp. 84, 86, 87.

10. Ibid., pp. 87–8; N. Murray, *The Scottish Handloom Weavers, 1790–1850: A Social History* (Edinburgh: Donald, 1978), pp. 4, 18–22, 23.

11. C. W. J. Withers, *Urban Highlanders* (East Linton: Tuckwell Press, 1998), pp. 86, 140.

12. Murray, *The Scottish Handloom Weavers*, pp. 31–5.

13. A. Webster, 'An Account of the Number of People in Scotland in the Year One Thousand Seven Hundred and Fifty Five', *Scottish Population Statistics including Webster's Analysis of Population 1755*, edited by J. G. Kyd (Edinburgh: Scottish History Society, 1975), pp. 77, 79.

14. R. Tyson, 'Contrasting Regimes: Population Growth in Ireland and Scotland during the Eighteenth Century', in S. Connolly et al., *Conflict, Identity and Economic Development* (Preston: Carnegie Publishing, 1993), pp. 64–7.

15. Ibid., pp. 66–7; R. Mitchison et al., 'The Eighteenth Century', in M. Flinn (ed.), *Scottish Population History from the Seventeenth Century to the 1930s* (Cambridge: Cambridge University Press, 1977), p. 302.

16. J. De Vries, *European Urbanisation 1500–1800* (London: Methuen, 1984), pp. 39, 45; Mitchison et al., 'The Eighteenth Century', p. 313.

17. C. Tilly, 'Did the Cake of Custom Break?', in J. M. Merriman (ed.), *Consciousness and Class Experience in Nineteenth-century Europe* (New York and London: Holmes and Meier, 1979), p. 27.

18. I. D. Whyte, 'Urbanisation in Eighteenth-century Scotland', in T. M. Devine and J. R. Young (eds), *Eighteenth Century Scotland: New Perspectives* (East Linton: Tuckwell Press, 1999), pp. 179, 184.

19. Fraser, *Conflict and Class*, p. 14.

20. J. Cleland, *Enumeration of the Inhabitants of Glasgow, etc.* (Glasgow, 1821), p. 6.

21. A. Dickson and W. Speirs, 'Changes in the Class Structure in Paisley, 1750–1845', *Scottish Historical Review*, 167, April 1980, pp. 160–1.

22. T. M. Devine, 'The Urban Crisis', in T. M. Devine and G. Jackson (eds), *Glasgow* (2 volumes, Manchester and New York: Manchester University Press, 1995), Vol. 1: *Beginnings to 1830*, pp. 402–17.

23. Fraser, *Conflict and Class*, chapter 2.

24. T. M. Devine, *The Scottish Nation, 1700–2000* (Harmondsworth: Penguin, 1999), p. 489.

25. Ibid., p. 487.

26. M. J. Mitchell, *The Irish in the West of Scotland, 1797–1848* (Edinburgh: John Donald, 1998), pp. 90–6.

27. T. Gallagher, *Glasgow: The Uneasy Peace* (Manchester: Manchester University Press, 1987), p. 2.

28. E. W. McFarland, *Ireland and Scotland in the Age of Revolution* (Edinburgh: John Donald, 1994), p. 244.

29. Mitchell, *The Irish in the West of Scotland,* p. 99.

30. Ibid., p. 104.

31. Ibid., chapter 2; McFarland, *Ireland and Scotland in the Age of Revolution*, chapter 6.

32. Devine, *The Scottish Nation*, pp. 196–7.

33. W. Straka, 'Reform in Scotland and the Working Class', *Scottish Tradition*, 2 (1972), p. 32.

34. M. Fry, *Patronage and Principle* (Aberdeen: Aberdeen University Press, 1987), p. 7.

35. Fraser, *Conflict and Class*, pp. 98–9.

36. Ibid., p. 109.

37. Murray, *The Scottish Handloom Weavers*, p. 99.

38. E. Knox, 'Between Labour and Capital: The Petty Bourgeoisie in Victorian Edinburgh', University of Edinburgh PhD thesis, 1986, p. 530.

39. J. D. Brims, 'The Scottish "Jacobins", Scottish Nationalism and the British Union', in R. A. Mason (ed.), *Scotland and England, 1286–1815* (Edinburgh: John Donald, 1987), p. 256.

40. W. M. Roach, 'Alexander Richmond and the Radical Reform Movement in Glasgow in 1816–17', *Scottish Historical Review*, 151–2 (1972), p. 4.

41. R. Brown, *The History of Paisley* (2 volumes, Paisley: Alexander Gardner, 1885), Vol. 2, pp. 184–5.

42. P. Holt, 'Review of *The Scottish Insurrection of 1820*', p. 35; National Library of Scotland, RB.m.145(8).

43. 'Address to the Inhabitants of Great Britain and Ireland', plate 29, p. 44.

44. Berresford Ellis and Mac a' Ghobhainn, *The Scottish Insurrection of 1820*, pp. 184–5; H. Henderson, 'Letter to *The Scotsman*', 5 July 1986, in *The Armstrong Nose*, edited by A. Finlay (Edinburgh: Hamish Henderson, 1996), pp. 267–8.

45. Holt, 'Review of *The Scottish Insurrection of 1820*', p. 35.

46. E. P. Thompson, *The Making of the English Working Class* (revised edition with a new preface, Harmondsworth: Penguin, 1980), pp. 760, 757–8.

47. T. C. Smout, 'Problems of Nationalism, Identity and Improvement in Later Eighteenth-century Scotland', in T. M. Devine (ed.), *Improvement and Enlightenment* (Edinburgh: John Donald, 1989), p. 12.

48. R. C. Gammage, *History of the Chartist Movement 1837–1854* (London: Merlin, 1969, facsimile of the 1894 edition), p. 33.

49. 'Song: The Deluge of Carnage at Length Has Subsided', *Radical Renfrew: Poetry from the French Revolution to the First World War*, selected, edited and introduced by T. Leonard (Edinburgh: Polygon, 1990), p. 91.

50. W. Aiton, *A History of the Encounter at Drumclog and the Battle of Bothwell Bridge in the Month of June 1679, with an Account of what is Correct, and what is Fictitious in* The Tales of my Landlord *Respecting these Engagements, and Reflections on Political Subjects* (Hamilton: W. M. Borthwick and Co., 1821), pp. 99, 7–8.

51. Scott to Croker, 19 March 1826, in *The Letters of Sir Walter Scott*, edited by H. J. C. Grierson (12 volumes, London: Constable, 1932–7), Vol. 9: *1823–1826*, pp. 471–2.

Index